Arch of History

Also by
Lola S. Kohen

First of a political thriller trilogy

Into The Arms of Danger
A Thriller in Future Israel
set around Israel's centennial

coming soon

Into Danger: Broken Promise
Second novel in the trilogy

Into Danger: Flashpoint
Third novel in the trilogy

Visit www.lolaskohen.com

Arch of History
through
Atlantis, Sumeria, Israel

Lola S. Kohen

ARCH OF HISTORY THROUGH ATLANTIS, SUMERIA, ISRAEL
Copyright © 2017 Lola S. Kohen

All rights reserved. No part of this book may be reproduced by any means whatsoever without written permission, except brief portions for purposes of review.

Published by
Whirlwind Publishing Group
Dallas, Texas 75233
www.whirlwindpublishinggroup.com

The star image on the cover is from a ceramic tile crafted by Fired Up Tiles, USA. Decorative ceramics were first made 26,000 years ago by an ice-age culture living in Central Europe.

Library of Congress Control Number: 2017950353
Whirlwind Publishing Group, Dallas, TX

ISBN: 978-0-9882643-2-8

1. Earth history—geologic—early humans 2. First societies—ancient empires 3. Hebraic history 4. Jewish history 5. World War history 6. Title

Book and cover design by Tim Brittain (twbrit@cox.net)
Author photo by Don Hoffman

Dedicated

To: George Lee Kahn ~ for your unwavering support in so many ways, and for your dedication to truth.
and
To: Laura, Nani, and Julia ~ three women of valor.

ACKNOWLEDGEMENTS

Syd Love and Dave Feldman for excellent editing and attention to detail; Ron Rexer and Dave Bedford for your moral support and encouragement.

For your critiques, research, fact checking, and suggestions I thank: Howard L. Dyckman PhD, Linda Sax Snaid, Agnes Lindstrom MD, Norma Posey PhD, John Robinson, Audrea Liszt, Caroline McCullough, George Keller PhD, Al Converse, Shirley San Nichols, Susan K. Burns, John Robinson, Rose Morrison, Dave Ward, Ken Yaros, Johnnie Thompson, Jerry Treadway, Maurice Kotzen, Natalie Freedman, Rafi Schutzer, and Harley Henley.

Your contributions helped make this a better book.

Contents

Author Notes
Introduction
1. Fragments and Clues 1
2. The Sumerian Creation Story 5
3. Earth: The Blue Planet 11
4. Early Human Culture 23
5. Toba Catastrophe 35
6. First Advanced Societies 41
7. Civilization X 55
8. The End of the Ice Age 71
9. Noah's Flood Marks a New Age 85
10. The First Empire 95
11. The Promised Land 107
12. The Egyptians and the Hyksos 113
13. Exodus 121
14. The Ancient World 131
15. Common Era 155
16. The Little Ice Age 175
17. Power and Control 185
18. The First Great War 193
19. No Peace in Our Time 199
20. The Second Great War 213
21. The Cause for Peace 227
22. Modern Israel 237
23. History Repeats 249
24. The Future 257

Appendix Earth Timeline 263
Appendix Climate Changes of the Last Ice Age 265
Appendix Canaan History at a Glance.. 267
Appendix Israel History at a Glance 269
Appendix Sumeria History at a Glance 272
Appendix Egypt History at a Glance... 273
Appendix The Balfour Declaration.. 277
Endnotes.. 278
Bibliography 312
Websites Utilized 318
Index 321

Author's Note

*A*rch of History is written in an interdisciplinary style to create an engaging, accessible narrative from the Big Bang and Earth's formation to the emergence of modern societies, through the centuries, and into today's world.

Dates and descriptions of events in antiquity offered in this narrative are based on the best evidence available to provide a frame of reference and to gain insight into ancient events.

The dating system used is the internationally recognized system of BCE (Before the Common Era) and CE (Common Era) in preference to BC (before Christ) and AD (*anno Domini*).

The Jewish calendar, also called the calendar of Nineveh, began in Mesopotamia around the time Sumerian city states formed a confederation on the plains of Nineveh. Jewish calendar dates are included in the latter part of this narrative as a reference point from Sumeria to modern times.

The year of publication for *Arch of History*, 2017, is 5,777 years from the beginning of the calendar.

ANCIENT LANGUAGES are sometimes difficult to translate accurately into English. Some disagreements about meaning may arise.

CANAAN is the region roughly corresponding to the territory first settled by Hebraic survivors of the Great Flood and later settled by Sumerians and others who became the Nation of Israel.

For ease of understanding and continuity the region is referred to as Early Canaan prior to the end of the last ice age in this narrative. After the end of the last ice age this land is called the land of Canaan, then Israel. Canaan/Israel is situated in the center between Africa, Europe, and Asia.

Early Canaan and Europe were the territories of the Neandertals, early Cro-Magnons, and later Cro-Magnon hybrids.

A NATION as used throughout this narrative is a community of people with a common ethnic origin and a distinctive way of life expressed through a shared background of traditions, beliefs, and language, whether or not they live together in one territory or have their own government.

For example, the Nation of Israel, or the Jewish Nation, is the collective Jewish population living inside or outside Israel; several Native American Indian nations live within the United States of America; and the Kurdish Nation lives in the four connecting corners of Turkey, Syria, Iraq, and Iran.

TORAH REFERENCES are from The Schocken Bible: Volume I, The Five Books of Moses: Genesis, Exodus, Leviticus, Numbers, and Deuteronomy—A New Translation with Introductions, Commentary, and Notes by Everett Fox.

INTRODUCTION

The following narrative, combining history, science, spirituality, and politics—called a Big History—is written from the perspective of a modern-day Jew looking back through time to the beginning. Finding a place to call "the beginning" became as daunting as trying to connect some of the puzzle pieces left behind.

A look at the creation of our world through its geologic evolution, the impact of natural disasters, and the progress of early human cultures lays the groundwork for how societies developed.

Patterns of archetypal cultures presented here will challenge Western history books which present a straight cultural line from primitive hunter-gatherers to farmers to our present state of highly urbanized peoples.[1] As in our present-day world, some ancient populations preferred different lifestyles. Some groups maintained mobile lifestyles, while others enjoyed farming, living in villages or in city states.

Great cultures such as the civilization of ancient Egypt that we admire and write about seemed to begin near their apex and then decline through political conflicts or natural disasters until their downfall or occupation. More realistically, the growth and decline of cultures indicate a cycle or a zigzag, not a straight line.

Technology, including the Internet, has enabled the current worldwide information explosion. Yet people are rapidly losing knowledge of their past. Personal journals and oral histories are fading. This is a good time to record our collective understanding of our past into a lasting account, a library of knowledge based on what we know today, to appreciate and protect ourselves and for the benefit of future generations.

Throughout recorded history when individual freedoms became increasingly restricted while populations grew crowded, hate crimes against minority ethnic groups increased. If history repeats, we must know about our past to accurately project into the future to understand what we might face.[2] For example, the rising level of worldwide violence against Jewish people in the twenty-first century is reminiscent of the rampant racism expressed during the buildup to World War II.[3]

Since the end of the last world war, countries around the world have moved steadily toward grouping into regions under the authority of the United Nations through the signing of treaties, secret international agreements, and international laws. The implications for the populations in a newly created regional unit like the European Union are increased surveillance, supervised behavior, and regulated activities.[4]

In ancient times, living conditions threatened by erratic climate or natural disasters often caused a nation to migrate to a favorable area. Other tribes sometimes moved into abandoned, developed areas. If the arriving people lacked an established spiritual system they sometimes adapted as much as they could understand of the previous culture's beliefs.

In ancient and in modern history, sometimes an aggressive people violently force another ethnic group out in order to acquire land and wealth. Predatory cultures usually eliminate or exile the intelligentsia of the target culture and rewrite the customs and spiritual system to the advantage of their own elite.

Even after the two world wars "to end all wars" our planet's populations still suffer violence from time to time and in place to place. In these and countless other tragedies, each life lost is like losing a library filled with rare books of knowledge and art available only to that life.

At the same time, we live in an age with a wealth of available knowledge coupled with expansive travel options allowing people to visit various sites of our shared ancient past. To have an opportunity to study the Sumerian culture, or look for clues to the existence of Atlantis, or analyze patterns of human civilizations, is remarkable.

1

FRAGMENTS AND CLUES

Modern humans have survived two major worldwide extinction events: the Toba supervolcanic eruption 74,000 years ago and the cataclysmic end of the last ice age 12,000 years ago.

Few early cultures lived through the Toba eruption and subsequent volcanic winter. A supervolcanic eruption or a major impact from space can fill the atmosphere with ash, debris, and dust that block the sun's warmth and light from reaching the planet's surface. Perpetual darkness causes plants to die off and results in starvation for species dependent upon vegetation for survival.

Scientists have calculated that an impact from space or a supervolcanic eruption equal to a 1,000 megaton explosion causes an impact or volcanic winter lasting weeks to decades.[5] Each megaton is equivalent to a million tons of TNT.

Thousands of years after the Toba supervolcanic eruption, people faced another life-threatening time, the end of the last ice. The survivors of both these events left clues for us to find and interpret.

Fragments of our past in the form of archaeological artifacts and geologic evidence are all around us. The following pages weave threads back through time into a tapestry of a great society living in a paradise during the last ice age. Possibly the first golden age, it could have been a place where people lived in prosperity, goodness, and knowledge.

Forming an arch across time, people carried knowledge from a society existing during the last ice age, through the disasters that ended that freezing cold period, and into the first Western civilization to form after the end of the last ice age, ancient Sumeria in Mesopotamia.

Archaeological artifacts connect ancient Sumeria to a highly developed society existing during the last ice age. That increases the possibility that another pre-Sumerian civilization, a Civilization X living in a golden age, may have also existed. A technologically advanced, sophisticated Civilization X, which we have come to know as Atlantis, represents a golden age society living in high prosperity and achievement. And that leads to questions about pre-Atlantean cultures.

The Athenian writer and philosopher, Plato, recorded in *Critias*, written around 2,400 years ago, a detailed description of the physical layout and location of Atlantis. He also described the nature of the society as a golden age. Plato's stories are considered fact, myth, or maybe a little of each.

Based on Plato's other writings, on those of his peers, and on oral histories, most researchers believe his account of the island paradise to be genuine. But even if he accurately recorded what he heard, there is no evidence to prove whether the original story of Atlantis, as told to Plato, is truth or myth.

Did Atlantis, or a technologically advanced Civilization X, exist? Geologic and archaeological records provide evidence for possible locations. An Atlantean culture will have to be discovered through patterns of cultural habits and recorded oral histories.

A culture represents a group of people with shared practices, beliefs, values, language, and social behavior. We can't know about the beliefs, values, or languages of the cultures existing during the last ice age, but interpretation of archaeological sites can provide evidence of group practices and social behavior.

Each new and exciting archaeological site discovered leaves many more still buried deep below civilization's encroachment or hidden within the last of our planet's wild areas. Each discovery has the potential to change scientific conclusions and to enhance historical timelines. One such discovery dated to 13,000 years ago in southwestern Turkey, the monolithic structure called Göbekli Tepe, indicates the presence of a technologically developed, sophisticated society or group of societies living there before the end of the last ice age.[6]

Some people surviving the cataclysmic worldwide destruction, flooding, and extinctions that ended the last ice age settled Mesopotamia and founded the ancient Empire of Sumeria. Thousands of years later severe droughts and hostile neighbors threatened their lifestyle. A core group of Sumerians fled to Canaan and eventually became Israelites.

Historians and archaeologists often refer to the confederation of city-states in Mesopotamia, Sumeria, as the "cradle of civilization," the beginning of our Western culture. So it seems fitting to begin with the Sumerian version of the creation of our world followed by a scientific perspective of world creation and the emergence of early cultures leading to today's modern world.

2

THE SUMERIAN CREATION STORY

Scientists and workers employed in Iraq by the British Museum excavated stone tablet fragments, and a few made of clay, from an archeological site containing the ruins of the ancient Babylonian Ashur-bani-pal Palace Library.

The tablets contained Sumerian stories, records, astronomical calculations, and other information. They were written in cuneiform almost 4,200 years ago, but the stories and information may be much older. The British Museum team transported the artifacts to London in 1952 and translated the inscriptions.[7]

Other historians and researchers translated the cuneiform after the British. Some translations refer to Earth, the Blue Planet, as Timat. Other tablets refer to goddess Timat. In some versions a destructive incoming astronomical body is referenced as Marduk.[8] Others refer to the planet Nibiru, sometimes called Neberu, as a star of the god Marduk, or as Nibiru, a place of crossing.[9]

The Babylonians referred to the planet Mercury as Marduk. The Sumerians referred to Marduk as son of Ea.[10]

The following is a compilation of translations published by the British Museum, the Electronic Text Corpus of Sumerian Literature Project, Stephanie Dalley, Samuel Noah Kramer, C. Leonard Woolley, Zecharia Sitchin, and E. A. Wallis Budge.[11]

IN THE BEGINNING

In our way of measuring time, it would be eons ago that a Great Consciousness existed in a primordial sea of breath, floating free, formless. Longing for experience, the awareness thought itself into formulas . . . and then into form.

A universe began.

Some misty new forms in transparent shapes could feel, and they could merge. But they couldn't grasp or hold. Drifting through space by the light of stars, they desired more. So, like a giant school of fish, sparkles of multicolored conscious lights flashed through the universe the way sardines glitter as they move synchronously through sharp turns and other sudden changes in direction. Along the way, they realized simultaneously that they searched for a home.

Excitement came slowly upon them for the first time. A new feeling. They liked it. A long time later the light sparkles found beautiful planet Timat covered with rippling blue water glistening under the rays of a suitably average star, a perpetual sun. The third planet out in a stable system. Home.

Some of the conscious light sparkles thought themselves around Timat and transformed into an invisible shield around her, pulsating toward the sun. The sparks of life remembered their expedition through the universe, and their thoughts etched the way into a path like an invisible current in a river.

Then they waited.

Out in the spans of the universe a large, dense planetary body in a dark corner gathered speed and mass, becoming Marduk. The planetary body took the path of least resistance and rolled along aimlessly through space. Marduk recklessly crashed into one terrestrial body after another on his unconscious journey, usually pulverizing each, hurling millions of new objects into the universe.

At some place in the void, Marduk slipped into the trail left by the light flashes on their way toward Timat. When Marduk reached the last solar system on the light route he didn't slow down as he entered a ring of dust at the outer edge. Marduk, only a few planets away from the center sun, perceived a pulsing force field. Fascination drew him closer.

In a high-risk, elaborate master plan the force field around Timat kicked out to push a nearby asteroid into a slightly different direction, crossing the path of incoming Marduk at the exact moment of his arrival at the designated location. Marduk destroyed the asteroid, turning it into many floating pieces. But the sacrifice of the asteroid changed Marduk's course enough to fulfill the requirements of the plan.

Timat waited as Marduk hurtled toward her. If she deviated even slightly he could miss her, ruining the plan. Moving in the wrong direction could cause Marduk to crash full on and destroy the ocean paradise she had created. Becoming dense in form in order to experience the physical ocean world, the light sparkles couldn't jump in and out between form and thought anymore. They needed Timat's protection.

Using her gravitational powers, she guided Marduk toward her.

Timat braced for contact.

The impact reverberated through the solar system as the dark planetary body smashed into Timat's side, ripping across her ocean floor causing a terrible deep wound. Her agony spiraled outward in all directions, causing a temporary whirlwind.

Marduk kept spinning forward on a new trajectory created by the collisions with the asteroid and with Timat. Trapped into an elliptical orbit inside the solar system, Marduk roams within his set path, moving close to Timat every few thousand years.

Timat's ocean rushed into the gashing, open wound to soothe her because water follows its nature, which is to equalize itself. As water filled the depths of her injury, part of the underwater landmass rose up above the waterline for the first time. A continent emerged.

Feeling delight, the Consciousness of the universe looked down on this creation.

Plants, grasses, and trees grew on the land. In the oceans plankton, coral reefs, and kelp forests thrived. Some of the sparks grew into physical beings, mighty creatures of the sea, swimming, playing, learning. For a long time, they thought and played in the water. The feel of the glittering blue wetness exhilarated them as they swam close to the sandy bottom of the sea and moved rhythmically in the warmth of the sun. Other physical beings lived on land and engaged in a variety of activities. Life on planet Timat was simple. And good.

A race of beings emerged in another part of the universe by taking physical forms on a virtual planet. They decided to call the universe their playground and they explored, and they collected resources. They became dense enough to grasp, and hold, and acquire.

The beings liked to travel through the cosmos. They decided to search the universe for their favorite new enchantment: gold. On their journey they learned they could travel by riding the wake of comets streaming through solar systems, one after another.

One time, moving along a familiar travel corridor, they followed a comet into a new, unfamiliar solar system. Curious, they stayed behind the comet and traveled deep inside the system. Eventually they found the Blue Planet.

These beings, among others for the first time, decided to name themselves the Annu.

The Annu became enchanted and amazed at the real landscapes and waters of Timat. Diverse forests, lush jungles with waterfalls, and steppes with grasses became their new playground. The landmasses, surrounded by turquoise-blue waters lapping white sand beaches, would provide them with everything they needed.

Eventually the Annu grew tired of looking for gold along riverbanks or depending upon chance findings in caves. They tired of physical labor. They needed a worker force to mine for gold and perform other tasks.

Time passed. Varieties of life forms lived on the continents. One day, the Annu watched as their Creator mixed blood with clay and brought humans to life. The Annu eventually merged with them to become modern humans.

Sumerian Influence

The Sumerian culture in Mesopotamia lasted from the first settlements 8,100 years ago to the fall of Ur 3,900 years ago. The Sumerian influence, however, may reach beyond the Middle East.

In the Sumerian/Akkadain language "Annu" has been translated to mean "royal blood," which may or may not be correct. The question arises as to whether this belief in the royal blood translation serves as the basis of authority for the so-called royal families in the days of ancient Egypt, Asia, and Rome up through the European, Asian, and other royals of today. Is a variation of the Sumerian Creation Story the basis for their claim to royal bloodlines?

The next chapter details the scientific creation story and explains the physical forces that shaped our planet.

3

EARTH: THE BLUE PLANET

The Sumerian Creation Story narrated in the previous chapter covered a time from the creation of the universe to the emergence of modern humans. The scientific account outlined in the following chapters follows roughly the same time period.

To calculate the age of our universe is a challenging task. Yet two distinctly different approaches have arrived at similar findings. The Maya Calendar, also called the Calendar of Nineveh, calculates the age of our universe to be 14.5 billion years. (As used in America, a billion is a thousand millions). Modern scientists have calculated the age to be 13.7 billion years.

In 2013, images and echo soundings from the Planck space telescope mapped background radiation from the early universe. Scientists recalculated the age, based on light and sound findings, to be 13.8 billion years.[12]

The scientific theory is called the Big Bang Theory. According to current Big Bang theory, the universe in the beginning may have been smaller than an atom, hot, dense, and compressed. In a split second it exploded, cooled, and expanded faster than the speed of light and to more than 100 trillion trillion times its size, separating time and space for the first time.[13][14] This "in the blink of an eye," expanding universe theory is based in part on Albert Einstein's 1915 Theory of General Relativity.[15]

Scientists hypothesize that four forces organize our cosmos. They are strong nuclear force that can bind atoms, gravity that can draw together particles of matter to form stars and planets, weak nuclear force that can cause our sun to warm us through a series of chain reactions, and electromagnetic force that can form a protective shield around Earth.[16]

The sun, an unexceptional star, is entirely plasma, called the fourth state of matter. The fusion of protons into helium nuclei at its core produces the energy equivalent of ten billion hydrogen bombs every second.[17] The electromagnetic shield surrounding Earth filters radiation from the sun.

The calculations of 4.6 billion years for the ages of Earth, the Blue Planet, and our solar system are based on analysis of lead isotope ratios in today's ores. The date may represent the age of Earth's core formation or the age of the material from which Earth formed.[18]

Geologists have divided Earth's past into eons, eras, periods, and epochs, usually based upon a geologic or mass-extinction event. Scientists consider the death of 75% or more of a species to be a mass extinction. Earth's history has four eons, each lasting half a billion years or more. Within the eons are ten eras, each lasting several hundred million years. An era can contain periods, epochs, and ages.

The Hadean eon began 4.6 billion years ago and represents the time the solar system and Earth formed. The Hadean eon ended and the second eon, the Archean eon, covers 4 billion to 2.5 billion years ago.

Earth is 8,000 miles (12,875 kilometers) in diameter and 25,000 miles (40,235 km) in circumference. The center of its core is approximately 4,000 miles (6,438 km) deep. The inner core is solid, approximately 70% the size of our moon, and it is lopsided, not spherical. It is 95% crystallized iron and 5% nickel. A hot, liquid iron outer core surrounds it. Between the core and the surface is Earth's mantle, a rocky shell about 1,800 miles (2,900 km) thick. Near the outer core the mantle becomes a viscous layer. On the top, Earth's crust covers the mantle. The continental part of the crust is granitic, and the crust under the oceans is basaltic.

In some places on Earth's surface the mantle is exposed. Tectonic activity pushed mantle rock to the surface in Newfoundland and Labrador. The third area of exposed mantle extends over thousands of square miles under the Atlantic Ocean. Scientists refer to this unexplained lesion as an open wound.[19] The Sumerians recorded in their Creation Story that a cometary impact early in Earth's history caused an open wound across an ocean floor.[20]

Successive volcanic eruptions and crust formation filled the first 2 billion years of Earth's history. Oceans covered Earth for about the first billion years. The last 2.5 billion years is about ice ages, asteroid impacts, supercontinents, supervolcanoes, and the emergence of life in many forms.

The oldest meteorites and lunar rocks found on Earth are 4.5 billion years old.[21] The oldest Earth rocks are in Canada in what is called the Canadian Shield. Repeated collisions of mineral-rich crust formed it 3.8 billion to 2 billion years ago.[22]

The magnetic field surrounded Earth 3.5 billion years ago in the shape of a pulsating spider at the same time that life began as organisms in an atmosphere lacking free oxygen (O_2).[23] Fossil remains of the anaerobic organisms are found in rocks.

Powerful solar outbursts and coronal mass ejections from the sun cause strong electrical discharges called plasma to hit

Earth in the form of hot, ionized gas. Ionized gas consists of electrically charged particles. Solar discharges can cause massive firestorms on Earth. Such plasma events cause auroras, that is, displays of colored lights present over the Arctic and adjacent regions. A geomagnetic storm is caused by a solar wind shockwave that interacts with Earth's magnetic field.

Asteroids are small planets, also called planetoids, usually consisting of a composite of mostly iron with some nickel. Some asteroids contain diamonds.

A meteoroid is a particle of space debris ranging in size from a grain of sand to a boulder.

A bolide is a generic, large crater-forming projectile such as a rocky or metallic asteroid, meteor, or comet, when the type of projectile is not known. A comet releases gases.

Scientists estimate that around 15,000 tons of meteoroids, micrometeoroids, and space dust enter Earth's atmosphere yearly. Micrometeoroids are small particles of space rock weighing less than a gram.[24]

When an asteroid, or a piece of an asteroid, or a meteoroid, or a comet survives the initial impact of Earth's atmosphere and crashes to the ground it is called a meteorite. Earth receives meteorite hits regularly. Based on data known today, Earth has had four major and hundreds of minor impacts. Each major strike caused a worldwide chain reaction.

Supercontinents form when floating continents are pulled together toward something radiating heat, such as a series of volcanic eruptions. The pieces of Earth's crust merge into a single landmass. The supercontinent breaks apart when volcanic activity or an impact from space weakens the crust and the continents drift apart. Between 3.1 billion to 2.8 billion years ago, Vaalbara, also called Ur, the theorized first supercontinent, formed and broke apart.[25]

The third eon, the Proterozoic, covers 2.5 billion years ago to 543 million years ago, and contains important geologic events in Earth's history. Continents stabilized over a billion years and complex multicellular organisms evolved.[26] This eon contains the Paleoproterozoic, the Mesoproterozoic, and the Neoproterozoic eras.

Paleoproterozoic Era 2.5 Billion to 1.6 Billion Years Ago

This era begins with the first extinction event, the first ice age, has two major impact events, and ends with the breakup of a supercontinent.

Excess free oxygen started to accumulate about 2.5 billion years ago in the atmosphere. Called the Great Oxygenation Event, it allowed a different type of bacterium to begin to grow. These blue-green algae, cyanobacteria, are formed by oxygenic photosynthesis, and this activity changed the atmosphere into oxidized air, toxic to the anaerobic organisms.[27]

The Great Oxygenation Event is also called the Great Oxygenation Catastrophe because the increase in oxygenation may have caused the extinction of the anaerobic organisms. The excess free oxygen may have reacted with greenhouse gases in the atmosphere. And this along with other factors such as Earth's rotation and sun activity may have led to the first ice age.[28]

Glacial periods, or ice ages, occur when ice sheets form in the Northern and Southern hemispheres. Intermittent warm periods occur during ice ages. An interglacial is a warm period lasting more than 10,000 years.

Sometimes an extreme cold period occurs during an interglacial warm period. An extreme cold period lasting less than 10,000 years and that occurs during an interglacial warm period is called a stadial.

Snowball Earth is a term used when Earth's surface becomes nearly or entirely frozen over during an ice age. A theory that

Earth, including the oceans, entirely froze over is controversial. Geoscientists in Scotland discovered evidence indicating that regions of Earth's oceans may have remained unfrozen during the Snowball periods.[29]

Greenhouse Earth is a time when warm tropical temperatures may reach the poles.

The first ice age occurred 2.4 billion to 2.1 billion years ago. One of the longest and severest, a Snowball Earth episode, it lasted 300 million years. It is named the Huronian glaciation because researchers discovered ice core evidence in the Lake Huron region of the United States and Canada.

An asteroid impact in South Africa formed the 6.2 mile (10 km) wide Vredefort Crater 2 billion years ago. It is one of the oldest and largest impact craters found on Earth. The crater is 186 miles (300 km) across.[30]

The first verified supercontinent, Nuna, also called Columbia, formed 1.8 billion years ago and broke apart 300 million years later. Researchers discovered evidence of the supercontinent in the Columbia River region of the northwestern United States.[31]

Mesoproterozoic Era 1.6 Billion to 1 Billion Years Ago

In this era, multicellular organisms emerged and continental plates developed. The second largest impact crater on Earth occurred in the Sudbury Basin in Ontario, Canada, from a bolide strike 1.5 billion years ago. The bolide is estimated to be 6.2 miles (10 km) wide which left a crater 39 miles (62 km) long, and 9.3 miles (15 km) deep, and may have broken the supercontinent Nuna apart.[32][33] Nuna, or Columbia, broke apart into three free-floating continents called Arctica, Atlantica, and Nena.[34]

A craton is a large block of Earth's crust that has been relatively stable for a billion or more years. A craton is hard enough and thick enough to withstand rifting (pulling apart). The North American craton, one of the fragments of the Arctica continent, forms most of North America. The Canadian Shield is the exposed part of the bedrock.

NEOPROTEROZOIC ERA 1 BILLION TO 543 MILLION YEARS AGO

The first deep-origin volcanic eruption happened a billion years ago fusing the Arabian and the Somalian tectonic plates to the Nubian plate expanding Africa into today's continent. Africa, Arctica, Atlantica, and Nena then moved toward volcanic eruptions forming mountain ranges in North America, Mexico, and Western Europe. The four continents became the supercontinent Rodinia for the next 300 million years.[35]

Something happened 720 million years ago that broke Rodinia apart and ushered in the next ice age. Scientists theorize that volcanic activity may have separated the supercontinent and resulted in a period of glaciation.[36] Arctica fragments are called Greenland, Laurentia (North America), Scotland, Siberia, and eastern Antarctica.

The second ice age, the Sturtian glaciation, occurred 720 million to 660 million years ago. The Sturt River Gorge of Southern Australia provided the evidence for this ice age, classified as a Snowball Earth episode because it reached tropical latitudes. Some scientists refer to this 60-million-year-long glaciation as a slushball episode.[37]

Animal life in the form of sponges began at the end of the Sturtian glaciation 660 million years ago.[38]

The third ice age occurred 650 million to 635 million years ago and lasted 15 million years. The Marinoan glaciation, also called the Elatina glaciation, is considered a Snowball Earth ice age. Scientists consider it the severest because glaciers may have reached as far as the equator. This ice age may have ended abruptly due to a massive release of methane from equatorial permafrost.[39]

Nearly a hundred million years after the Marinoan glaciation, a rapid emergence of flora and fauna marks the beginning of the fourth eon, the Phanerozoic. It began 543 million years ago and continues today. This fourth eon contains the Paleozoic, the Mesozoic, and the Cenozoic eras.

PALEOZOIC ERA 543 MILLION TO 250 MILLION YEARS AGO

Plant and animal life started emerging 543 million years ago in an intense period of activity lasting 5 million to 10 million years called the Cambrian Explosion. Scientists determined that most of the plant and animal organisms emerged fully developed because ancestral forms from earlier periods have not been discovered.[40]

The fourth ice age, the Andean-Saharan glaciation, occurred 460 million to 430 million years ago, lasting 30 million years. Ice covered only part of Earth.

The fifth ice age, 360 million to 260 million years ago, is named the Karoo Ice Age from evidence found in the Karoo region of South Africa. This ice age lasted 100 million years and did not cover the entire planet.

Massive volcanoes erupted over a million-year period in Siberia 252 million years ago creating a region today called the Siberian Traps. Toxic gases and debris from the eruptions raining down may have caused Earth's oceans to turn acidic. Researchers have linked the ocean acidity to a mass extinction lasting 60,000 years and devastating life at the time of the Siberian eruptions.[41]

Mesozoic Era 250 Million to 65 Million Years Ago

The supercontinent Pangaea formed at the beginning of this era 250 million years ago. Plant and animal life recovered, developed, and expanded. A large magma flow, a superplume, erupted in Pangaea 30 million years after the supercontinent formed. Volcanic eruptions weakened the crust for its entire length.[42]

The superplume that erupted 220 million years ago through the center of Pangaea created the Mid-Atlantic Ridge, the longest mountain range in the world. Volcanic eruptions occurred over the next million or more years from the middle of Pangaea north to the Arctic Ocean and south to a junction of three tectonic plates near Antarctica. Pangaea separated into two halves and then into present-day continents. The splitting created the Atlantic Ocean.

The Mid-Atlantic Ridge is part of a continuous system of ridges on Earth's ocean floors, and it is a boundary between tectonic plates. Magma from Earth's molten mantle reaches the seafloor and erupts as lava through the surface to form new layers of crust along this boundary.[43]

In this era the first primates developed as early as 85 million years ago in Africa. The oldest recorded primate fossil is dated at 55 million years ago; however, scientists have calculated the earlier emergence date from other evidence.[44]

Another mass extinction occurred at the end of this era. A gigantic asteroid had broken up in a space collision 160 million years ago, and one or more massive pieces hit the Yucatán Peninsula, Mexico, 65 million years ago. Called the (K-Pg) Chicxulub extinction event, it may have been the cause or a major factor of a mass extinction known as the end of the dinosaur age, when 90% of species were wiped out.[45]

Apiece of the asteroid 6 miles (10 km) wide entered Earth's atmosphere and struck Earth as a meteorite, causing tremendous damage. Upon impact, it left a crater 112 miles (180 km) wide and 12 miles (20 km) deep.[46]

CENOZOIC ERA 65 MILLION YEARS AGO TO PRESENT

A worldwide impact winter blocking the sun's warmth and light from Earth's surface and lasting years or decades followed the meteorite strike in the Yucatán Peninsula 65 million years ago.

Between 37 million and 24 million years ago a series of volcanic eruptions formed the Alps and the Carpathians in southern Europe and the Atlas Mountains in northwestern Africa.

A superplume begins in the mantle of Earth. The African and the Pacific superplume fields are Earth's two sources. Both run laterally for thousands of miles and might, in some places, rise as much as 620 miles (1,000 km) vertically. This creates hotspots where cracks in Earth's crust exist or where plate movement occurs.

Sometimes volcanic eruptions eject magma so quickly that the surrounding land collapses into the emptied magma chamber causing a depression called a caldera.

The magma plume under eastern sub-Sahara Africa 30 million years ago weakened fault lines. The Arabian Plate split off from the continent 30 million to 25 million years ago to form the Arabian Peninsula.[47]

Yellowstone National Park is part of the Yellowstone Plateau in the Great Plains of the United States. The park sits over a hotspot where molten mantle rock rises toward the surface. The hotspot originates deep in Earth's crust and it may be a superplume. The Yellowstone hotspot has generated eruptions over millions of years, some massive enough to be classified as supereruptions.[48]

One of the largest known volcanic eruptions occurred in North America 23 million years ago forming La Garita Caldera in Colorado. Major volcanic eruptions such as La Garita have global consequences. Extinction events occur because of the dust and chemicals pumped into the atmosphere, screening the sun and cooling the planet. For several years after La Garita, Earth experienced a perpetual volcanic winter, like an impact winter, which could have caused plant and animal species to die out.[49]

At the time of the La Garita eruption, the Strait of Gibraltar closed for the first time, sealing off the Tethys Ocean, site of today's Mediterranean Sea. Over the next several million years it broke open and closed a few more times.

Ten million years ago the Great Rift Valley formed when the magma plume under western Africa weakened fault lines along the edges of the Nubian and Somalian tectonic plates and they began pulling apart from western Africa up through Israel.[50]

The Strait of Gibraltar closed again 5.6 million years ago and the Tethys became isolated. The Tethys evaporated over the next thousand years and the Mediterranean basin became mostly an arid region such as Death Valley in present-day California. Seafloor spreading in the Atlantic caused a channel to break open through the Strait of Gibraltar creating a megaflood around 5.3 million years ago.[51] The basin filled into today's Mediterranean Sea.

(See Appendix: Earth Timeline)

4

EARLY HUMAN CULTURE

TIMELINE (y.a. = years ago)

4 million y.a. .... Stone tools in Great Rift Valley, Africa
4–3 million y.a. ....*Australopithecus* genus, Africa
3 million y.a. ....*Homo* genus, Africa
2.6 million y.a. ....Sixth ice age, Quaternary glaciation
2.3–1.5 million y.a. .... *Homo habilis*, Africa
2 million–12,000 y.a. .... *Homo floresiensis*, Indonesia
1.85 million–70,000 y.a. ....*Homo erectus*, West Central Asia
800,000-11,500 y.a. .... *Archaic Homo sapiens*, worldwide
200,000–30,000 y.a. .... *Homo sapiens Neandertalensis*, Early Canaan
160,000 y.a. ....Anatomically modern, *Homo sapiens idaltu*, Africa
130,000 y.a. .... Cro-Magnon, *Homo sapiens sapiens*, Early Canaan
74,000 y.a. .... Supervolcano reduces world population

By 4 million years ago the Great Rift Valley had widened into an enormous, sediment-filled valley approximately 3,700 miles (6,000 km) long with rivers, lakes, and a variety of lush vegetation.[52] It starts in the Bekaa Valley, Lebanon, and goes through Israel's Lake Kinneret (Sea of Galilee) and the Dead Sea to the Gulf of Eilat and the Red Sea. The Great Rift Valley is not continuous in Africa. It is a series of valleys from the Horn of Africa to Mozambique in West Africa.

The first stone tools and the first toolkit industry developed in the Great Rift Valley around 4 million years ago. *Australopithecus*, a short, slender, bipedal hominid, emerged in the Afar region of Ethiopia around 4 million years ago and lived until around 3 million years ago. The first find, nicknamed "Lucy," indicated that adults of this group stood 3 feet to 4 feet tall (about 1 meter).[53] *A. afarensis, A. deyiremeda*, and other bipedal primates shared parts of the Great Rift Valley and used early stone tools.[54]

The Homo genus, which modern humans belong to, emerged around 3 million years ago in and around the Great Rift Valley. Archeologists discovered a piece of a lower jawbone in the Afar region of Ethiopia dated to 2.8 million years ago. The fossil has both *A. afarensis* and Homo features of a hybridized individual.[55]

Stone tool technology changed in Africa before the onset of the last ice age. By 2.6 million years ago the toolkits contained choppers, scrapers, and pounders.[56]

Around 2.6 million years ago tectonic plate movement formed the Isthmus of Panama connecting North America and South America. The narrow strip of land separated the Atlantic and Pacific oceans and created the Gulf Stream. Formation of the Gulf Stream may have been one of the factors causing the sixth, or present, ice age.[57] This ice age called the Quaternary glaciation started 2.5 million years ago, beginning the Pleistocene Epoch. Changes in climate caused by several factors, including periodic variation in solar radiation reaching Earth, resulted in a series of glacial periods and interglacial warm periods lasting until 11,700 years ago, ending the Pleistocene epoch.

Each time a glacial period developed during this sixth ice age huge volumes of water became frozen as part of continental ice sheets and glaciers. This resulted in dramatic sea-level drops. Then, during interglacial warm periods, coastlines drowned as sea levels rose quickly from melting ice.

Scientists have identified eleven major glacial events and many minor ones during this ice age. Climate change causing glacial advancement and retreat is related to different factors such as major impact or eruption events and the effects of solar radiation. Cycles of the sun affecting ice ages are called the Milankovitch cycles named for Milutin Milankovitch.

Short African humans called *Homo habilis* lived in the African part of the Great Rift Valley from 2.3 million years ago to 1.5 million years ago. *Homo habilis* in Africa used small, distinct stone tools.

H. habilis, or a close relative, may have migrated during a warm period to Indonesia 2 million years ago to become *Homo floresiensis*, nicknamed Hobbit People, who lived on a remote Indonesian island. *H. floresiensis* also used small, distinct stone tools. On Flores, a large, remote Indonesian island, an expedition from Australia's University of Woollongong in 2004 discovered bones of small primitive people in a vast limestone cavern. The team named them *Homo floresiensis* and called them Hobbit People because adults stood about 3 feet high (1 meter) and they had long flapper feet. Their feet and wrists resembled those of African hominids. Their facial structure matched that of *H. habilis*, who lived in Africa 2.3 million years ago.[58]

Small stone tools dating from 2 million years ago to 12,000 years ago have been found on Flores and on a nearby island. *H. habilis* died out in Africa 1.5 million years ago while *H. floresiensis* lasted until 12,000 years ago during the catastrophic end of the last ice age.[59]

During an interglacial warm period, *H. erectus* emerged 1.85 million years ago in the Caucasus Mountain region and lived on every continent until 70,000 years ago. *H. ergaster* emerged 1.8 million years ago in Africa and lived until 1.4 million years ago. Some paleoanthropologists consider *H. ergaster* to be a separate species. Others define both groups as African and Asian populations of *H. erectus*. The African group coexisted with *H. habilis* for 300,000 years.[60]

Stone tools consisting of choppers, scrapers, and pounders, changed about 1.7 million years ago.[61] In the 1940s, archaeologist Hallam Movius studied human toolkits dated from a million years ago to around 500,000 years ago. On a map, he drew a line, now called the Movius Line, to separate the two lithic toolkit areas.

Lithic toolkits contain stone tools. Bifacial means the tools had two edges, each different. The tools were sharpened on two sides and used as a multipurpose knife or hand axe.

People in northern India, Pakistan, northern China, Myanmar (Burma), Indonesia, and Malaysia, north of the Movius Line, used stone chopping tools and may have used bamboo tools. South of the Movius Line, bifacial implements such as picks, cleavers, and hand axes have been found in Western Europe, the Middle East, Africa, and southern India. The Movius Line suggests that two early cultures developed simultaneously and that *H. ergaster* settled north of the Movius Line, *H. erectus* south of it. Fossil evidence supports a difference in the two cultures.[62]

Also called Upright Man, *H. erectus* lived in hunter-gatherer societies, controlled fire, and may have been first to have a human voice. Scientists think they were capable of language. *H. erectus* manufactured a sophisticated stone tool technology around 1.6 million years ago until about a million years ago. *H. erectus* settled throughout Africa, the Caucasus Mountain region, Western Europe, Turkey, Russia, the Middle East, India,

Indonesia, China, and Southeast Asia. They may have migrated to continents and islands all over the world by using rafts to travel over oceans.[63]

In northern Israel, *H. erectus* excavations dating from 790,000 to 690,000 years ago show evidence of production and use of stone tools and controlled use of fire. The sites suggest that they could light fires. Israeli archaeologists reported that the Gesher Benot Ya'qov site, situated along the Dead Sea rift in the Hula Valley in Israel, contains eight layers of occupation. The Hula Valley is near the source of the Jordan River. Each layer spans several generations. All layers had remnants of ancient hearths.[64]

Anthropologists in China discovered a site near Beijing with at least four layers of occupation indicating controlled use of fire. One of the first *H. erectus* discoveries, called Peking Man, is dated to 680,000 to 780,000 years ago. At the site they excavated remains of *H. erectus* and, in another layer dated 500,000 to 300,000 years ago, a cache of stone tools.[65]

Israeli archaeologists excavated a *H. erectus* site in France with evidence of controlled fire dating to around 300,000 years ago.[66]

H. erectus is not known for producing jewelry or art objects, but two items have been found that were altered by *H. erectus* people. They are called Venus figurines because their appearance has the morphology of the later Cro-Magnon Venus figurines. Some scientists dispute the classification because the figurines may be natural formations with some carving marks found on them.[67]

One, the Venus of Tan-Tan, is from a small piece of quartzite rock. Found in Morocco by a visiting German archaeologist, it is at least 300,000 years old. Scientists found remnants of red ochre pigments and a greasy substance indicating paint smudged on it.[68] Ochre is the earliest pigment used for dye. It is derived from naturally tinted clay containing mineral oxides.

The other, the Venus of Berekhat, is a modified red tufic pebble (compressed volcanic ash) found at Berekhat Ram in the Golan Heights, Israel. It is dated at 265,000 to 230,000 years old. The Venus of Berekhat is displayed at the Israeli National Museum.[69]

Archaic humans first appeared between 800,000 and 500,000 years ago and died out or merged with other humans at different times. The last archaic humans may have been the Red Deer Cave People who lived in China until around 11,500 years ago.[70] Scientists debate how to classify *archaic H. sapiens*. Some include them in the *Homo sapiens* group, while others classify them as a separate species. A variety of *archaic H. sapiens* human fossils have been found representing several types.

Scientists don't know when spoken language started. Scientists studying *archaic H. sapiens* fossils from Spain have produced a computer model of the bones to determine what kinds of sounds would be transmitted. In the fossils they found middle ear bones capable of hearing sounds that humans use to differentiate speech sounds.[71]

In North America, the Yellowstone Caldera, one of the four overlapping calderas in the Yellowstone Plateau volcanic field, formed from a supereruption around 600,000 years ago.[72]

In Europe, Western Asia, and Africa, archaic modern humans called *Homo heidelbergensis* lived 500,000 to 250,000 years ago. They used ochre and they buried their dead. *H. heidelbergensis* in Europe and Western Asia stood about 5 feet 5 inches tall (1.6 meters) and in South Africa they averaged around 7 feet tall (2.1 meters).[73]

Neandertals lived in caves in Early Canaan from 200,000

years ago to 45,000 years ago. They may have shared caves with early Cro-Magnons 90,000 years ago to 80,000 years ago. Canaan Neandertals occupied a limited range of territory from northern Israel to the southern coastline of the Black Sea.

Another, more primitive group of Neandertals occupied territory in central Europe, the Balkans, France, and the Iberian Peninsula from at least 176,000 years ago until they went extinct 30,000 years ago.[74] Some European Neandertals engaged in cannibalism.[75] They lived in small, isolated groups of 100 to 200 individuals with a combined population of around 70,000 at any given time.[76] Neandertal sites have not been found in Africa.

They were short, the males averaging less than 5 feet 5 inches (1.6 meters). They were extremely strong, they probably had red hair, and they had rounded eye sockets that would have given them a wide-eyed appearance. The most distinctive physical feature is a protrusion, shaped like a bun, on the back of their skulls.[77]

A Neandertal site in Croatia has yielded over 1,000 tools dated between 120,000 and 130,000 years ago. An important find at that site is an eagle talon necklace. Neandertal jewelry and art artifacts are rare.[78] Neandertals engaged in rituals and created art.[79] They buried their dead with the arms crossed over the chest, like ancient Egyptians.[80] The name Neandertal derives from the Neander Valley in Germany where scientists excavated one of the first fossils. Most scientists now classify this group as *Homo sapiens Neandertalensis* and think they had complex language skills.

Scientists in 2010 published the results of a project that sequenced Neandertal genes from recovered DNA. The scientists found between 1% and 4% Neandertal DNA in modern-day European, Middle Eastern, and Siberian populations.[81]

The Basque people of Spain and France share DNA markers with Celts, Scandinavians, and North African Berbers. The

Basque population has 40% RH negative blood type. Caucasians have an average of 15% RH negative blood type, while Africans, Asians, and Indians have only rare cases.[82] The Basque population also has the characteristic Neandertal "bun" on the back of the skulls. These are indicators of interbreeding between Cro-Magnon and Neandertal people.[83]

Shared qualities exist in appearance and behavior among today's populations and Cro-Magnons, archaic modern humans, and Neandertals.

Anatomically modern humans, *Homo sapiens idaltu*, emerged in the southern part of the Great Rift Valley. Their sites have been found throughout Africa. The oldest known *H. sapiens idaltu* fossil site is 155,000 to 160,000 years old in Omo National Park near the village of Herto in southwestern Ethiopia. Paleontologists refer to this anatomically modern human group as a possible transition from hominid to modern human. *H. sapiens idaltu* may also represent a group of hybrid humans.[84]

Dry, freezing-cold ice age conditions kept the planet locked in a full glacial world from 150,000 years ago until a rapid warming phase began the Eemian interglacial around 130,000 years ago.[85] The global climate became warmer and moister than today, and a group of modern humans may have left Africa in a wave of migration during the 20,000-year Eemian interglacial.[86]

Early Cro-Magnon people, *Homo sapiens sapiens*, first appeared in the area of Early Canaan 130,000 years ago at the beginning of the warm period.[87] Stone tools found on Crete mean they probably inhabited Aegean islands 130,000 years ago.[88]

The name Cro-Magnon derives from the name of a rock

cave in southern France where the first fossils were discovered in 1868.

Early Cro-Magnons also resided in the area of Morocco. An important archaeological site in Morocco, Jebel Irhound Cave, is known for numerous hominid fossils discovered there. Two different testing methods dated early Cro-Magnon remains in the cave to be either 190,000 or 90,000 years old. Before additional tests were conducted, the Islamic Moroccan government allowed the cave to be quarried for two decades, destroying the site.[89]

An excavated site, Skhul Cave on the slopes of Mount Carmel in Israel, contained remains of ten early Cro-Magnon individuals. Four had clearly been buried. The others may have been buried but the site had been disturbed and scientists couldn't be sure. Early Cro-Magnon occupation is evidenced there from 130,000 to 90,000 years ago.[90] Another early Cro-Magnon set of remains at this site is dated to 80,000 years ago.[91]

A similar site in Israel, the Qafzeh Cave in a rock shelter in Lower Galilee, contained early Cro-Magnon remains dated to between 115,000 and 90,000 years ago. The Qafzeh site yielded several human graves, flint artifacts, animal bones, red ochre, and necklace shells brought from the Mediterranean coast. Similar shell beads found at the Pigeon Cave site in Morocco are 82,000 years old and those in Blombos Cave, South Africa, are 73,000 years old.[92]

The skulls found at the Qafzeh and Skhul caves have a modern human appearance with possible archaic traits. The skulls have been variously classified as hominid, as Neandertal hybridization, and as robust Cro-Magnons. Scientists now generally agree that these skulls represent a separate lineage from the Neandertals.[93] The Moroccan early Cro-Magnon remains from Jebel Irhound Cave were from the same *H. sapiens sapiens* group as the Qafzeh and Skhul finds.[94]

In southern China at the Zhiren Cave site, archeologists in 2007 identified a jawbone and several molars of an early Cro-Magnon individual dated 100,000 years old.[95]

Early Cro-Magnons occupied the Tabun Cave at Mount Carmel in northern Israel 90,000 to 80,000 years ago. They may have shared the cave with Neandertals.[96]

The British government claimed Israel as its de facto territory after World War I. English archaeologists, researchers, and treasure hunters between 1929 and 1934 ran all over Israel collecting artifacts and shipping them back to London to store, sell, or display in British museums. The Tabun Cave site yielded a 120,000-year-old female Neandertal skeleton and a set of seven teeth. The scientists who discovered the teeth classified them at first as belonging to a Bronze Age individual (around 5,000 years old).[97]

Tests revealed the teeth dated to 90,000 years ago. English scientists reclassified the specimens, all from one individual, to be baby Neandertal teeth. Some scientists now believe the teeth to be early Cro-Magnon. Chronology is part of the evidence for classifying the teeth as Neandertal, and because British scientists did not accept that modern humans lived in Early Canaan 90,000 years ago they concluded that the teeth must therefore be Neandertal. The teeth have been in storage at the London Natural History Museum since 1955.[98]

British scientists published *The stone age of Mount Carmel: Report of the Joint Expedition of the British School of Archaeology in Jerusalem and the American School of Prehistoric Research* at the conclusion of the 1929-1934 excavations.[99] British scientists considered the matter of modern human emergence in Early Canaan closed because they considered themselves to be the final authority on the subject. British and American scientists disregarded the importance of Early Canaan as the birthplace of modern human occupation and development. In their reports the region east of the Mediterranean Sea is referred to only as "the gates of Europe."[100]

Following the end of the long, warm Eemian interglacial period 110,000 years ago, a huge ice mass called the Laurentide Ice Sheet formed 95,000 years ago covering hundreds of thousands of square miles of North America. The water trapped in the ice sheet, in some places over 2 miles (3.2 km) thick, lowered sea levels and exposed extended continental shelves and formerly submerged islands worldwide.[101]

The climate cooled and warmed slightly after the Eemian interglacial until a massive explosion 74,000 years ago plunged Earth into a full glacial world again.[102]

(See Appendix: Earth Timeline)

5

TOBA CATASTROPHE

Three major volcanic eruptions occurred over the last million years in Indonesia. The third and largest eruption blasted out of Sumatra 74,000 years ago. Called the Toba supervolcanic eruption because the force of it formed massive Lake Toba, it affected human and animal populations worldwide.[103]

It ejected magma into the air that covered an estimated 200,000 square miles (518,000 km^2) of land and oceans, and sent an estimated 6 billion tons of sulfur dioxide, ash, and debris into the atmosphere. Sulfur dioxide is a toxic gas with a caustic, irritating smell. This eruption may have caused a decade-long volcanic winter followed by thousands of years of dry, cold climate.[104]

Environmental events such as floods, volcanoes, and droughts, or human activities such as war or genocide can sharply reduce a population. The human gene pool is limited to a small group of survivors after an extinction event. That is called a bottleneck because a smaller population can concentrate unfavorable genetic traits.

The Toba catastrophe theory is that a bottleneck of the human population occurred following the eruption and volcanic winter. The extreme environmental conditions forced the survivors to adopt new survival strategies, including migrating to places where food sources existed or could be developed while Earth became freezing cold for thousands of years.[105]

Scientists estimate that the event reduced the world population to around 15,000 people. Genetic evidence shows that today's humans descend from a small population from around the time of the Indonesian eruption.[106]

Vegetation die-off from the darkened skies and lack of rain destroyed food sources for humans and animals. The Eastern chimpanzee, the Borneo orangutan, the cheetah, the tiger, and many other animals have genetic variations tracing to around the time of the Toba eruption. The gene pools of eastern and western lowland gorillas reveal that those populations also suffered a bottleneck at that time.[107]

Before the explosion Earth's climate had been in a long, mild period. Imagine people watching the sky darken with ash and debris. The traumatized survivors, living in darkness through the volcanic winter while inhaling sulfur dioxide and foraging for dwindling food sources and clean water, would have to endure life-threatening dangers to stay alive. Infections would be rampant because of emergency living conditions, lack of nutrition, and exposure to parasites and insects.

What would life be like under these uncontrollable circumstances? Inhaling sulfur dioxide is associated with difficulty in breathing and premature death. Also, exposure to sulfur dioxide and infections may be factors in preterm birth, when a baby's organs are not mature enough to allow normal postnatal survival. Preterm infants are at greater risk for complications including disabilities and impaired mental development.[108]

Homo floresiensis, the three-foot-tall hobbit-like people on the isolated Indonesian island of Flores, may have survived the initial effects of the massive eruption because they were upwind of the explosion. After the eruption they moved into their limestone cavern refuge for the next thousand or more years.[109]

The island of Flores is their only known habitat. Sophisticated stone tools associated with these small people were found in the cavern. Skeletal remains indicate *H. floresiensis* lived underground 74,000 years ago, 38,000 years ago, and 13,000 years ago. Similar stone tools dated 2 million to 1.1 million years old have been found on the island.[110]

The tools and skeletal remains are evidence that *H. floresiensis* survived the effects of the Toba eruption.

Refuges near oceans provided marine food sources. Fossil and artifact evidence indicates that early Cro-Magnon people may have migrated after the eruption from Early Canaan through the Great Rift Valley to South African coastal caves.

Blombos Cave on the coast of South Africa may have been a refuge during disasters. Scientists have found evidence that three different groups of people lived for brief periods in the cave between 140,000 to 100,000 years ago. People occupied the cave again 78,000 years ago, and 73,000 to 71,000 years ago. Over 8,000 pieces of ochre and some stone tools were found in the oldest layer. Many ochre pieces had been rubbed smooth, probably to make pigment powder, perhaps for decorative body paint. Ochre is frequently found at sites less than 100,000 years old.[111]

Teeth from five to seven people and bone tools including grinding stones have been uncovered in the middle and youngest levels of the cave. The youngest layer, 73,000 years old, contained bone and stone tools, marine shell beads, and a piece of engraved ochre a few inches long. One side, rubbed smooth, is covered with a complex geometric design of overlapping lines, some parallel, some triangular. It is considered the oldest known object of prehistoric art.[112]

In the center of the engraving, and part of the geometric design, is an image that looks like "The Star of David" or the "Shield of David." Before the reign of ancient Israel's King David, the Hebraic people called that symbol the "Morning Star" or the "Shield of the Morning Star." Some scientists thought the carefully etched marks represented a random doodle. However, thirteen more stones with the same pattern have been found.[113]

Distinct pressure-flaked tools were also found at this layer.[114] Pressure flaking is a method of shaping a stone into a tool by pressing a sharp animal bone or antler on the stone instead of striking it. The pressure-flaking technique, a complicated shaping method, produces finely detailed and sharper tools.

Similar pressure-flaked artifacts had first been found dating to 22,000 years ago in Spanish caves. Anthropologists thought the distinctive arrowheads and other unique tools and artifacts to be a European culture named Solutrean that emerged across southern Europe and disappeared around 17,000 years ago.[115] However, the recent finds at Blombos Cave in South Africa dating similar pressure-flaked tools to 73,000 years ago disproved that theory.

Shell necklace beads from the Mediterranean Sea found in early Cro-Magnon cave shelters in Israel and in Blombos Cave at the 73,000-year-old level suggest that early Cro-Magnon people migrated from Early Canaan to Blombos Cave in South Africa after the Toba supervolcanic eruption. Early Cro-Magnons occupied the cave for a thousand years.[116]

The Solutrean people may have already been in Africa or they may have migrated there after the Toba eruption darkened Earth's skies. They might have used the cave shelter at the same time or a different time than the early Cro-Magnon people from Early Canaan.

The South African Still Bay culture settled close to and in the Blombos Cave area 78,000 years ago and also left 71,000 ago. A later culture, called the Howiesons Poort culture, arrived in South Africa 65,000 years ago, lived near Blombos Cave and left 60,000 years ago when the climate began to warm.[117][118] Their artifacts have not been found after they abandoned their rock shelters in South Africa.[119]

Sub-Saharan Africa became a large refuge for many of Earth's peoples after the Toba supervolcanic explosion and subsequent volcanic winter. Neandertals survived in cave shelters in southern Europe and in Early Canaan.

Human populations also survived in the Himalayan Mountains and in southern India. More early Cro-Magnons entered the plains of India 73,000 years ago and may have lived as farmers and foragers until around 55,000 years ago.[120]

By 70,000 years ago thick ice sheets covered much of northern Europe, Siberia, and North America. *H. erectus* became extinct 70,000 years ago at the peak of the dry, cold, glacial aftermath of the Toba supervolcanic eruption. Forests had turned into grasslands, and in some areas grassland had turned to desert.[121]

The warmer climate 60,000 years ago brought the Cro-Magnon people back to Early Canaan where they interbred with Neandertals for thousands of years.[122]

The following chapter is about development of the highly organized Cro-Magnon Aurignacian culture. The term "Cro-Magnon" is used by the archaeological community. Other scientists prefer the term "Early Modern Human" and use the designation EMH.

6

FIRST ADVANCED SOCIETIES

TIMELINE (y.a. = years ago)

55,000–20,000 y.a. .... Cro-Magnons in Early Canaan
44,000–26,000 y.a. .... Cro-Magnons settle in Europe, Russia
42,000–39,000 y.a. .... Cro-Magnon/archaic/
Neandertal hybrids in China
30,000 y.a. .... Neandertals become extinct
20,000 y.a. .... Kebaran nomads occupy northern Canaan
13,000 y.a. .... Natufians from North Africa
occupy southern Canaan

Around 60,000 years ago Earth began to warm intermittently, ice sheets partially melted, and some grassland steppes became wooded.[123] A large group of modern humans migrated out of Africa around 60,000 years ago.[124] They may have been the descendants of the peoples who journeyed into Africa after the Toba supervolcanic eruption.

A stable warm period called Oxygen Isotope Stage 3 began 57,000 years ago. Oxygen isotope stages record warm and cool periods in Earth's climate. Evidence of climate change is found in pollen and plankton remains and in calcite.

The warm weather gave life forms an opportunity to grow and flourish. An abundance of vegetation promoted human migrations. Human populations surviving the Toba supervolcanic eruption, the subsequent volcanic winter, and the following cold climate period began to expand.[125]

Tabun Cave at Mount Carmel in Israel showcases the longest-known time of intermittent human occupation. Neandertals lived in the cave beginning 200,000 years ago, early Cro-Magnons shared the cave 90,000 to 80,000 years ago, and Cro-Magnons returned to share the cave again 55,000 years ago.[126] Cro-Magnons began to occupy cave shelters, including known Neandertal sites, in Early Canaan along the Mediterranean coastline around 60,000 years ago.[127] These Cro-Magnon people living after the Toba supervolcanic event show features indicating a slightly less robust physique than do the early Cro-Magnons.

Genetic studies indicate that Neandertals and Cro-Magnons first interbred in Early Canaan between 60,000 and 50,000 years ago. Archaeologists found a Neandertal site occupied from 61,000 to 48,000 years ago at Kebera Cave in northern Israel. Israeli scientists have identified a female Cro-Magnon partial skull dated 55,000 years ago, found in Manot Cave in Israel's Western Galilee.[128] The Cro-Magnon-Neandertal culture that developed in Early Canaan and later spread to Europe is called Aurignacian after the first discovered site in the French town of Aurignac.

Archaeologists found Neandertal tools, Aurignacian ornaments, and a Cro-Magnon skeleton dated to 45,000 years ago, possibly earlier, in a large rock shelter below a steep limestone cliff northeast of Beirut at Ksar Akil Cave. Quarrying operations in Lebanon destroyed Ksar Akil Cave, making further testing impossible. It is now buried under tons of soil sludge from the gravel-making machines which operated on the site until 1964.[129]

The Neandertals had Rh-negative blood type; the Cro-Magnons had Rh-positive blood. Neandertal females, therefore, could not produce offspring with Cro-Magnon mates, but Cro-Magnon females could produce offspring with Neandertal mates.[130] Neandertal finds in Early Canaan stop at 45,000 years ago.[131] The remaining Neandertals merged with the more dominant Cro-Magnon culture at that time, became so few in numbers that they died out, or they may have moved to Europe to join the more primitive Neandertals living there.

A few Cro-Magnon Aurignacians moved from Early Canaan to the coastline of Italy 44,000 years ago.[132] And at the Tianyudian Cave site in China near the Pacific Coast, in the same caves *H. erectus* previously occupied, a band of Cro-Magnon/ archaic/Neandertal hybrids lived from 42,000 years ago until 39,000 years ago.[133]

Another archaic modern human group is called Denisovan. The few fossil fragments found, dated to 41,000 years ago, reveal interbreeding with Neandertals and modern humans. Denisovan DNA is found in modern-day populations living in Southeast Asia. The name derives from the Denisova Cave in Siberia where archeologists found a bone fragment fossil. The cave, also used by Neandertals and Cro-Magnons, is situated in the Altai Mountains, a range that connects Russia, China, Mongolia, and Kazakhstan.[134]

The Aboriginals of Australia have been isolated for 40,000 to 60,000 years. They have a high concentration of Denisovan DNA and may have Denisovan features. No Denisovan skull has been found so those features are unknown.[135]

By 40,000 years ago Cro-Magnon Aurignacians had

settlements throughout Early Canaan, including the Jordan Valley and the Syrian Desert. In Europe by 40,000 years ago they expanded their population and occupied a vast territory from the Mediterranean coastline up to the line of glaciers separating southern Europe from ice-covered northern Europe and Russia. They settled in Spain, Portugal, throughout southern Europe, in the Balkans, and in Ukraine around the Black Sea.[136]

The Neandertal people lived in small, isolated matriarchal family groups. The Cro-Magnon people lived in large patriarchal communities spread throughout a wide territory. Matriarchal societies often live in small, frequently nomadic independent bands. Central leadership of large settlements is a trait of patriarchal societies.[137]

European Cro-Magnon Aurignacians coexisted with Neandertals until Neandertals became extinct. Except for evidence found along the coasts of Spain and Portugal, European Neandertal evidence stops around 30,000 years ago.[138]

The highest-elevation Aurignacian site is in an Alpine mountain range, the Karawanks, between Slovenia and Austria. Evidence at Potok Cave, Slovenia, dates Aurignacian Cro-Magnon use from 40,000 years ago to 26,000 years ago. The cave, at an elevation of 5,500 feet (1,675 meters), may have been used as a hunting camp. There, archaeologists found arrowheads, a bone flute, a bone sewing needle, and bones of various animal species.[139]

People of the Aurignacian culture fashioned works of art and jewelry. Venus figurines, found in many Aurignacian sites throughout Europe and the Middle East, are a few inches high. The earliest were usually carved from stone or ivory, later ones often fashioned from clay. They are similar in shape and represent a variety of female figures with large breasts, bellies, and hips. Most of the figurines lack feet and cannot stand on their own. People likely used them as amulets.[140]

Thousands of Venus figurines have been found. The archaeologists who discovered the first ones named them Venus figurines, perhaps after the mythical goddess of love. The Sumerians named the first historical "Venus" Inanna, also called Innini, their goddess of love.[141]

The oldest verified Venus figurine, called the Venus of Hohle Fels, is between 35,000 and 40,000 years old, sculpted from a woolly mammoth tusk. Archaeologists found it in southwestern Germany. The oldest known musical instruments are flutes found near this site. One flute is carved from a vulture wing bone, one is made from the wing bone of a swan, and two are carved ivory.[142]

The southern tip of Germany on the border of Austria is called Swabia. It has a high concentration of Aurignacian sites dated to around 36,000 years ago. Numerous small stone Venus figurines have been found in this region. Other artifacts from this area include ivory flutes and stone tools.[143]

These early societies built villages, produced ceramic objects, developed high-level works of art, and played musical instruments. The Cro-Magnon cultures of Early Canaan, North Africa, and Europe may have developed a sophisticated, golden age civilization in a warm interglacial period during the latter part of the last ice age.

Cro-Magnons developed a culture named Gravettian and established a site in Aurignacian territory in the Crimean Mountains in southern Ukraine around 32,000 years ago. By 28,000 years ago Gravettians also occupied a settlement in Spain.[144]

A period called the Last Glacial Maximum began around 26,500 years ago. The climate turned cold. Ice sheets and permafrost began to advance on most of North America, northern Europe, Siberia, and parts of Asia. Sea levels dropped significantly as water turned to glacial ice. Ice sheets and permafrost extended steadily into the European Aurignacian territory for around 500 years after the Last Glacial Maximum began.[145]

A major European Aurignacians population center, after several thousand years, moved northeast from Swabia to today's Czech Republic. A Venus figurine named the Venus of Dolni Vestonice found in the Czech Republic is an abstract female form with smooth lines. It is the oldest known ceramic article in the world, around 26,000 years old. This is one of the last known Aurignacian sites in Europe.

At the same site with the Dolni Vestonice, archaeologists excavated stunningly beautiful stone or ivory figurines of bears, lions, mammoths, horses, foxes, rhinos, and owls. The site also had over 2,000 balls of burnt clay, probably used for cooking food by placing the hot clay balls inside containers with uncooked food.[146]

The Aurignacians abandoned their homes 26,000 years ago when the ice sheets and glaciers of the Last Glacial Maximum crept into their northern territories. Known sites do not display evidence of a major war or other disaster. Scientists and researchers classify their disappearance from Greece to Italy, up through Crimea, Eastern Slovakia, Swabia, Austria, Transylvania, Russia, the Balkans, France, Spain, and Portugal as unexplained and mysterious.[147]

After the inexplicable Aurignacian departure from Europe, the Gravettian culture rapidly expanded. The Western Gravettian culture until the end of the Last Glacial Maximum 22,000 years ago occupied parts of Spain but lived mostly along the Mediterranean coastline of southern France. The Eastern Gravettians lived and hunted mammoths in Central Europe and Russia. The population of this culture occupied a much smaller territory than the Aurignacian.[148]

The Aurignacians may have influenced this culture because the Gravettians produced hundreds of Venus figurines and carvings similar to those of the Aurignacians. One is the Venus of Lespugue, dated to around 25,000 years ago. Discovered in 1922 in France in the foothills of the Pyrenees, it is approximately 6 inches (15 cm) tall, carved from an ivory tusk, and has large breasts, hips, and buttocks. Elizabeth Wayland Barber, a textile expert, found the earliest representation of spun thread in a skirt carved on the figurine.[149]

The most famous of the Venus figurines, dated to 23,000 years ago, is the Venus of Willendorf, also called the Woman of Willendorf, found in 1908 near Willendorf, Austria. Carved from limestone that is not local, and tinted with red ochre, the statuette is 4.3 inches (11 cm) high and has curly or braided hair.

The Gravettians lived in the region for at least 6,000 years, then left their territory during a cold snap at the end of the Late Glacial Maximum. Their artifacts have not been found in Europe later than those dated to 22,000 years ago. Cro-Magnons, likely the Western Gravettians, settled in Morocco 22,000 years ago and lived there until 5,000 years ago when they became the Beaker culture.[150]

The last-known European Neandertal remains are dated to around 30,000 years ago. However, Neandertal fire evidence discovered on the coast of Portugal dates to 24,500 years ago, and one Cro-Magnon skeleton with Neandertal traits, discovered in Morocco, dates to 24,000 years ago.[151] Scientists found a necklace shell and a piece of red ochre buried with the Cro-Magnon/Neandertal hybrid.[152]

The fire remains on the coast of Portugal are 5,000 years past the extinction date for Neandertals in Europe. The hybridized Cro-Magnon Neandertal fossil is in the time of and in the territory of the Western Gravettians.

Periods of intense cold, terrible droughts, and generally erratic weather in the Northern Hemisphere caused populations to seek refuge from the harsh environment of northern Europe and Russia during the last ice age. Because scientists identified the last evidence of Neandertals and a hybrid on the Atlantic Coast, it is possible that a band of remaining Neandertals and Cro-Magnons took refuge near the ocean from Portugal to Morocco.

It is also possible that Neandertals or hybrids lived on the Mid-Atlantic Ridge while a Cro-Magnon Atlantis-type civilization flourished there. If people lived on the Mid-Atlantic Ridge from the Azores to Iceland, cataclysmic events at the end of the last glacial period would have destroyed all traces of their culture.

The European and Russian settlements abandoned by the Aurignacians 26,000 years ago and the Gravettians 22,000 years ago were unoccupied or used only sporadically until the Solutrean culture appeared on the coastline of Portugal at the end of the Last Glacial Maximum 22,000 years ago. They occupied the Mediterranean coastline from Spain to France, and settlements have also been found in Germany, Poland, the Balkans, and England.[153]

The Solutrean people may have lived on an exposed North Sea continental shelf during the Last Glacial Maximum before the warming trend caused increased sea levels. That may have triggered a Solutrean migration into Europe. They occupied former Aurignacian sites in southern Spain, Portugal, and southern France for 5,000 years.[154] They are possibly the same culture identified in South Africa 73,000 years ago.[155]

While the Solutreans occupied parts of Europe, a culture identified as the Epigravettian arrived 20,500 years ago and occupied central and east Europe, Italy, the Balkans, and the Aegean mainland.[156] A similar culture, called the Magdalenian, moved into northwestern Europe around the time of the Epigravettians. The Magdalenians lived in caves or tepees on the vast glacial tundra of northern Europe and Russia. They occupied and expanded the territory of the Solutreans and used tools different from those of the Solutreans.[157]

In Early Canaan and Mesopotamia a severe regional drought 20,000 years ago caused famine. The Canaan Aurignacians left at the beginning of the drought. Artifacts from this culture stop after this time and have not been found in other regions.[158]

DNA research reveals that the ancestors of Ashkenaz Jews and Flemish people share a common Middle Eastern ancestor that split into two groups 20,000 years ago. The Aurignacians, a people with light-colored hair and blue eyes, could be the genetic link between Ashkenaz Jews and the Flemish people of Belgium, northern France, and the Netherlands, formerly called Flanders.[159]

Shortly after the Aurignacians left Early Canaan during the severe drought a group of nomads called the Kebaran culture moved into the area 20,000 years ago. They were highly mobile hunters and gatherers. They collected and ground wild cereals. Archaeologists found stone and bone tools, clay ovens, red ocher, and marine shell beads from both the Mediterranean Sea and the Red Sea at Kebaran sites.[160]

Groups of Cro-Magnons also lived in China on the Pacific Coast 20,000 years ago.[161]

The Oldest Dryas stadial that began around 19,000 years ago was the coldest of the three Dryas stadials (freezing cold periods occurring during interglacial warm periods). It took over 1,000 years to settle across the northern hemisphere and then lasted 4,500 years. Forests across Europe became tundra, a nearly level treeless plain with frozen subsoil. At the same time, the Sahara plain in Africa became too dry for human habitation, and people once again migrated to areas of refuge. Dryas stadials are named for an alpine/tundra plant, *Dryas octopetala*.

Geological surveys reveal that 18,000 years ago, when oceans were much lower than today, a very large area of dry land stretched from Britain's east coast to the Netherlands, Germany, and Denmark. Archaeologists have named it Doggerland after the North Sea sandbank Dogger Bank. The land connecting the United Kingdom (British Isles) and the rest of the European continent consisted of uninhabited frozen tundra until the Last Glacial Maximum receded. The ice melted, and for thousands of years this area became a vast low-lying plain where tens of thousands of people lived.[162]

Researchers are investigating underwater human burial sites, stone fire circles, and a burial ground for mammoths in ancient Doggerland. Artifacts from the underwater landscape where people once lived include woolly mammoth bones, reindeer bones, an axe made from an antler with part of the wooden shaft preserved, a tool made from the bone of a large type of extinct bovine, a tool made from a red deer antler, human skeletons, and a human skull. The skull artifact has distinctive round eye sockets.[163]

One of the first known Doggerland artifacts, which the captain of a British fishing trawler found in 1931, is a harpoon point with carved barbs along one side. The harpoon point, fashioned from an antler, is on display at a museum in Norwich, UK.[164]

North Sea oil companies have provided geophysical surveys that helped scientists map the rivers, lakes, hills, coastlines, and estuaries of the once-fertile landscape. Scientists in Scotland refer to Doggerland as a Stone Age Atlantis because it represents an authentic ice age society that flourished in the heartland of Europe.[165]

European Solutrean artifacts stop 17,000 years ago during the Oldest Dryas, the first of the freezing cold Dryas stadials. The

Solutreans occupied their last active colonies on the coastline of Portugal.[166]

However, archaeologists have found distinctive arrowheads and other unique artifacts of the Solutreans on the East Coast of the United States. Both used a pressure-flaking technique resulting in elaborate barbed arrowheads unique to the Solutrean and North American pre-Clovis cultures. The Solutrean stone tool artifacts found in Europe are dated 22,000 to 17,000 years ago, and they match American pre-Clovis stone tools found in Cactus Hill, Virginia, dated 18,000 years ago. Cactus Hill is the oldest verified pre-Clovis archaeological site in North America.[167]

The hypothesis that the two cultures are the same people is contested for lack of evidence that the Solutreans could have crossed the Atlantic Ocean. However, archaeologists Dennis Stanford and Bruce Bradley suggested that the Solutreans moved from Iberia and southern France across the North Atlantic along the edge of an ice sheet to North America using traditional Eskimo travel methods.[168]

Stanford and Bradley's hypothesis of an Atlantic Ocean crossing is further strengthened by the timing of the extremely cold Oldest Dryas stadial that began 19,000 years ago, intensified 18,000 years ago, and lasted until 14,500 years ago, significantly lowering sea levels.[169]

Evidence indicating a violent or catastrophic event has not been found at the time the Solutreans abandoned their settlements in Portugal, Spain, and France 17,000 years ago. Like the Aurignacians and the Gravettians before them, when the climate turned very cold with the beginning of the Oldest Dryas, the area they occupied became crowded by refugees pouring in from the freezing northern regions.[170]

Competition for food resources may have caused the Solutrean people to leave. They could have migrated to the

Mid-Atlantic Ridge by taking advantage of lowered sea levels and exposed continental shelves during the Oldest Dryas stadial. If a civilization existed on the Azores Platform at that time, the Solutreans may have lived near it or joined it for a time.

Then, by walking on ice sheets and continental shelves and using rafts when necessary, they could have continued migrating to North America and settled at Cactus Hill, Virginia. Blade and spear artifacts similar to those found at the Virginia site and dated around 500 years later were discovered in Pennsylvania, Wisconsin, and Texas. The site at Buttermilk Creek Valley, Texas, is the largest settlement and has yielded 16,500 artifacts.[171] This evidence indicates that a group of people with a distinct culture arrived on the East Coast of America and migrated to the middle of the continent over a 500-year-period.[172]

The Magdalenian culture in Europe seems to be related to or influenced by the former Aurignacian and Gravettian cultures because the Magdalenians produced the characteristic Venus figurine amulets as well as other artworks. Found in Swabia in southern Germany and dated to 15,000 years ago, the Venus of Engen is a Magdalenian stylized figurine carved from jet, a dense, black lignite mineral. Many Cro-Magnon cave art finds including the well-known Lascaux animal cave paintings of southern France are from this culture.[173]

A warm, stable period lasting several hundred years followed the Oldest Dryas stadial when it ended 14,500 years ago. A group of archaic-modern hybrids identified as Red Deer Cave people arrived in southern China 14,500 years ago at the beginning of the warm period.[174] Cro-Magnons, probably of the Magdalenian culture, began migrating back into northern Europe when the cold period subsided.

An artistic Cro-Magnon culture occupied a cave complex

in the Basque region of today's northern Spain from 14,500 years ago to 12,500 years ago. Deep inside the Atxurra cave site archaeologists discovered an estimated 70 engravings and paintings on ledges 1,000 feet underground. The art depicted horses, goats, deer, and buffalo hunting scenes. One painting showed 20 lances stuck in a dying buffalo.[175]

People living on Doggerland, the landmass connecting the British Isles to the European mainland, thrived after the Oldest Dryas stadial gave way to a stable warm climate.[176]

The Natufian culture from Northern Africa migrated 14,500 years ago into parts of Kebaran territory in Early Canaan. Their main archaeological site is in Judah, Israel. Fossils identified as Kebaran have round skulls; fossils identified as Natufian have elongated skulls.[177]

A 140-year-long glacial period—The Older Dryas stadial—interrupted the warming trend 14,140 years ago. Early Canaan and Mesopotamia suffered through drought while Europe reverted to a glacial landscape.

The Natufians stayed and the Kebarans left drought-stricken Early Canaan during the freezing Older Dryas cold snap 14,140 years ago. The Magdalenians remained in Europe. The Epigravettians abandoned their settlements 13,500 years ago.[178]

7

CIVILIZATION X

The existence of a historical Atlantis, a Civilization X, requires evidence of a society in a physical location during a specific time period. Physical evidence has not been found at any of the proposed locations except for possible evidence found in North Africa. Early writings, oral histories, references, tales, and myths form the basis for theorized idyllic golden age societies.

Sudden and destructive Earth changes occurring for over a thousand years at the end of the last ice age 12,800 years ago to 11,700 years ago left only those stone structures that could withstand natural disasters. If the site of a Civilization X—an Atlantis—can be established, researchers can consider that the Atlantean society was the advanced culture, or at least one of the advanced cultures, responsible for engineering monolithic structures in lands around the Mediterranean Sea.

Plato situated Atlantis in the Atlantic west of the Pillars of Hercules. He described an island paradise with a glittering city and luxurious gardens that sank under the Atlantic 11,500 years ago.[179]

One or all of the theorized locations could have been part of an ice age civilization whose population possessed advanced technological skills.

Thera and Crete

Several researchers believe Plato is inaccurate about the location of Atlantis and the year of its destruction. Some surmise he referred in his writing to the supervolcanic eruption 3,650 years ago on Thera Island (later called Santorini) in the Aegean Sea because it destroyed the advanced civilization on nearby Crete in the Mediterranean Sea.

Supporters of this theory believe the demise of Atlantis occurred 3,650 years ago and that the island of Atlantis is Crete.

The Yucatán Peninsula

Situated between the Gulf of Mexico and the Caribbean Sea, the Yucatán Peninsula is a theorized location for being part of an Atlantis-type empire. Its supporters believe an Atlantean civilization stretched from the Yucatán across the ocean to the West Indies and the Azores Archipelago (the Mid-Atlantic Ridge). Then, the settlement continued from the Azores across land bridges to the Strait of Gibraltar and included the territory of Spain, Portugal, and Morocco.

Supporters note that Yucatán native oral history records a story about an ancient civilization suddenly destroyed by a torrent of water.[180]

Spain

Spain, a mountainous region with high plateaus, is also one of the theorized locations of Atlantis. The mountain plateaus have cave shelters where people lived during the glacial age in times of harsh weather. The Atlantic Ocean and the Mediterranean Sea border Spain.

Northwestern Africa-Atlas Mountains

The Atlas Mountains are another theoretical site for Atlantis. The mountain range extends through Morocco, Algeria, and Tunisia and separates the Mediterranean and Atlantic coasts from the Sahara Desert, one of Earth's largest and driest deserts. The mountain range drops to the coastline on the Atlantic side. Cold periods exposed continental shelves and significantly extended the African shoreline.

During the last glacial period, refugees from colder regions occupied a network of caves in the Atlas Mountains.[181]

North Africa-Egypt

Evidence has convinced some researchers to conclude that a technically sophisticated civilization may have sculpted the Great Sphinx and the Valley Temples while flourishing in North Africa 40,000 years ago.[182]

A recently discovered underground city, carved out of the bedrock, is about 55 miles (90 km) south of Cairo. Each layer of occupation is approximately the size of 11 football fields side by side. Romans constructed the top level and the next level down is Macedonian. Archaeologists have discovered at least 2 additional levels but have not been able to explore them.[183]

Plato recorded that Solon, a friend of Plato's grandfather and a famous Athenian lawgiver, traveled to Egypt where he met high priests in Sais. The high priests revealed to Solon that they knew or were themselves descendants of the survivors of Atlantis.[184]

Some Egyptologists speculate that, along with Plato's account of Solon meeting descendants of Atlanteans in Sais, Egypt, a 40,000-year-old civilization and an ancient underground city could be evidence that Atlantis was in Egypt.

THE CANARY ISLANDS

The Canaries, an archipelago of 13 islands south of the Azores Archipelago and west of North Africa, are a theorized location for Atlantis because of their proximity to Morocco and to the Azores. The islands sit 62 miles (100 km) southwest of the coast of Morocco. Over 2 million mostly Spanish and native Canarians (formerly called Guanche) currently live on the islands.

Some researchers believe the ancient, blond, blue-eyed Guanche population to be direct descendents of Cro-Magnons who may have left Canaan or Europe 22,000 years ago to 14,000 years ago during severe freezing cold periods when sea levels were low enough to expose continental shelves and form land bridges on islands now submerged.[185] Or, the original Guanche people may have taken refuge in Morocco during the catastrophic end of the last ice age 12,800 years ago to 11,700 years ago. With raft or canoe technology they could have sailed to the Canaries after the end of the last ice age.

MID-ATLANTIC RIDGE

Examining the Mid-Atlantic Ridge may be the key to understanding the most likely location of an Atlantis-type Civilization X. Sections of this mountain range stretching from the Arctic Ocean to Antarctica became exposed during this last ice age.

Underwater hydrothermal vents are found near areas of active volcanoes. The Mid-Atlantic Ridge has several hydrothermal vent groups. Vents at ground level are called hot springs, geysers, or fumaroles. Vents found near volcanoes are fumaroles, emitting steam and gases in a plume through the earth's crust. Subterranean superheated water turns to steam and creates pressure, enabling fumaroles to last from weeks to centuries.

Active volcanoes and geysers release an abundance of geothermal energy, which could have been utilized by a technologically skilled civilization.

Part of the ridge widens from the Azores to Iceland, an island situated where the North Atlantic and Arctic oceans meet. Iceland is a theorized Atlantis location. It has an environment suitable for human habitation, even during the last glacial period. The island is an exposed part of the Mid-Atlantic Ridge above a mantle plume, a hotspot. Lava from volcanic eruptions built up the landmass over time.

The landscape is varied and dramatic. Mountains, valleys, lakes, and glaciers cover the interior. Waterfalls provide hydrodynamic energy. The North Atlantic Current runs past Iceland and keeps ice from forming along the island's coasts.

The Azores Platform

The Azores Archipelago is a group of nine islands that are exposed mountaintops of a 2 million-square-mile (5,180,000 km^2) area called the Azores Platform. The platform sits on top of the Mid-Atlantic Ridge. When sea levels lower enough to expose the platform during times of glaciation, it forms a small continent-sized landmass in the Atlantic Ocean directly west of the Strait of Gibraltar.

The Azores are situated about 1,200 miles (1,900 km) from Newfoundland to the west and about 900 miles (1,450 km) from

Portugal and Morocco to the east. The islands extend about 235 miles (375 km) across the Atlantic. The landscape of the Azores includes mountains, valleys, volcanic crater lakes, and grassy plateaus.

The Strait of Gibraltar, where the Atlantic Ocean and the Mediterranean Sea meet, is a narrow opening only 9 miles (14 km) wide separating Europe on the north from Africa on the south. In ancient writing the Rock of Gibraltar on the north and a mountaintop in Morocco on the south represented the Pillars of Hercules. Plato described Atlantis as in the Atlantic, west of the Pillars of Hercules.[186]

During North American glaciation, including the Laurentide Ice Sheet, the Azores Platform remained exposed. The giant platform, together with floating and stationary ice masses, extended continental shelves, and formerly submerged islands would almost create a bridge connecting the Mid-Atlantic Ridge to Europe on one side and North America on the other. This fits the description of Atlantis given by Plato.

The landscape and pleasant climate of today's Azores Archipelago create a paradisiacal environment with grassy pastures, thick forests, rolling hills, picturesque mountains, valleys, rivers, and lakes. Plato described Atlantis as an island paradise rich in natural resources, such as metals.[187]

Mysterious Stone Structures

A society needed to understand engineering concepts and have specialized tools or machines to carve or build the monuments and structures occupied before the end of the last ice age. An ancient advanced society may have developed construction methods not known today. This level of skill implies the need for writing and may also require some form of farming or organized food collection.

Scientists, researchers, and others have speculated for years that ancient monuments and structures were built for religious worship. Popular opinion is that these edifices were constructed well after conventional history began around 7,000 years ago. A few scientists, however, suggested they may be much older.[188] Then, the discovery of the 13,000-year-old Göbekli Tepe complex in Turkey extended the timeline to before the end of the last ice age for skills and technical ability to construct monumental structures and carve massive stone columns.

While most posit that enormous ancient structures may have been designed for religious purposes, survivors (or descendants of survivors) of natural disasters may have constructed massive stone compounds for protection. Only deep caverns, underground cities, or large-scale stone structures could shield a group of people from the effects of a wildly variable climate or life-threatening disaster.

Exploring evidence of these mysterious places may give clues to the societies that created them.

Egyptian Pyramids

Who built the great pyramids of Egypt? This question has been analyzed in detail, and hundreds of books have been written on the subject. The commonly held scientific opinion that workers constructed them around 4,500 years ago may be unrealistic because a population with skills to create these monumental structures did not exist at that time.

Egyptologists generally opine that the oldest pyramids were designed as tombs for pharaohs of the Old Kingdom period. The pyramids-as-tombs explanation lacks evidence. Egypt's Old Kingdom Period, from 2575 BCE to 2150 BCE, saw the introduction of a new solar religion and had a weak central government.[189] Severe droughts began causing mass famine toward the end of this period.[190]

It does not seem likely that extensive national building projects, like the kind initiated in the later New Kingdom Period, would be possible. How could workers move millions of stone blocks weighing 50 tons to 70 tons each into the construction area in order to build precisely engineered structures? Also, copper implements and stone hammers were the common tools of the Old Kingdom. Most of the stone blocks used to construct the Great Pyramid on the Giza Plateau fit so perfectly together that even a piece of paper cannot be inserted between them.[191]

Modern tests have not been conducted to demonstrate that this construction feat could have been accomplished using the known tools of that time. Some researchers speculate that today, even using modern tools and technology, the Great Pyramid could not be built with the same precision that exists in the ancient monument.

The pyramids at Giza, Sakkara, and Dashur were engineered and constructed by designers and builders with technical math skills and who possessed the tools and equipment needed to complete these projects. Some of the quarries were in Abydos, 600 miles (965 km) away. Scientists do not know how the hewn stones were transported.[192]

Huge granite stones cut into blocks approximately 4 feet (1.2 meters) high and weighing around 50 tons each are at the base of the third pyramid in Giza. They fit together to form a paved surface like a road built for giants. The paved surface in front of the Giza pyramid has the same appearance as the megalithic underwater Bimini Road near the Bahamas.[193]

The Mystery of the Great Sphinx

The famous Egyptian carved lion body with a human head placed on top, called the Great Sphinx, has been written about since ancient times as one of the world's greatest wonders. The name Sphinx derives from a Greek word meaning to strangle or bind tight. The name early Egyptians used, *shesep-ank*, probably translates as "living image." Egyptian writings of 4,500 years ago referred to the monument as Horus in the Horizon, Place of Horus, and Ra of Two Horizons.[194]

A limestone mound sculpted in place became the body of the Great Sphinx. From the limestone removed to carve the Great Sphinx, blocks estimated to weigh 100 tons each were obtained and used to construct two nearby structures called the Sphinx Temple and the Valley Temple.[195] Evidence of how or when Early Dynastic Egyptians could have accomplished this feat has not been discovered.

Egyptologists generally believe the Sphinx may have been carved around 4,600 years ago by order of Pharaoh Khafre at the end of the Early Dynastic Period or at the beginning of the Old Kingdom Period. The Egyptians of that time were making the transition from wood to using stone for building materials, and they built a military-and-trade base south of Egypt in Nubia. No mention is made about carving one of the world's greatest monuments.[196]

Egyptologists also make the connection to Khafre because artifacts mentioning him were found near the monument. No other evidence of a connection to pharaohs and the Sphinx has been found.[197]

Another common explanation is that both the Great Sphinx and Khafre had square chins, which dates the Great Sphinx's age to Khafre. The head of the Great Sphinx is not part of the carved-in-place lion body. It is constructed from a more durable limestone. The head does not show the same type of water erosion as the body, indicating that the head may have been added later. Some researchers speculate that the head, which is proportionally too small for the body, may have been a lion's head originally and it could have been carved into its present form during the early dynasties.[198]

Many scientists have studied the Great Sphinx's water-erosion patterns. Most point to heavy rainfall to explain the weathering, but a few insist on flooding as the source.

Robert M. Schoch, Scottish geologist, geophysicist, and anthropologist, estimates the weathering on the Great Sphinx could date to at least 11,000 years ago. The last heavy sustained rainfall in North Africa occurred around 9,000 years ago, and Schoch points out that the North African region has been mostly arid for the last 5,000 years. Egyptian structures that definitely date to the Old Dynastic Kingdom show only wind-and-sand erosion.[199]

Edgar Cayce, a famous American psychic who died in 1945, developed a worldwide following because of his abilities and because his clients included famous people, among them Woodrow Wilson, Thomas Edison, and Irving Berlin.[200] Cayce predicted that a chamber he referred to as a "Hall of Records," possibly from the age of Atlantis, would be found underneath a paw of the Great Sphinx.[201] Scientists, Egyptologists, and researchers of his time laughed at the idea.

But recently, while conducting studies on the erosion patterns of the core limestone body, Schoch discovered evidence of a large cavity or chamber under the left-front paw, of smaller cavities under and around the body, and a possible tunnel along the length of the body. Schoch did not know of Cayce's predictions.[202]

The best evidence for dating the Egyptian pyramids, the Great Sphinx, and the two nearby valley temples is the complexity of the technical engineering and skills necessary to create these monuments. Evidence of such skills during the early dynastic periods of ancient Egypt has not been established. Though the dynastic rulers recorded their greatest accomplishments, records of creating these monuments have not been found.[203]

Stone monuments and buildings are usually dated by examining nearby organic materials. However, dating the time period for the construction of the Great Pyramid and the carving of the Great Sphinx is difficult because it is based on analysis of erosion patterns.

BIMINI ROAD

The Commonwealth of the Bahamas consists of around 700 islands in the Atlantic Ocean north of Cuba and Hispaniola and east of the Florida Keys. Bimini is a chain of islands in the Bahamas about 50 miles (80 km) due east of Miami, Florida. The two largest islands are North Bimini and South Bimini.

Edgar Cayce had also predicted that evidence of Atlantis would be found near the Bahamas in the 1960s. In 1968 close to North Bimini near a coral reef, scuba divers discovered three parallel underwater rock formations composed of flat-lying irregular blocks. The largest is called the Bimini Road, or Bimini Wall, because it resembles a half-mile-long underwater stone highway. Its limestone blocks range in height from 7 feet to 13 feet (2–4 meters).[204]

Cayce's prediction about Atlantis and the discovery of the rock formations near North Bimini have fueled hundreds of books on the subject of whether or not the Bimini Road and the two other nearby rock features were constructed or altered by humans, or if they are simply unique natural rock formations.

Scientists and researchers have studied the Bimini Road to determine its origins and to establish a date for the blocks. Scientists estimate the age anywhere from 125,000 years to 15,000 years. Most geologists and archaeologists consider Bimini Road / Wall to be a natural feature.

It may be a coincidence that the megalithic granite paving-stone "road" lying at the base of a pyramid in Giza has the same appearance as the underwater Bimini Road in the Bahamas. If a connection can be discovered that links the Bimini Road to an ice age society in Egypt, a case could be made for an Atlantean-type empire with a territory much larger than the area of the Azores Platform, now an archipelago.

Due to erosion of the Bimini Road, this is a question that may never be answered until definitive evidence is found or existing evidence reinterpreted to prove the nature of the Bimini Road to be constructed, modified, or natural.

GÖBEKLI TEPE

During the warm period following the Older Dryas stadial, a technologically advanced group of people with highly developed engineering skills came together in Anatolia to construct an extraordinary 30-acre compound.

Göbekli Tepe, discovered in the 1990s in southwestern Turkey under a mound, has been described by scientists and researchers as a Neolithic place of worship, or the world's first known temple.[205] The reasons for building this massive stone compound are unknown. It may have been constructed as a refuge for protection against the ravages of a wildly fluctuating climate and the natural disasters during the devastating stadial, 12,800 years ago to 11,700 years ago. The purpose for its construction may be evidenced in the timing of the construction and occupation of this complex. Archaeologists estimate habitation to be 13,100 years ago until 10,200 years ago.

Several distinct cultures occupied Europe, Anatolia, and Canaan before and during the construction of Göbekli Tepe, however, the Anatolian culture that occupied this magnificent compound has not been identified.

The complex has at least 3 layers, each circular. It is 2,500 feet (760 meters) above sea level at the top of a mountain ridge near the Syrian and Iraqi borders.[206] Archaeologists have uncovered, in each layer, huge T-shaped stone pillars with carved, detailed reliefs depicting animals, birds, and symbols. Some have carved images of human arms and hands. Others display strange, humanlike dancing figures.[207]

The site has been only partially excavated, and geophysical surveys show 16 more compounds with another 200 columns. Relief images on T-shaped pillars are precisely carved without scratch marks or even an occasional chisel mark or gouge. Where are the "practice" pillars? If master craftsmen worked the massive stone pillars into sophisticated images, where did these craftsmen come from?

Dozens of limestone pillars are arranged in a circle enclosed by a circular stone wall. The pillars have reliefs of animals including gazelles, snakes, foxes, scorpions, boars, lions, and vultures. The tallest pillars are 18 feet (5.5 meters) high and weigh an estimated 16 tons each. Stone benches connect some of the pillars.[208]

The oldest pillars at over 13,000 years are the biggest, tallest, and most artistic. Later pillars became smaller and simpler. The pillars came from bedrock limestone pits found near the site. Most of the pillars weigh between 10 tons and 20 tons. Workers at the quarry found one column weighing 50 tons.[209]

The oldest, deepest layer partially excavated had charcoal in four circular compounds with T-shaped stone pillars standing within interior walls of stone. High-relief sculpturing is found on some of the pillars.[210]

On one column, two perfectly straight parallel lines run its entire length. On one side, the image of an arm wraps around the pillar with a five-fingered, no-opposing-thumb hand grasping the front edge. On the other side, another arm wraps around with a hand that looks modern, four fingers and an opposing thumb. Below the hands, a belt image wraps across the front and sides with what looks like a three-fingered hand with fingernails carved at the end of the three tips pointing down the middle from underneath the belt.[211]

The three hand types might represent three different human groups. Or it may be merely an abstract carving in the midst of other pillars showing realistic representations of animals, birds, and insects.

More Stone Structures

An Israeli governmental sonar survey in 2003 of the southwest portion of Israel's Lake Kinneret revealed a cone-shaped underwater stone structure 32 feet (10 meters) high with a diameter of about 230 feet (70 meters). It is built of basalt cobbles and boulders and resembles the size and shape of the stone-covered monument of Göbekli Tepe in southern Turkey. Scientists suppose it could be 12,000 years old.[212][213] People built this structure on land before the waters of Lake Kinneret rose to cover it. An underwater archaeological expedition is needed to search for artifacts and to try to determine the date and purpose of the structure.[214]

Ancient massive structures have been built in various places around the world. For instance, ancient pyramids have been discovered in Bosnia, India, China, Cambodia, and the Canary Islands. Those structures may have been constructed during the last ice age. Dating tests have not been performed at those sites because scientists lack funds to conduct excavations in most of those locations.[215]

The mathematical precision exhibited in building the Great Pyramid, the erosion on the Great Sphinx, the massive compound of Göbekli Tepe, and other structures offer credible evidence of the possibility of one or more technically skilled societies operating between 50,000 years ago to around 10,000 years ago.[216] The construction methods and purposes of most these monuments are not known. A reasonable explanation is that a technically advanced society operating during the last ice age built them.

Populations with engineering skills survived the catastrophic beginning and end of the Ice Age and then build new civilizations in Canaan, Mesopotamia, Anatolia, and Egypt.[217]

8

THE END OF THE ICE AGE

The end of the Older Dryas stadial 14,000 years ago ushered in a warm period for over a thousand years. Flora and fauna thrived, forests returned, and human populations expanded on every continent. But then a catastrophic event or series of events 12,800 years ago resulted in a return to ice-age conditions for over a thousand years. The transition to such extreme conditions may have taken up to a decade or the onset may have happened in a few days. Greenland ice core samples show that the climate changed rapidly instead of gradually.[218]

The Younger Dryas stadial is considered an extinction-level event. Scientists refer to this stadial as the Younger Dryas Boundary impact event. The third and last of the Dryas stadials is also called the Big Freeze.

The Laurentide Ice Sheet that had formed 95,000 years ago and covered hundreds of thousands of square miles of North America began to melt during the warming trend that began 22,000 years ago. The meltwater became trapped behind a thick, frozen section below Hudson Bay and along its northeastern edges. The 170,000-square-mile (440,298 km²) body of water that formed is called Lake Agassiz.[219]

Most glacial and interglacial periods can be linked to cycles of sun activity, but 12,800 years ago something caused part of the frozen edge of Lake Agassiz to break. Huge volumes of fresh water entered the oceans and, along with worldwide glacier and ice sheet melt, caused sea levels to quickly rise.[220]

Water with high salinity is heavier and drops to the ocean floor causing warmer water to move across the top of the colder water. This movement creates a current that moves the top layer of warmer water to distant coastlines. The large amount of glacial water entering the Atlantic 12,800 years ago diluted the ocean's salt content, stopping the North Atlantic Current for a thousand years.

Glaciers advanced worldwide while a drought swept across Canaan and Mesopotamia.[221] Many species of large animals, including the woolly mammoth and saber-toothed tiger, died out in this time of massive environmental destruction. In fact, nearly half of all megafaunal species became extinct at this time.[222]

Europe became colder and wetter. Desertification began in Asia and North Africa. The Clovis Culture declined in North America as glaciers advanced.[223]

The Younger Dryas stadial brought an end to many cultures. The Red Deer Cave People in southern China and the band of Cro-Magnons living on the western coast of China perished by the end of the Younger Dryas.[224] Solutrean artifacts in North America stop at this time. The small Hobbit people living in Indonesia died out in their limestone cavern. The Cro-Magnons of the Iberian Atxurra caves did not return after the cataclysmic events of the Younger Dryas.

Other cultures survived the catastrophic stadial. Natufian nomads living in Canaan began setting up camps 12,000 years ago in Jericho near the Jordan River.[225] The El Khiam people moved into Canaan 12,000 years ago and expanded across the Jordan Valley to Mesopotamia and into the Sinai. Their main settlement area may have been around the Dead Sea. The El Khiam culture produced fired clay objects and carved small bone and stone female figurines similar to those of the earlier Aurignacian, Gravettian, and Magdalenian cultures.[226]

Extinction events can usually be linked to a specific cause. Something dramatic happened to bring about the initial collapse of the Laurentide Ice Sheet, worldwide destruction of flora and fauna, and a sudden return to glacial conditions. Some scientists disagree, but evidence that a cometary explosion occurred over North America 12,800 years ago is becoming widely accepted. A massive space-rock impact or comet swarm strike could explain what happened to plunge Earth back into a freezing cold period.[227]

A solar flare strike could have caused extensive damage, but that would be specific to one area, and massive destruction occurred on every continent. Most scientists agree that a bolide (unidentified cometary object) impact from space is a likely cause for the kind of worldwide destruction that occurred. The impact from a comet swarm or other major bolide strike, similar to a major nuclear explosion, could destroy civilizations without leaving a trace of the culture. A dust-and-debris cloud could have enveloped Earth in darkness for years or decades, devastating plant life and causing mass starvation.

Space Impact Evidence

Tektites, tree-ring dating, and Greenland ice core samples are used to identify bolide impacts. Tektites—gravel-sized, smooth-surfaced pieces of high-heat, high-pressure glass—represent impact events. Tektite is a type of natural glass that is chemically and structurally unique. Its qualities indicate meteoric origin.[228]

Researchers and scientists use evidence from several tektite fields. Most known tektite fields are linked to specific events. Central European tektites result from an impact crater formed in Germany 150 million years ago. A North American tektite field covers parts of Texas and Georgia in the United States from an impact in Chesapeake Bay 34 million years ago. Ivory Coast tektites are from the Lake Bosumtwi impact 1.3 million years ago.[229]

Most tektites are black or dark green. Those found on the Libyan-Egyptian border are a light yellow-green. They are dated to between 26 million years and 29 million years ago, and usually called Libyan Desert Glass.[230]

An Australasian tektite field covering Australia, New Zealand, and New Guinea has been attributed to an impact 800,000 years ago in the Indochinese Peninsula. Archaeologists found several tektites at Tikal, a well-known, partially excavated Maya city in Guatemala, in a display of objects inside a possible temple structure. Two of the Tikal tektites were dated to 820,000 years ago.[231]

Another dating method, analyzing tree rings, can provide evidence that a catastrophic event occurred without identifying a source. Tree-ring evidence, through dendrochronology, counts the number, width, and space between rings in tree trunks as a way of determining past climatic conditions. Narrow, close-together rings are a sign of a very cold, dry climate while wide rings spaced far apart indicate fast growth in warmer, moist periods. Live or dead trees up to about 14,000 years ago can be analyzed.

Ice core samples from Greenland contain ash evidence that may be caused by volcanic sources or impacts from space.

Scientists also look for inland marine deposits as evidence that a megatsunami, a wave hundreds or thousands of feet high, has occurred. Regular tsunamis result from sea-floor movement. A megatsunami results from a giant landslide or an impact from a meteorite striking an ocean. The space impact theory was at first rejected by most scientists because evidence of a megatsunami at the end of the Ice Age has not been found.

Diamond is the hardest material on Earth. Natural diamonds are formed in Earth's interior or in space. Synthetic diamonds are usually produced in a high-pressure, high-temperature process that simulates Earth's mantle, that region between the crust and Earth's core.[232] Natural diamonds from carbon-containing minerals take 1 billion years to 3.3 billion years to form.

Two deep-origin volcanic eruptions 100 million years and a billion years ago may be the source for ejecting diamond-bearing magma-turned-lava to the surface. Deep-origin volcanic eruptions are rare because most volcanic eruptions carry magma from around 30 miles (50 km) underground. Diamond-bearing magma originates at 93 miles (150 km) below Earth's surface.

The volcanic eruption blows open a channel, a long passage that the magma erupts through. Diamonds are deposited in the channel during the eruption. Once ejected, the lava cools into igneous rocks, and in rare occurrences it cools into diamond-bearing rocks.

The De Beers brothers found a large, diamond-filled channel on their farm in South Africa in 1871. From 1871 to 1914 miners dug out the channel (42 acres wide) to a depth of 790 feet (240 meters). The hole became a tourist attraction called "The Big Hole." The World Heritage Society is considering a proposal to designate it a protected site.[233]

Carbonado diamonds are black, found only in central Africa and Brazil. They are harder and more porous than other diamonds. Black diamonds are found in sedimentary rocks dated to around 3 billion years ago. Their origin is controversial. Some scientists believe they are Earth-formed natural diamonds. However, evidence has not been found to support a volcanic source for black diamonds. Others think they came from a large, diamond-bearing asteroid created from a supernova 2.3 billion years ago.[234]

When atmospheric contact heats a projectile entering Earth's atmosphere, it usually explodes before ground impact. If an object is larger than a mile (1.6 km) in diameter, a concussion from the explosion can result in damage on Earth.

Some scientists theorize that an object up to 3 miles (5 km) in diameter hit the northern ice cap or exploded above it, and that the thick ice cap covering the underlying ground absorbed the impact.[235]

Nuclear physicist Richard Firestone and geologist Allen West theorize that a 6.5-mile-wide (10 km) comet exploded over the North American Midwest around 13,000 years ago, melted vast amounts of glacier ice, and devastated plants and animals. The impact from the comet would have triggered earthquakes, volcanic eruptions, and intense firestorms from rocks and debris falling on land. Rocks and debris falling on Earth's oceans would have triggered megatsunamis.[236]

Nanodiamonds, diamond dust, found scattered across North America dated 13,000 years ago are the primary evidence of impacts from space, but the evidence is controversial because diamonds can also be ejected during a supervolcano explosion.[237]

Evidence from 25 North American archaeological sites confirms that an enormous space rock exploded on or above North America 12,900 years ago, showered debris across the continent, and caused temperatures to plunge.[238]

The sites contained spherules of glass (tektites), carbon, and high levels of the element iridium. The explosion would likely result in wildfires if the event happened over land. Rocks from the sites showed black layers of carbonized material from wildfires that swept across the continent. Greenland ice cores showed that a massive burning event occurred across North

America 12,800 years ago.[239] Solar discharges, coronal mass ejections from the sun, also cause massive firestorms when hot, ionized gas hits Earth.

A series of dramatic events began the sudden Younger Dryas glacial period. Plato may have recorded those events, including the massive burning event across North America, in the Helios Myth.

According to Plato, when Solon traveled to Egypt the wise men of Sais spoke about an allegorical story that had become a myth to the Athenian people of Solon and Plato's time. The story bears a striking resemblance to the style of the Sumerian creation and flood stories. The myth follows as an excerpt from *Critias*, written by Plato in 360 BCE.[240]

> The wise men of Egypt, called High Priests of Sais, told Solon: There have been, and will be again, many destructions of mankind arising out of many causes; the greatest have been brought about by the agencies of fire and water, and other lesser ones by innumerable other causes. There is a story, which even you have preserved, that once upon a time Phaethon, the son of Helios, having yoked the steeds in his father's chariot, because he was not able to drive them in the path of his father's chariot, burnt up all that was upon the earth, and was himself destroyed by a thunderbolt. Now this has the form of a myth, but really signifies a declination of the bodies moving in the heavens around the earth, and a great conflagration of things upon the earth, which recurs after long intervals; at such times those who live upon the mountains and in dry and lofty places are more liable to destruction than those who dwell by rivers or on the seashore. And from this calamity the Nile, who is our never-failing savior, delivers and preserves us.
>
> When, on the other hand, the gods purge the earth with a deluge of water, the survivors in your nation are herdsmen and shepherds who dwell on the mountains,

but those who, like you, live in cities are carried by the rivers into the sea.

The "Sinking" of Atlantis

Another series of dramatic events ended the 1,100-year-long Younger Dryas glacial period. Those events may have been recorded in the allegorical story of Atlantis.

The earliest written mention of Atlantis may be in Homer's *Odyssey*, written around 2,800 years ago in Ionia, on the coast of Anatolia, now Turkey. The most common references are from Plato in the fourth century BCE. Plato described Atlantis as a mountain island, larger than Libya and Anatolia combined, in the Atlantic Ocean west of the Pillars of Hercules (Strait of Gibraltar).

Atlantis is defined in English dictionaries as an idyllic island in Greek mythology that sank below the sea in an earthquake. The exposed Azores Platform on the Mid-Atlantic Ridge, above sea level during the Last Glacial Maximum, could have been the "idyllic island" referred to by Plato.

Greenland ice core data shows that the Younger Dryas cold period may have ended in a few years or, according to some scientists, it may have even happened in a day and a night 11,700 years ago.[241]

The destruction of Atlantis, as told by Plato, records that a massive sea battle fought in the North Atlantic 11,500 years ago between two major civilizations, the Atlanteans and the Athenians, ended with the demise by sinking of an island continent and the near extinction of the civilizations at war. The story of Atlantis could contain allegories to record information for future generations.

Ice sheets in North America broke off and dumped massive amounts of water from glacial lakes into the Atlantic Ocean

11,700 years ago. Water swept across the Azores Platform about the time Plato said Atlantis sank under the Atlantic.[242] The Azores Archipelago, currently home to 246,000 Portuguese citizens, may be all that is left of a former ancient island paradise, home to a Civilization X, which could have been Atlantis.

Plato also wrote that in Egypt in the temple of Neith at Sais secret halls containing historical records of a distant golden age society had been kept for 9,000 years at the time Solon visited Sais. That places the time of the records at around 11,500 years ago, the end of the last glacial period, which coincides with the "sinking" of Atlantis as described by Plato.[243]

Doggerland also seemed to "sink" at the end of the last ice age. The rising sea levels at the end of the Younger Dryas stadial left an archipelago of islands in the North Sea and finally submerged them.[244]

A Rare Space Event

The Younger Dryas stadial ended with devastation on every continent. The calamitous destruction of the Younger Dryas that began 12,800 years ago and ended 11,700 years ago may have resulted from a rare space event. Scientific theories of a massive space rock exploding above North America, a comet swarm strike, solar flares, and solar storm blasts may all be accurate. The effects of a supernova could account for a variety of disasters.

A star maintains equilibrium between inward forces of gravity against an outward force of energy released by nuclear fusion. Eventually, after millions or billions of years, depending on the size of the star, the nuclear fusion fuel, hydrogen, is exhausted. Massive stars burn faster. The star then contracts, gets hotter, and begins to fuse in stages, burning through elements in the periodic table up to iron.

When fuel up to iron is exhausted, the star implodes. The

implosion event is dramatically sudden, taking only minutes. Small stars contract into a solid ball of neutrons (elementary particles without electric charge) and glow for a very long time as they cool.

A supernova is a catastrophic implosion of a massive star. Large stars implode with such violence that the contraction sends (explodes) into the cosmos a shockwave that synthesizes heavier elements beyond iron. The implosion/explosion event is ten- to a hundred-million times more luminous than the sun. Luminosity is the energy radiated per second by an astronomical object.

Elements including iron, carbon, and oxygen blast into space, the core of the star collapses, and blue plasma gases surrounded by four plumes of orange gases stream into space. The gases release a brilliant burst of gamma rays.[245] Astronomers estimate up to three supernovas per century are occurring in our Milky Way galaxy.[246]

Carbon dating is a scientific technique used in dating plant and animal fossils by measuring carbon-14 decay in organic material. Carbon-14 is a radioactive isotope of carbon found in organic matter.

This method of dating is useful in providing age estimates for archaeological, geological, and hydrogeological samples. Willard Libby and his colleagues at the University of Chicago developed the method in 1949.

Solar rays originate from our sun. Cosmic rays originate outside our solar system. Cosmic rays that interact with nitrogen in the atmosphere are the main source for carbon-14 found on Earth. Nuclear testing above ground between 1955 and 1980 increased atmospheric carbon-14. Gamma rays from a major solar storm can also increase carbon-14 in Earth's atmosphere.

Establishing a date for archaeological samples is the main use of the technique. Plant and animal samples have approximately the same levels of carbon-14 as the atmosphere at the time the plant or animal died. An age estimate determined by the rate of decay, the carbon-14 level for the sample, can be compared with an age estimate provided by direct comparison with known year-by-year tree-ring data.

Scientists recorded differences of up to 10,000 years in samples from the Younger Dryas period. Some samples had more carbon-14 than should be present, according to dendrochronology. Excess carbon-14 in the atmosphere could be explained by an immense nuclear explosion on Earth, but no known civilization capable of producing nuclear technology existed that long ago. Scientists concluded that carbon-14 must have entered our atmosphere 13,000 years ago from a solar source. Scientists Richard Firestone, Allen West, and Simon Warwick-Smith suggest a series of cataclysmic events resulting from a supernova caused the carbon-14 increase and the massive worldwide destruction that occurred around 13,000 years ago and continued for over a thousand years.[247]

After a supernova event the star that remains is sometimes (depending on mass) a pulsar: a small, dense star that emits regular, intense bursts of radiation such as radio waves and X-rays.

Scientists have found radiocarbon (carbon-14) measurements that provide evidence of a nearby supernova explosion. Icelandic marine sediment samples show radiocarbon peaks that can only be caused by cosmic rays from a supernova-type event. The radiocarbon spikes occurred at 41,000, 34,000, and 13,000 years ago.[248] The spikes could represent the supernova explosion, the initial shock wave, and a subsequent energy wave.

The Geminga pulsar is the closest known pulsar to Earth. It became a supernova 41,000 years ago. The initial shockwave from the Geminga supernova hit Earth 7,000 years later. The shockwave impact date is derived from Icelandic ice core sample evidence.[249] Mammoth tusks dated to 34,000 years ago were found in North America peppered with tiny holes produced by an intense, high-speed blast of iron-rich grains. The grains may be evidence of the supernova. Their composition is similar to lunar meteorites that fell to Earth in Canaan and Mesopotamia 10,000 years ago.[250]

A supernova will wreak havoc on other star systems in its vicinity. The shockwave from the Geminga supernova implosion/explosion would have disturbed cosmic debris from the Oort cloud, a huge collection of comets and debris at the edge of our solar system. The shockwave and debris from the Oort cloud would have hit the Kuiper Belt, the ring of dwarf planets and comets around the solar system, and then struck the asteroid belt.[251] The asteroid belt circles between Mars and Jupiter and contains asteroids and minor planets.

Debris from one or both belts striking the sun would have produced a series of solar flares. One or more solar flares may have hit Earth. The disturbance could have sent one or more comets toward Earth and caused solar storms. A major solar storm could cause earthquakes, volcanic eruptions, raging wildfires, tsunamis, megatsunamis, and drowned coastlines on Earth. Sea levels would rise again from massive amounts of ice and meltwater entering oceans. The aftermath of the supernova blast likely plunged Earth back into an ice age for over a thousand years and then brought a cataclysmic, abrupt end to the freezing cold period.[252]

Robert M. Schoch suggests that the change may have literally happened overnight when a major astronomical event ended the freezing cold climate. According to Schoch, plasma hitting the surface of Earth could heat and fuse rock, melt ice caps, and vaporize shallow bodies of water, thereby creating extensive rain and causing a sudden warming event. He also notes that a rapid melting of massive ice sheets can result in enough pressure relief to cause earthquakes and volcanoes.[253]

The Younger Dryas stadial ended 11,700 years ago in a series of disasters that threatened humankind with extinction. The worldwide devastation that occurred may be recorded in the biblical story of Noah and the Ark.

9

NOAH'S FLOOD MARKS A NEW AGE

The biblical account of Noah and the Great Flood may be mythical, symbolic, based on a true event, or it may be a combination of those. If biblical Noah and his family were real people, the flood event could represent any one of many disasters.

The Torah is the first section of the Jewish Bible. The five books of the Torah, sometimes referred to as the Written Law, are Genesis, Exodus, Leviticus, Numbers, and Deuteronomy. The narrative in Genesis explains the need for a disaster on Earth because of misdeeds, and declares that a deluge-type flood will end the biological mixing of divine beings with human women.

Before the Great Flood, the *bene ha'elohim* took Earth women, and through those unions the *nefilim* were born. The Hebrew phrase *bene ha'elohim* is translated as sons of the gods, or sons of the rulers, or sons of divine beings. In this case, "sons" means they are members of a category of beings with common characteristics.[254] Genesis refers to the *nefilim* as the heroes of ancient times, men of renown. In Hebrew, the root word for *nefilim* (also *nephilim*) means "to fall." The word *nefilim* is sometimes mistranslated as fallen angels.

In Second Temple Judaism the reference to the divine beings who are sons of the rulers taking advantage of the daughters of men became a discourse on the subjugation of the weak by the powerful.[255] The Torah mentions that before the Great Flood the giants were on the earth in those days but only directly addresses the devastation caused by mankind.[256]

GENESIS 6:1 ~ Now it was when humans first became many on the face of the soil and women were born to them,
6:2 ~ that the divine beings saw how beautiful the human women were, so they took themselves wives, whomever they chose.
6:4 ~ The giants were on earth in those days, and afterwards as well, when the divine beings came in to the human women and they bore them (children)—they were the heroes who were of former ages, the men of name.

Giants are described in detail in a Jewish manuscript collection found at Qumran, an archaeological site in the Judean Hills about a mile inland from the northwest shore of the Dead Sea. Essene Jews flourished there for hundreds of years until Roman soldiers destroyed the community during the Great Revolt of 66-70 CE.[257]

Essene Jews were a sect of Second Temple Judaism, one of three main denominations established after the destruction of the First Temple in Jerusalem in 722 BCE. The name "Essene" is a Greek spelling from the Hebrew "Osey hatorah" found in some of the scrolls. Osey hatorah is the name the "Essene" people called themselves. Osey hatorah means "observers of Torah."[258]

Bedouins in 1946 found seven scroll fragments by accident hidden inside sealed clay jars in a cave at Qumran. Between 1946 and 1956, Bedouins and archaeologists found hundreds more in caves in the Judean Hills. Over 900 Qumran texts written in Hebrew and a few written in Aramaic or Greek were recovered. Most are written on parchment, a few on papyrus sheets.[259]

Collectively they are called the Dead Sea Scrolls. Several complete Torahs, other related writings, and extra-biblical manuscripts make up the collection, which is dated from 408 BCE to 50 CE. The scrolls are commonly thought to be an Osey hatorah (Essene) library. The Jewish community at Qumran may have written some or all of the scrolls or may have collected them.[260]

In the Qumran scroll known as the Book of Giants, written around 100 BCE, Gilgamesh is referred to as an antediluvian giant who protected the Jewish people. Another antediluvian giant, Humbaba, also called Huwawa, may have also protected the Jewish people. Humbaba is called the guardian of the cedar forest and is sometimes referred to as The Terrible. Gilgamesh and Humbaba may have fought each other.[261]

Children or descendants of giants in the Hebraic Empire are referenced after the Great Flood, but the giants themselves are apparently gone.

Tablet fragments found in 1914 at an archaeological site in Iraq identified as ancient Nippur in Sumer contained a Great Flood story. The most famous Sumerian version, used during the Uruk period 6,100 years ago to 4,900 years ago, is the *Epic of Gilgamesh*.[262]

In the narrative, the hero of the story, Gilgamesh, travels a long distance to meet the primeval man Ut-na'ishtim, who tells him about the Deluge caused by a sun god that had destroyed the world. Ut-na'ishtim, his family, friends, and animals survived the Great Flood because the god Ea had instructed him to build a huge vessel made of reeds to protect them. The reed ship rested on a mountain after the flood.[263]

The name Ziusudra is a Sumerian translation of Ut-na'ishtim, the original Akkadian flood story hero's name. The abbreviation, Na'ish, means "he found life."[264]

In Hebrew, Noah is pronounced Noach with a hard "ch" at the end. The English pronunciation sounds more like No'ah. Noach is probably the Hebraic pronunciation of the Akkadian Na'ish.

Several versions of the Great Flood story have been recorded. The Judaic version is called Noah and the Ark.

Before the Great Flood, what kinds of societies existed in the Mediterranean and Mesopotamian regions? The Torah refers to Enoch, Noah's grandfather, as a man who walked with G-d. That reference may hint at a highly developed society. After leaving the ark and receiving G-d's blessing, Noah planted a vineyard and produced wine. That knowledge implies he came from a society with skills such as winemaking.

The Noah-and-the-Ark story, first recorded on stone tablets in Sumeria and later written in the Torah, may be an eyewitness record of actual events. The narrative describes the flood as the last worldwide catastrophe before the settling of Mesopotamia. Many cultures were destroyed during the Younger Dryas period. The Hebraic culture may be one of the few to survive.

Some researchers believe fossilized remains of a huge wooden ark are resting under ice and snow on Mount Ararat in Anatolia, now Turkey. Satellite photographs show a large, angular object, mostly under snow and ice, near the peak of the mountain.²⁶⁵ Other researchers have discovered remnants of what appears to be a massive reed ship on a nearby mountaintop.²⁶⁶ One of those artifacts may be Noah's ark.

If the Torah narrative about Noah and the Ark is historical, it could be about a related group of people who survived the ravages of the Younger Dryas stadial. If it is a representational story, the destruction described in the Torah might correspond to a combination of events. Either way, Noah and Na'ama's descendants kept the genealogical record of the Hebraic people before and after a natural disaster that resulted in a ruined Earth.

The biblical narrative of Adam and Havva (Eve) is a story of beginnings. Noah's family surviving the Great Flood is a story of new beginnings, of humanity starting over. In the Torah narrative, Adam and Havva are the "parents of humanity." Adam's name in Hebrew, Adom, means "humanity," and Havva means "mother of all the living." Noah is described as an Adam-like "father of humanity."

The Great Flood story would have been part of an oral history before the Sumerians recorded the story on tablets. Blending historical with mythical events and people into an allegory is a method used by tribal cultures worldwide to preserve their history for future generations.

How reliable are oral histories? Jews throughout history have insisted on the absolute integrity of the Torah because the word of G-d must remain unchanged. Scribes are men who copy Torah scrolls to create new ones. They study and practice for years before they are allowed to produce their first scroll. The collective Jewish belief is that the Torah given to Moses by G-d at Mount Sinai during the Exodus from Egypt to Israel has remained unchanged.²⁶⁷

This belief remained an unsubstantiated claim until 1903

when an Egyptian artifacts dealer sold to an English collector a papyrus sheet containing the Ten Commandments and a liturgical prayer. The find, called the Nash Papyrus, dated to around 100 BCE. The Ten Commandments and the priestly benediction on the Nash Papyrus are as used, word for word, today.[268]

Construction workers discovered a treasure stash of artifacts in 1979 outside Jerusalem in the only intact tomb found in a field of robbed First Temple tombs. Among the articles recovered were two small, silver amulets inscribed with a prayer. The amulets, originally worn as necklaces around 2,700 years ago in the First Temple period, have been displayed in Israel's museums. One amulet contains a benediction, again, word for word, still used today. The other, smaller amulet contains a shortened version of the same prayer.[269]

Oral history may be more accurate, and therefore even more important, than written history because written history can be, and is, interpreted in different ways. With oral history the interpretation is built into the story.

For example, Plato wrote that in Egypt Solon met the High Priests of Sais and they recounted the oral history of Atlantis and explained the Athenian Helios myth. In the myth, a thunderbolt killed Helios after he became angry at his father, climbed into a chariot, and burned up the world. But when the High Priests of Sais explained the deeper meaning of the myth, it became clear that the story is a warning about what can happen when solar activity, asteroids, and other cosmic agents affect Earth.

In the Sumerian flood story version, a "sun god" caused the Great Flood. The Sumerian reference to the sun god may hint that a solar event caused the Deluge.

The supernova blast that some scientists theorize hit Earth 11,700 years ago would have caused massive rain, flooding, and tsunamis that match the descriptions in the Torah narrative.[270] The severity of the rainstorm, the flooding, the ruined Earth, and the time it took Earth to recover from the event as depicted in the Torah suggest the Great Flood could have happened during the catastrophic end of the last glacial period.

Scientists have found evidence that events between 12,800 years ago and 11,700 years ago left Earth in a state of nearly complete destruction.

Wildfires burned out of control across North America, skies darkened from massive volcanic eruptions, and collapsed ice sheets resulted in megatsunamis and coastlines suddenly submerged by rapidly rising sea levels. When it ended, piles of strewn debris could be found on every continent. Worldwide monumental flash floods left small mountains of animal carcasses mixed with debris such as tree trunks, clearly a time of death and destruction.[271] This could be characterized as a ruined Earth.

In the biblical story, in the time of Noah and his wife, Na'ama, the world had come to ruin. Each verse in Genesis 6:11 through 6:13 uses the words "ruin" and "earth" in the narrative. The repetition emphasizes the story's message.[272]

The warning suggests humankind will be destroyed with the exception of Noah's family and representatives of every animal in existence. After the birth of his sons, Noah built a large ark for his family and the animals. As predicted, the ensuing flood devastated Earth.

The violent surging of the water subsided after 150 days when the "rushing wind" abated and the Ark came to rest on Mount Ararat. Noah opened the Ark's window 40 days after that. Weeks later, after a raven flew out and did not return, Noah's dove flew out and brought back a bitter olive leaf in its mouth. Noah, his family, and the animals waited a year for the land to recover. Then they left the Ark.[273]

The use of certain Hebrew words in the narrative indicates that a partial flood destroyed a particular world and that Noah's Flood did not cover the entire planet. The partial world described or alluded to in the narrative is sometimes referred to as the "World of Torah." The narrative does not describe the physical World of Torah.[274]

Noah's Great Flood is understood by many to be a literal description of an actual worldwide flood that occurred thousands of years ago. Others believe that the story of Noah and the Ark may be an allegory recording historical events fused with a message for future generations.

The Ark is estimated to be the length and width of two football fields and three stories high. Four men and four women would probably not be able to manage a vessel of that size filled with animals and supplies.

From the geological record, violent storms and upheavals during Earth's formation and again during the Younger Dryas glacial period are known to have occurred. A "rushing-spirit" during creation is mentioned in Genesis 1:2 and is similar to a "rushing-wind" after Noah's flood, also mentioned in Genesis 8:1. The rushing-spirit/wind is mentioned only twice in the Torah.

The similarity of the "rushing-spirit" during creation and the "rushing-wind" during the Noah-and-the-Ark story may hint at the severity of Earth changes during both those times. The scientific term for the Younger Dryas cataclysms is Terminal Pleistocene Extinction because nearly half of all species of mammals became extinct.[275]

In the Torah, the genealogy of Noah's descendants appears to be both a family bloodline and a story of a human repopulation of a flood area. The ten generations from Adam and Havva to Noah and ten more to Abraham may represent the order of the descendants more than the number of years. Or the mention of the generations may represent actual time spans. It is possible that the length of time between Adam and Havva to Noah may be much longer than the time span between Noah and Abraham.

Adam lived 930 years, according to the Torah narrative. Eight generations later, Adam and Havva's descendant Methuselah, son of Enoch, fathered Lamech, who fathered Noah. Enoch lived 365 years. Methuselah lived to be 969 years old and is the oldest person in the Torah. Lamech lived 777 years.[276]

The Ramban, born Moshe ben Nahman, lived in thirteenth-century Spain, and became a rabbi, philosopher, physician, Kabbalist, and Torah commentator who provided an explanation for the long lives of people living before the Great Flood.

He said that before the Great Flood, Adam and Havva and their descendants were physically perfect and so naturally they lived hundreds of years. But after the Great Flood a deterioration of the atmosphere caused a gradual shortening of life. By the age of the Patriarchs Abraham, Isaac, and Jacob, and the Matriarchs Sarah, Rebecca, Rachel, and Leah, a normal lifetime had become 70 to 80 years.[277]

The Ramban pointed out that after the Deluge only the most righteous lived longer than the normal lifespan of 70 to 80 years. Abraham lived 175 years, Sarah lived 127 years, and their son Isaac lived 180 years. Isaac and Rebecca's son Jacob lived 147 years. Jacob and Rachel's son Joseph lived to age 110.[278]

Scientific theory may support the Ramban's explanation. Modern scientists theorize that the deep-space plasma event that may have hit Earth 11,700 years ago would have melted ice caps and vaporized shallow bodies of water, creating a sudden downpour of rain. A plasma burst consisting of electrically charged particles could have been caused by a coronal mass ejection from the sun. Powerful plasma events have happened occasionally in Earth's history.[279]

Robert M. Schoch and other scientists are analyzing theories that the electrically charged particles caused by these events could have enhanced mental abilities and extended the lifespan of humans and other life forms.[280]

A "deterioration" of the atmosphere, as suggested by the Ramban in the thirteenth century, could have actually happened with the dissipation of the electrically charged particles from a solar or deep-space event ending the Younger Dryas stadial 11,700 years ago. Such an event may also have been the proximate cause of, or in the time of, the Great Flood as described in the Torah and in the Sumerian flood story.

The story of Noah and Na'ama may represent several family lines who survived massive flooding and worldwide destruction. The wives of Yefet, Shem, and Ham bore children after the Great Flood and began distinct and separate nations. The next chapters trace Noah and Na'ama's descendants as they repopulate the recovered Earth.

10

THE FIRST EMPIRE

TIMELINE (y.a. means years ago)

11,800 y.a. .... First village in Mesopotamia is built
11,700 y.a. .... Younger Dryas glacial period ends
11,400 y.a. .... Nomads settle Jericho in Canaan
10,200 y.a. .... Villages built on Cyprus
6,900 y.a. .... City-state Mari built
5,900–4,900 y.a. .... Severe worldwide aridification
5,800 y.a. .... Sumerian confederation begins
5,600 y.a. .... Bronze Age begins in Sumeria
4,200 y.a. .... Severe regional droughts
3,950 y.a. .... Sumeria falls, becomes Babylonia

The scientific record indicates the transition to a warm climate happened rapidly 11,700 years ago. Survivors began to emerge from refuges around the world. Forests and vegetation started to grow back, even though the enormous ice sheets and glaciers covering the northern latitudes took around 2,000 years to melt back to present glacier lines.[281] Survivors resettled familiar territories or traveled to new areas.

In the biblical account, Noah's family survived a flood disaster that ruined Earth. No other worldwide disaster is recorded after the Noah and the Ark story. After the Great Flood the descendants of Noah and Na'ama formed nations throughout Mesopotamia, Canaan, Egypt, seacoast nations from the Greek peninsula to the Black Sea coastline, and island nations in the Mediterranean Sea.

The Hebraic descendants of Shem created an empire throughout their territory based on an original, fundamental belief system later recorded in the Written Torah and sometimes referred to as Judaic principles. This blueprint reflects an ethical, moral way of living and a path to spiritual awakening.

The Judaic principles may have been handed down to Noah's family from an ice-age culture existing before the "ruined Earth." The Great Flood destroyed the society that Noah and his family came from when it flooded the World of Torah.

The territory of the nations of Noah may represent the rebuilt World of Torah after Earth recovered from the Great Flood. The Torah records that following the disaster, Noah became the father of a new humanity with new beginnings. Noah and Na'ama's three sons, Yefet, Ham, and Shem, became the fathers of 70 nations after the Great Flood. Their nations began in certain territories. Societies developed all over the world, but the Torah lists only the nations connected to each other by Noah and Na'ama's bloodlines.

The Torah links a society of people living before the Great Flood, that is, Noah and Na'ama and their families, to, after the Great Flood, Mesopotamia through their descendants.

Descendants of Shem settled in Mesopotamia and built the city-states of Sumeria, the first advanced civilization to form after the end of the freezing cold Younger Dryas.

The archaeological record after the Younger Dryas begins with the first village built in northern Mesopotamia (future Sumeria) on the border of today's Iran and Iraq. This village culture of early Mesopotamia developed east of the Tigris River from around 11,800 years ago until 9,400 years ago. The area repopulated about a thousand years later.[282]

The Natufians left Canaan and migrated back to North Africa.[283] The hunter-gathers living near the Jordan River built the town of Jericho (Yeriho in Hebrew) 11,400 years ago.[284]

A site discovered 20 miles (32 km) southwest of Göbekli Tepe called Nevah Cori (also called Nevali Cori) is smaller, but similar in construction and design. Constructed 1,700 years after the original (first) layer of Göbekli Tepe, it is dated 11,400 years ago at the oldest layer to 10,200 years at the youngest layer.[285]

Göbekli Tepe-type massive T-shaped pillars found at Nevah Cori were carved in relief. Some pillars had hand depictions, others had animal images.[286] Hundreds of small, 2-inch-high (5 cm) ceramic figurines, most depicting humans, were found at the site. The figurines, fired at temperatures between 500-600 degrees Centigrade, suggest advanced firing technology.[287]

The Cro-Magnon Aurignacian culture first used ceramic technology 26,000 years ago to produce the Dolni Vestonice Venus figurine and other objects. This may be a connection to the people at Nevah Cori. The Dolni Vestonice figurine, discovered at an Aurignacian site in the Czech Republic, is considered the oldest ceramic in the world. Other ceramic objects were found at nearby Aurignacian sites.[288]

The Dolni Vestonice date is significant because the next known use of ceramics is the discovery of ceramic figurines from the Nevah Cori archaeological site in Turkey dated to 10,500 years ago, and ceramics dated to around 10,000 years ago from the Korean Peninsula.[289]

Master craftsmen constructed the middle layer of Göbekli

Tepe in Turkey, dated to 10,800 years old, after the Younger Dryas stadial. It contains several adjoining rectangular buildings with polished limestone floors. The buildings do not have doors or windows. People may have entered through openings in wooden roofs. A Venus figure is carved deeply and sharply into the stone surface on a bench between two pillars. Two of the columns have bas-relief carvings of two lions. The top layer is not as tall as the two other (older) layers.[290]

People carefully buried Nevah Cori 10,300 years ago and Göbekli Tepe 10,200 years ago by backfilling each site into a mound of small limestone fragments, stone vessels, stone tools, and animal and human bone debris. The mounds, thought to be natural geologic features by local populations, protected Göbekli Tepe and Nevah Cori until their recent discoveries.[291]

The similarity of building materials and construction style connects the people of Nevah Cori and the nearby Göbekli Tepe compound. Nevah Cori has a unique connection to the Aurignacian culture because of the production of ceramic Venus figurines.

Did the people who constructed and used Göbekli Tepe also construct Nevah Cori? Did another culture build a similar complex in a better location 20 miles (32 km) away, or did one group split into two related cultures?

The cultures of Göbekli Tepe and Nevah Cori have not been identified, but the recurrence of the Venus figure as an amulet or as a symbol connects both to the Aurignacian, the Gravettian, and the Magdalenian cultures in Europe. The Aurignacians and the Gravettians had left their settlements in Europe well before the end of the ice age. The last distinct Magdalenian artifact is a Venus figurine discovered in Monruz, Switzerland, called the Venus of Monruz pendant. It is a stylized figure of a woman dated to 11,000 years ago and carved from jet.[292]

The Kebaran culture in Canaan, the El Khiam culture of

Canaan and Mesopotamia, the cultures of Sumeria, ancient Israel, the Nile Delta in Egypt, and the pre-Harappa in the Indus River Valley continued the practice of producing female figurine amulets after the end of the last ice age.[293]

Nevah Cori is credited with evidence of plant domestication, such as Einkorn wheat, making it an important site of human occupation after the last glacial period. Unfortunately, the Turkish government built the Ataturk Dam. The rock-lined dam on the Euphrates River covered the Nevah Cori compound and many other archaeological sites with water.[294]

Villages with roads and wells scattered across Cyprus by the time Göbekli Tepe and Nevah Cori were abandoned 10,200 years ago.[295]

Polar ice samples show that a series of seven massive volcanoes erupted 9,900 years ago. Scientists don't know where the volcanoes exploded, but the skies would have darkened for an extended time. Earth experienced cooler temperatures for 300 years to 800 years afterwards.[296]

People in the town of Jericho abandoned their territory around the time of the multiple volcanic eruptions 9,900 years ago, and the village culture east of the Tigress River abandoned their territories 9,400 years ago. Both areas remained unsettled for the next thousand years. Settlements dotted the Jezreel Valley in today's northern Israel by 9,000 years ago, perhaps from the Tigress River people.[297]

Vegetation covered North Africa, the Arabian Peninsula, and northern Mesopotamia by 9,000 years ago.[298] Nomads moved into the Arabian Peninsula 9,000 years ago and claimed the interior region while sedentary tribes settled along the coastlines.[299]

Jericho repopulated 8,800 years ago as tribes throughout Canaan expanded their territories. For the next several thousand years after the end of the last ice age, archaeological evidence, legends, and stories reveal a growing territory of settlements along the northeastern Mediterranean coastline (Anatolia) into Canaan (Syria, Lebanon, Israel, and the Jordan Valley) and up around the Black Sea, parts of the Caspian Sea, and through the Caucasus Mountains. Villages developed in Mesopotamia (Iraq, parts of Iran), northern India (now parts of Pakistan, India, and Afghanistan), the Hindu Kush (now part of China, Pakistan, and India), and Mediterranean islands Cyprus and Crete. Southwest from Canaan people settled North Africa along the southern Mediterranean coastline and they settled in the Horn of Africa.[300]

The remaining Laurentide Ice Sheet on the edge of northeastern North America collapsed 8,200 years ago and twin glacial lakes Agassiz and Ojibway quickly drained into the North Atlantic Ocean. This raised worldwide sea levels significantly, perhaps by as much as 9 feet (2.8 meters).[301]

The ice sheet collapse resulted in a climate change to a cool and dry period that lasted 200 years worldwide and up to 300 years in Mesopotamia and surrounding regions.[302]

People in northern Canaan spoke an original Semitic language 8,100 years ago and they moved east into Mesopotamia. Archaeologists named the dominant early cultures of Mesopotamia the Halaf and the Samarra followed by the Ubaid and Uruk.[303]

Around the time people began building towns in Mesopotamia 8,000 years ago, nomads migrated into India, and farmers on the central plains of China formed villages while nomads and farmers, probably descendants of the Kebaran and Natufian cultures, staked out territory in Egypt.[304]

The settlements of early Mesopotamia changed over time. Sumer (also called Shumer) meant "the land" in Sumerian. Early Sumerians constructed city-state Mari 6,900 years ago, with its round, white limestone buildings. In the city-state Kish, people built a magnificent palace complex 6,000 years ago.³⁰⁵

A worldwide period of intense dry climate with little rainfall, called aridification, began 5,900 years ago and lasted over 1,000 years. A vast area in Africa turned to desert and is known today as the Sahara.³⁰⁶ Cultures around the world migrated toward rivers and lakes during the aridification period.

The organization in Mesopotamia of city-states into a confederation began at the time of the hot, dry climate change. The Ubaid culture on the Plains of Nineveh merged with another culture and began building round, walled cities like Mari with complex water storage and distribution methods. Sumeria became a group of connected city-states such as Nineveh, Mari, Kish, and Ur with a highly organized central leadership or kingship system of government. The city-states formed the confederation of Sumeria around a sophisticated collective irrigation system.³⁰⁷

The Jewish calendar, also known as the Calendar of Nineveh, started at the beginning of the Sumerian Empire around 5,800 years ago. It is based on a complex Sumerian mathematical calculation, a formula employing the Constant of Nineveh.³⁰⁸

Archaeologists working in Iraq found the computations on tablet fragments excavated at the site of the ancient Babylonian Ashur-bani-pal Palace Library. In the Constant of Nineveh calculation, the orbits of the planets can be expressed by one number, an unusual shared common denominator that is the product of seventy multiplied seven times by sixty.³⁰⁹

The Jewish calendar is based on coordinating three independent astronomical phenomena: the rotation of Earth about its axis, the revolution of the moon around Earth, and the revolution of Earth around the sun representing, respectively, a day, a month, and a year.

It is a lunar calendar comprising 354.37 days. The Julian/

Gregorian calendar is a solar calendar comprising 365.24 days. The lunar Jewish calendar is adjusted to the solar cycle to ensure that Jewish holidays occur at the time of year specified in the Torah. Sumerian astronomers added intercalary months as needed to adjust the lunar calendar year to coincide with solar years.[310] The Sumerian calendar year started with Nisan, as does the modern Jewish calendar, and each lists the same month names.

At the time the Calendar of Nineveh began and Sumerian city-states formed a confederation, the Akkadian language developed 5,800 years ago as a variant of proto-Semitic Hebrew, the ancestor to historic Hebrew and other Semitic languages of the Middle East. Sumerians and Akkadians used cuneiform writing for 3,000 years.[311]

Sumerians developed advanced metallurgy skills and began using bronze around 5,600 years ago, bringing in the Bronze Age. They established long-distance trade routes throughout the region, including Crete. Evidence excavated from the ancient Sumerian city of Mari, birthplace of Sarah, referred to the island of Crete as Kaptara.

The Torah describes one of the many tribes of Canaan (people descended from Noah and Na'ama's son Ham) settling first in Egypt, then on Crete (Genesis 10:13-14). Archaeological sites of the first farming settlements on Crete dating to 9,000 years ago could be evidence of these early Hamites. The Sumerians were trading partners with people living on Crete. A contingent of Sumerians ("people of the land") from Mesopotamia arrived on Crete 5,650 years ago to become Kaptarans ("people of the island"). English archaeologists named the culture Minoan after an imaginary Greek king, Minos, son of Zeus.

About 5,000 years ago the Minoan/Kaptarans, experienced

seafarers, invented the galley, a sailing vessel powered by men handling a row of oars on each side. The Sumerians in Mesopotamia kept a close relationship with their cousins, and trading partners, on Crete. An Egyptian relief from the Old Kingdom Period around 4,400 years ago depicts trade between Egypt and Crete. The Egyptians of that time used a Minoan/Kaptaran-type galley ship to transport wood and slaves from Canaan to Egypt.[312]

The Minoan/Kaptarns believed their first leader and teacher to be a huntress; her symbol was a pomegranate, her constant companion a lion.[313] The Israelite tribe of Judah became a tribe of leadership during the Exodus, and the flag of Judah depicts a lion. King David and King Solomon from the tribe of Judah are ancient Israel's most famous monarchs. A carved ivory pomegranate dating to the time of Solomon is among modern Israel's artifacts. King Kubaba, a famous woman ruler of ancient Sumeria mentioned on the King List, carried a mirror and a pomegranate as her symbols.[314] (Sumerians, Egyptians, and Israelites had male and female kings.)

Sumerians developed a complex culture that thrived for thousands of years. The Sumerian King List hints that this culture may have developed from an earlier society that flourished during the ice age.[315]

Some of the tablet fragments excavated from the Ashurbani-pal Palace Library site in Iraq, when pieced together, contained a Sumerian King List. The list and accompanying narrative describe a succession of kings of Kish who ruled their people for 24,510 years, three months, and three and a half days, then kingship transferred to Uruk 5,000 years ago.[316] The narrative records Kish as the first city to have kings after the deluge. Kish may have been the first ruling city-state of ancient Sumeria.[317]

The tablets recorded that Aka, son of Enmebaragesi, who reigned for 629 years, completed the list of 23 kings of Kish.

Most researchers have concluded that the period of 24,510 years is a fantasy or a misinterpretation. The life span of the initial kings on the list lasted an average of 1,000 years and decreased to the 629 years listed for the last king before the kingship transfer. The unusually long lives may represent the reign of a family line instead an individual; however, the Torah also records longer lives occurring before the Great Flood. For example, as mentioned, Adam lived 930 years and Noah's grandfather Methuselah lived 969 years.

Also, evidence has not been found that a civilization existed in Mesopotamia until after the end of the last glacial period. The King List could reference a civilization that operated with a kingship system in another location during the ice age because the list references over 24,000 years of royal rulers prior to the founding of Sumeria. That time frame coincides with the beginning of the Last Glacial Maximum 26,500 years ago.

Hundreds of small female figurines made of clay have been excavated from sites in Nineveh in Sumeria and northern Mesopotamia. The figurines connect Sumeria to ice-age cultures that produced similar small female statuettes, or amulets.

Some features of the Göbekli Tepe complex and the smaller Nevah Cori complex hint that the people who engineered these sites could have been related to the Sumerian culture of Mesopotamia. At Göbekli Tepe, the roughly incised female figure on a stone bench may be a link between the cultures because female-figurine amulets were common in Sumeria, and hundreds of them were found at Nevah Cori.[318] Also at Göbekli Tepe is a 12,000-year-old life-sized stone statue of a mother giving birth. It is called by some researchers, referencing the Sumerian Creation story, "the emerging human" statue.[319]

A thousand years after the confederation of Sumeria formed, societies based largely on craft-trade began to form in the Indus River Valley in India around 5,000 years ago. Grasslands and thick forests covered the Indus River Valley at that time, unlike today. The culture, called pre-Harappa, that settled into the Indus River Valley grew grains and produced hundreds of female figurine statutes.[320]

In Egypt by 4,800 years ago villages and city-states may have coalesced into a distinct culture under a single dynasty.[321] By 4,800 years ago people in Mesopotamia and Canaan began speaking Hebrew, Ugaritic, and Aramaic.[322]

A series of kings ruled Sumeria from the capital of Kish until Sargon of Akkad unified the Sumerian city-states of Akkad, Kish, Lagash, Uruk, Mari, Yarmuti, Elam, and Ur from 4,270 years ago to 4,215 years ago. During his 55-year reign, Ur, in southern Sumeria, became the power center of the empire.[323]

One of the severest droughts in ancient history began 4,200 years ago and lasted 100 years across the entire Middle East and North Africa.[324] When the drought intensified, the rulers of Ur built a western wall as a security measure to prevent the tide of refugees from the northern territories from overwhelming Ur. Akkad fell to invading mountain people 4,100 years ago.[325] At the time Akkad was overrun, the first central government, the Xia Dynasty, formed in China.[326]

For the next several hundred years, intermittent rain, food shortages, and dwindling water sources from repeated droughts in Canaan, Mesopotamia, and Asia caused neighboring tribes to wage war against one another.[327]

11

THE PROMISED LAND

In an austere time of dwindling resources and tribal violence, Abraham, the father of Judaism, and Sarah, first Jewish Matriarch, were born in Sumeria. Their ancestors had lived in Mesopotamia during the golden age of Sumeria and Akkadia.

Judaism's greatest rabbis have debated the birthplace of Abraham based on their knowledge of the settlement of Noah's descendants. The Torah mentions the town of Harran as the location for the House of Terach, Abraham's father. Rabbis and scholars agree that the family of Terach's son moved from Ur to Canaan, then to Egypt.

Noah, his second-born son, Shem, and Shem's great-grandson, Ever (Ivri in Hebrew), were known to be monotheists before Abraham and Sarah reintroduced monotheistic concepts to their Sumerian family and followers.[328] By the time Abraham and Sarah married and established their home in Ur, the Amorites, a nomadic, predatory Hamite tribe, began threatening Sumeria.

Around that time Abraham and Sarah left Ur with his father, Terah, and nephew, Lot, to move to the land of Canaan.

Lot's father, Haran, died in Ur before they made the journey. Abraham's other brother, Nahor, stayed in Sumeria.

Abraham and his family traveled as far as Harran where Terah had a house. Harran was an important city and center of moon observation and study, like the city of Ur. Many Sumerians fled their homeland to join Abraham and Sarah's tribe in Harran during the Amorite invasion. A large group of skilled craftsmen, artists, and engineers left Harran for Kaptara (Crete). At the time Ur fell 3,950 years ago, the Kaptarans began building elaborate palaces, developed community water supply and sewage systems, and started using kilns and potter's wheels to produce refined, artistically stunning ceramics.[329]

Abraham and Sarah's tribe stayed in Harran until Abraham's father, Terah, died and G-d commanded Abraham to take his people to the Promised Land, the land of Canaan (Genesis 12:5).

The story continues through Genesis. The migrating Sumerians, led by Abraham and Sarah, left Harran and traveled to the Judean Mountains where they stopped in the town of Shechem. Sumerians who left Mesopotamia built the town around 4,000 years ago. In Hebrew, Shechem means "shoulder" and describes the view of the Judean Mountains.

Israelis have discovered several third-millennium BCE megalithic structures close to Lake Kinneret. One is Bet Yerah, 19 miles (30 km) northeast of Lake Kinneret. People built Bet Yerah, a large, well-fortified third-millennium town, with round buildings enclosed by large concentric circular stone walls like Göbekli Tepe in Anatolia and Mari in Sumeria.[330]

Abraham assembled his tent in Shechem, the tribe rested, and Abraham prayed. Then they journeyed continually until they came into the Negev, the southern desert region. Unfortunately, mass starvation from a drought afflicted Canaan (future

Israel) so they traveled on to Egypt where they planned to live temporarily.

Abraham became wealthy in Egypt, the regional drought ceased, and the time came for Abraham, Sarah, and their people to return to Canaan.

The tribe of Abraham and Sarah settled parts of Canaan (in Israel and the Jordan Valley). Years later, Abraham and Sarah had a son, Isaac. Thirty-seven years later Sarah died in Hebron and Abraham buried her there. He mourned for three years before turning his attention to their son.

Abraham sent a trusted servant, the elder of his household, to Sumeria to find a wife for Isaac among his and Sarah's tribe, not from the local Hamite tribes.

The servant traveled to Aram Of-Two-Rivers, the town where Nahor, Abraham's brother, lived. He returned to the Negev with a beautiful, kind woman named Rebecca. Isaac and Rebecca met and fell in love.

G-d's promise to Abraham that he and Sarah's descendants will inherit the Promised Land is close to fulfillment.[331] Before Abraham's death, he made inheritance arrangements. He had children with women other than Sarah. But only the descendants of Isaac, the child of Matriarch Sarah and Patriarch Abraham, will inherit the Promised Land.

Rebecca and Isaac lived in the Negev. G-d's plan was revealed to Rebecca during her difficult pregnancy. They raised their twin sons, Esav and Jacob. When the time came, Rebecca chose Jacob, the second-born twin, to be the leader of their now-large tribe and to see that G-d's plan would be carried out properly.

Jacob received a blessing from G-d to inherit the Promised Land, described as the land of Canaan. The blessing combined words and phrases found in the Genesis Creation verses, the new start after the Great Flood, and the covenant with Abraham.

The message to Jacob is clear that the advent of the nation of Israel for the benefit of humanity is near.[332]

Jacob moved to Harran where he married two sisters, Leah and then Rachel. Rachel died giving birth to her second son, Benjamin, on the family's move from Harran back to Canaan. Jacob fathered twelve sons and a daughter with Leah, Rachel, and Leah's maid, Zilpa, and Rachel's maid Bilha.

Genesis then reveals the origin of the name Israel. One day on a journey to meet his estranged brother Esav, Jacob had a vision and met a mysterious stranger. The stranger, an angel, changed Jacob's name from Yaakov (second-born twin) to Yisrael (G-d Fighter).

The family lived in Israel while the children matured. Joseph, Rachel's firstborn, was secretly sold into Egyptian slavery by his jealous brothers. Many years later, Leah died, and another regional famine swept across Israel, Egypt, and other lands.[333] Jacob heard that Egypt had extra rations so he sent ten of his sons to go buy rationed grain.

Joseph, the brother sold into slavery, had done well in Egypt, had married, and become governor over the land. Joseph's position included supplying rationed grain to the people so his brothers came to him, not recognizing him.

The regional famine continued and the sons of Jacob journeyed a second time to Egypt to buy additional provisions. Joseph then revealed his identity. Joseph had a joyful reunion with his repentant brothers, and then explained to them that G-d made a plan for him to be sold into slavery and taken to Egypt in order to save the family from the famine. He informed them that they must immediately move to Egypt because he believes the drought will cause another five years of severe famine.

The brothers returned to Canaan and told all to their father, Jacob. The family and their relations, with their livestock and possessions, moved to Egypt's Nile Delta to reunite with Joseph and wait out the famine.

The clan became successful and stayed after the famine ended. Jacob died seventeen years after the tribe entered Egypt. His dying wish, to be buried in Hebron with Abraham, Sarah, and Leah, is fulfilled with a royal-type funeral procession, complete with chariots, from Goshen to Hebron.

The last part of Genesis recounts how powerful Joseph became in Egypt by receiving silver and gold from people both in Egypt and in Canaan in exchange for rationed grain during the first part of the famine. When the famine continued, Joseph agreed to accept livestock for the grain, and finally, during the last of the famine they traded their land for grain.

When the famine ended Joseph had control of, or ruled, the Egyptian people and all of Egypt. The people praised Joseph for saving them. Joseph told them to keep their land and work it, but to give to pharaoh one-fifth of everything produced on their land as a grain tax.

During the reign of Joseph, the Hebrew people lived lives of prestige and wealth. The book of Genesis ends with the death of Joseph at age 110. Joseph also wanted to be buried in Israel, so his relatives embalmed him and put him in a coffin in Egypt to be taken to Israel later.

After Joseph died, the Egyptians forgot or discounted that he had saved their lives during the great famine. The first chapter of Exodus, the second book of the Torah, recounts the death of Joseph and how, after his death, the Hebrews fell on hard times in Egypt.

The phrase in the first chapter of Exodus, "rise up from the ground," is the excuse the pharaoh used to enslave the Hebrew people. The phrase means they will improve their wretched condition or that the pharaoh fears Jacob's descendants will gain ascendancy over all of Egypt.[334]

The Hebrew people, once proud and wealthy, became enslaved by the Egyptian government as a workforce. The Hebrew word *perekh* used to describe the labor inflicted upon the Children of Israel can mean "crushing-labor," or ruthlessly, or with vigor, or it can denote a legal term. In Near Eastern languages the Hebrew word *perekh* is equivalent to the Akkadian word *pirku*, a legal term describing unjust and unreasonable demands. When the term is applied to nonslaves it means extended forced labor, treating a free person as a slave. Ancient Egyptian documents describe a king's right to press his or her free subjects into forced national labor for a reasonable time; beyond that time would be a violation of the subject's natural rights and would therefore be perekh.[335]

Through the period of wealth and prosperity as well as the enslavement, the Hebrew people, the Children of Israel, kept their tribal identities intact.

The Egyptians agreed to exempt the tribe of Levi from work so they could spend their time in study and prayer. Use of the word perekh to describe the type of labor and the work exemption for the Levites indicates the Children of Israel were free subjects forced to work on national building projects under unjust conditions and for an unreasonable length of time.[336]

The Torah describes the 110 years of hard labor the Children of Israel (except for the Levites) endured while they built monumental brick-based national projects throughout Egypt.

The Torah story of Joseph's rise to power in Egypt and Jacob's royal-type funeral has led some researchers to conclude that the Hebrews of the Torah are the Hyksos of ancient Egypt. The next chapter explores the origins of the mysterious Hyksos culture.

12

THE EGYPTIANS AND THE HYKSOS

TIMELINE (BCE/CE used for timelines after 3,900 years ago)

1900 BCE	Hyksos begin migration to Nile Valley, Egypt
1807 BCE	Dynastic Hyksos family rules Lower Egypt
1710 BCE	Hyksos rebuild Avaris into fortified capital
1710 BCE	Hyksos build in Canaan
1640 BCE	**Supervolcano Aegean Sea**
1640 BCE	Dynastic Hyksos family rules all of Egypt
1550–1520 BCE	Hyksos-Egyptian war, Avaris falls

Egyptians recorded a King List of their dynastic rulers. In the Middle Kingdom Period, Egypt experienced prosperity and political stability in the Twelfth Dynasty. One of the last rulers of that dynasty, a woman named King Sobekneferu, died in 1802 BCE (Jewish calendar: 1958) and with her death a peaceful age of a united Egypt ended.[337]

King Sobekneferu did not leave an heir. A series of royal

family members ruled Upper Egypt following her death. Lower Egypt became autonomous. During the reign of the last king of the Twelfth Dynasty, work in copper and turquoise mines in the Sinai stopped. Artifacts provide evidence that a foreign dynast and his followers began settling in the Nile Delta before King Sobekneferu's reign.[338]

Dynasts are hereditary monarchs or founders of a dynasty, a prominent and powerful family group whose members retain their position through several generations. Examples of dynasts are Abraham and Sarah.

According to Egyptian records, around 1900-1850 BCE (Jewish calendar: 1860-1910), a mixed Semitic tribe with horses and chariots migrated from Canaan to Egypt due to drought-caused famines.[339]

A painted wall of an Egyptian tomb dated around 1900 BCE depicts a Semitic tribe entering the Nile Delta. The groups of men and women entering Egypt travel with children, livestock, and bundles of possessions, and most wear fine clothing. Some of the children ride donkeys. The women have long, dark hair and walk with the children between groups of men carrying spears, bows, and sheathed arrows. The men have dark, shoulder-length hair and trimmed beards. The arrivals have light skin and are greeted by dark-skinned Egyptian men with long, dark hair and goatees.[340]

A Theban historian, Manetho, in 300 BCE (Jewish calendar: 3460) referred to the Fifteenth Dynasty Semitic rulers of Egypt as the *heqa-khase*, meaning "rulers of foreign lands." First-century CE Greek translators called heqa-khase "Hyksos." Flavius Josephus, a first-century CE Jewish historian, identified the Hyksos people as the Hebrews of the Torah.[341]

The Second Intermediate Period in Egyptian dynastic history, the Hyksos Period, includes the Fourteenth and Fifteenth Dynasties. Egyptian records document that the Hyksos dynasties started in 1807 BCE (Jewish calendar: 1953) and lasted until the fall of their capital, Avaris, 286 years later.³⁴²

King Jakbim, founder of the Fourteenth Dynasty, ruled for twenty-three years. His son, Y'annui, reigned after him. Burials in the Nile Delta at the beginning of Hyksos rule suggest possible attacks by Egyptians from Thebes. Later the Hyksos of Avaris and the Egyptians from Thebes allowed each other to travel across their territories.³⁴³ The Hyksos kings of the Fourteenth and Fifteenth Dynasties traded with Nubia, a kingdom to the south.³⁴⁴

By 1710 BCE (Jewish calendar: 2050) the Hyksos had built a fortified city in the Nile Delta, Avaris, as their capital. Some buildings had Minoan/Kaptaran frescoes from Knossos on Crete.³⁴⁵ Archaeologists also date to the same time a Hyksos fortified city discovered near Tel Aviv, Israel.³⁴⁶

A supervolcanic eruption in the Aegean Sea in 1620 BCE (Jewish calendar: 2120) shook the region and darkened the skies with debris. The tsunami that followed likely destroyed the Minoan/Kaptaran civilization on nearby Crete. Minoan/Kaptarans who escaped the Aegean Sea supervolcanic eruption in 1620 BCE had sailed away from Crete to the Aegean mainland in the northeastern Peloponnese 56 miles (90 km) southwest of Athens when the volcanic warning signs started.

They were likely joined by Hebrews from Egypt escaping the devastation of the volcano's aftermath. Together these two groups of Sumerian descendants founded the advanced Mycenaean culture. An intact Mycenaean grave discovered in 2015 (Jewish calendar 5775) yielded a treasure of items including a gold ring with an engraved likeness of King Kubaba, the most famous Sumerian king, holding her mirror.³⁴⁷ The widespread damage to property and famines from crop failures following the supervolcanic eruption caused regional migrations and a great scattering of peoples.

Mass graves were used in Avaris after the supervolcanic eruption. The Hyksos provided grain to the Egyptians through the volcanic winter. Archaeologists found in Avaris huge ancient granaries in the palace complex. When it ended, the Hyksos kings ruled all Egypt and the Abydos city-state to the south.[348] The ability to store enough grain to feed Egypt's and Canaan's populations through years of famine is part of the Torah story of Jacob and Rachel's son, Joseph.

The Hyksos rulers, Hebrew kings, seemed to have brought Egypt back to prosperity for the next hundred years after the supervolcanic eruption. But near the end of the Fifteenth Dynasty the stable economy and peaceful relationships with neighboring nations tempted the Theban elite who wanted the power and wealth of the Egyptian kingdom for themselves.[349]

A Theban from one of the four ruling families in 1571 BCE (Jewish calendar: 2189) declared himself king of a newly created Seventeenth Dynasty, which he ruled from Thebes. Hyksos King Apophis traded land for peace and allowed the Theban Seventeenth Dynasty to coexist and rule Upper Egypt. The two dynasties may have established trade agreements after initial confrontations. Twenty years of peaceful coexistence passed, but then the House of Thebes wanted more. Theban King Kamose raided and plundered Hyksos villages and the neighboring Nubian Kingdom. Then he initiated a war against them.[350]

The Hyksos had been in Egypt for 270 years by the time King Kamose came to power in Thebes. In the first historically recorded aggression based on ethnic cleansing, the Theban king began propagandizing the need to expel them because they were a foreign race, not Egyptian. Hyksos defenders killed Kamose when he attempted to raid their village. Theban King Ahmose succeeded him and continued the war against the "foreigners."[351]

In 1521 BCE (Jewish calendar: 2239) the Hyksos capital, Avaris, fell to the army of King Ahmose. The age of individual freedoms and fair taxation, the age of the Hyksos kings in Egypt, closed abruptly. King Ahmose changed his title to Pharaoh Ahmose and became absolute ruler of Egypt, including newly conquered Nubia and Abydos. In five years the army of Ahmose plundered North Africa, Canaan, southeastern Anatolia, and western Arabia. Egypt became a regional military superpower. Egyptian records say that the government enslaved a former free and powerful people, a separate nation living among Egyptians, to build national monuments and temples from stone and brick.[352]

The Torah describes the same work the Egyptian rulers exacted from the Hebrews in the same time period. Plunder financed the projects in Karnak, Thebes, and several other places throughout Egypt. Massive brick-based building projects began shortly after the fall of Avaris and continued for over a hundred years.[353]

Kamose and, after his short reign, his successor, Ahmose, used the same excuse—national pride—to attack the foreigners, strip them of their possessions, and enslave them. Ahmose, after destroying the Hyksos capital, declared Egypt liberated from foreigners. He then instituted strict government controls over the Egyptian people. The pharaohs who followed Ahmose in the Eighteenth Dynasty continued the harsh totalitarian rule. They used plunder and tributes provided by their army to finance their own national building projects.[354]

Were the Hyksos the Children of Israel? The Hyksos began their reign in 1807 BCE (Jewish calendar: 1953) in the Nile Delta. The Torah time frame of Jacob and his sons migrating to the Nile Delta during a drought would put the Hebrew tribe with Jacob entering the Nile Delta around the same time.

The Torah story of Joseph and his brothers in Egypt could be a combination of events, such as the regional famines and the Aegean Sea supervolcanic eruption, which created circumstances for a rise to power by the dynastic family line of Abraham and Sarah through Jacob, his sons, and their descendants.

The Hyksos introduced horses, chariots, and advanced fortification techniques to Egypt. The first mention of chariots in the Torah is Joseph leading the funeral procession for his father, Jacob, from Goshen to Hebron. Horse-drawn chariots were in the procession. Chariots, first designed for transportation, were later produced as implements of war, especially by the Egyptians.

Joseph's father, Jacob, lived in Goshen, in the Nile Delta, a short time before his death. Yet, the pharaoh's entire household and all the elders of Egypt joined Joseph, his brothers, and the Hebrew households for the journey to Hebron in Israel. The funeral procession began after all of Egypt wept for Jacob for seventy days. The Egyptian national bereavement and involvement in the procession to Hebron seem extraordinary for anyone other than a royal family member.

Near the end of Genesis, Joseph asked the royal household to put in a good word for him to "Pharaoh" so he could get permission to go to Hebron to bury his father. In a seemingly contradictory statement after the funeral in Hebron, Joseph told his brothers that in order to save the Children of Israel during the famine G-d had made Joseph "Father to Pharaoh" and lord of all his household and ruler over all the land of Egypt. That could imply that Joseph became a king of Egypt.

Before the Aegean Sea supervolcanic eruption, Hyksos kings ruled Lower Egypt while Theban kings ruled Upper Egypt. Joseph, as a Hyksos king, might have asked the Theban king, or House of Pharaoh, for permission to cross territory or grant certain other considerations for his father's funeral procession.

When the people agreed to give Joseph one-fifth of their harvests "over to pharaoh," the harvest "tax" could have gone to one of Joseph's giant storage warehouses like the kind found at

Avaris, or it could mean the harvest portion belonged to a king whom Joseph served.

The earlier Egyptian dynasties, including the period of Hyksos rule, used the word "pharaoh" to mean the "great house," or building associated with the government. When the Hyksos rule came to an end in Egypt, the word became associated with a king as an absolute, or divine, ruler.[355]

Egyptian records say the Hyksos kept apart from the Egyptians. The Torah also records that the Hebrew population, the Children of Israel, kept apart from the Egyptian population. In the Torah, the pharaoh perceived the Egyptians to be the native nation and the Children of Israel to be a foreign nation. According to Egyptian historian Manetho, the Hyksos kings ruled Egypt for 286 years, and after they left they moved north and founded the Temple in Jerusalem.[356]

The Hyksos, foreign rulers of Egypt, were clearly the Hebrews of the Torah.

13

EXODUS

After the fall of Avaris, during the time the Hebrews were enslaved as a workforce, pharaohs of the Eighteenth Dynasty exploited the conquered territories of Nubia and Canaan.

When leaders in Canaan rebelled against high taxes and lengthy conscriptions into the Egyptian military, the ruling pharaoh took the rebel leaders' children from Canaan to "reeducate" them in Egypt.[357] The next pharaoh continued the punitive rule, collected tributes, and engaged in building projects. Severe working conditions imposed on the national laborers intensified.[358]

The Egyptian government, drunk with power and arrogance, was out of control. The only relief for the enslaved workers would be to leave Egypt and return to their homeland.

The timeline for the Exodus is derived from a combination of Jewish Bible records and archaeological evidence. The Torah records

430 years as the length of time in Egypt for the dynastic family line of Jacob, his sons, and their descendants. The Nevi'im, the second section of the Jewish Bible, records 480 years from the Exodus out of Egypt to the construction of the Temple in Jerusalem during King Solomon's reign.

The time from completion of the Temple going back 480 years is 1440 BCE (Jewish calendar: 2320), the proposed date for the Exodus.

The second book of the Torah, Exodus, is about the political and religious origins of Israel. The Torah doesn't mention the name of the pharaoh who overworked the Hebrew descendants of Jacob's twelve sons. The narrative does describe how the workload increased until the Children of Israel cried out to G-d for help.

Yocheved and her husband, Amran, both from the Tribe of Levi, had Moses, Aaron, and Miriam. Moses, raised by a pharaoh's daughter, arose to challenge the ruling pharaoh to release the Children of Israel.

Following a series of dramatic and prolonged negotiations with the pharaoh, Moses received permission to leave Egypt with the Children of Israel. Before their departure Moses instructed the Israelites to go among the Egyptians and ask for compensation for the unjust slave labor. They asked and received payment in the form of precious gold and silver jewelry, fancy linens, and gems.[359]

One group of Jews headed south along the familiar Nile River. They established a Jewish community around 1400 BCE (Jewish calendar: 2360) on the island of Yebu, named Elephantine by historians, in northern Nubia, now Aswan, Upper Egypt. Yebu would thrive as a Jewish city-state complete with a Temple for nearly a thousand years.[360]

Another group left to join their relatives on the Aegean mainland, the Mycenaeans. At the time of the Exodus, the

Mycenaeans built a stone block, walled fortress called by historians the Palace of Nestor. Enormous stone block construction, similar to the later Israelite's Western Wall in Jerusalem, was used for the nearby Lion's Gate. Linear B script appeared in the Palace of Nestor. This form of writing is an adaptation of Linear A script, a twenty-two letter system used only by the Minoan/Kaptaran palace class.[361]

The main group, led by Moses, Aaron, and Miriam, then began the Exodus to Israel. Egyptian soldiers followed the Israelites to retrieve gold they may have taken from Egyptian temples, or to murder the Israelites, or to return the workforce of three million people to Egypt.

A week after they left Egypt, at the Sea of Reeds in the Sinai Desert, the Israelites crossed the marshland before a supervening torrent of water drowned the soldiers. After losing the soldiers at the Sea of Reeds, the Egyptian government left the encampment of Jews alone, and Moses led the Jewish people to Mount Sinai.

Some men (Midianite converts) in the encampment fashioned a golden calf while Moses prayed on the mountain. The women of the tribes, including Moses's wife, Zipporah, refused to take part in the golden calf project. Moses returned from the mountain with Ten Commandments mystically written on stone tablets. The ground opened up under the men who made the golden calf. They died. Moses rewarded the women for refraining by giving women the holiday of Rosh Khodesh, a monthly celebration of the New Moon. Jewish women today still celebrate Rosh Khodesh.

The entire encampment of three million people on Mount Sinai heard the revelation of the Oral Torah directly from G-d.

During their time in Egypt, the descendants of Jacob's sons kept their family lines intact. At Mount Sinai the Israelites took the first census of the Jewish Nation by counting every military-able male over the age of twenty as the head of a household. Each head of household identified his family's lineage. Moses and the other leaders arranged the entire encampment by tribe.

The census counted adult males by the donation of a half-shekel coin. Shekel in Hebrew refers to measuring. The people of Sumeria first used the shekel as a currency.[362]

Moses and his brother, Aaron, designated a space in the center of the encampment for the Tent of Meeting, also called the Mishkan, or Tabernacle. People from each tribe brought gifts to build and supply the Tabernacle. The primary items needed, and generously donated, included gold, copper, linen, goat hair, animal skins, acacia wood, olive oil, spices, gems, and wool. They dyed the wool aqua, purple, or red.[363]

Silver used in the Tabernacle to make some of the ceremonial objects came solely from the half-shekel coin collection gathered from the head of each household during the first census taken on Mount Sinai.[364] The Tabernacle housed the Ark of the Covenant during the Exodus and the early settlement of Israel and became the spiritual center for the people.[365]

Moses, a year after leaving Egypt, sent twelve men to scout the Land of Israel. When they returned, Caleb ben Yefuneh representing the tribe of Judah, and one other scout, Hoshe's ben Nun (later called Joshua) from the tribe of Ephraim, told the truth and encouraged the people. The other ten scouts reported that the land's inhabitants were fierce and unconquerable. They also reported seeing offspring of Anaks, primeval giants. Children or descendants of giants in the Hebraic Empire are referenced after the Great Flood, but the giants themselves are apparently gone.

Even though the funeral procession for Jacob had taken only a few days to reach Hebron from Goshen, Moses stayed with the Israelites in the wilderness for forty years preparing for the settlement of Israel. They left Mount Sinai and wandered, meaning they moved their encampment many times. They traveled with herds of cattle and sheep so they camped in places where their animals could graze.

When they traveled or camped, the tribes were divided into four groups of three tribes each. The groups surrounded the tribe of Levi, and the Levites surrounded the Tabernacle. Each tribe carried a flag.

For those four decades the Israelites were vulnerable, encamped in the Sinai Desert. During that time the pharaohs of the Eighteenth Dynasty of Egypt were absorbed with internal power struggles and busy managing national building projects.[366]

During the Exodus, the Tribes of Israel used flags for identification while in the wilderness. Each tribe carried a flag with a specific color and emblem. The flags of Reuben, Shimon, Levi, and Joseph represent historical events.[367]

Some Jews today use the unique and colorful tribal flags of Israel as a motif for art, jewelry, clothing, quilts, and other items.

The sky-blue flag with a lion belonged to the tribe of Judah. As the tribe of leadership, Judah led the tribes in the Wilderness.[368]

The tribe of Reuben had a red flag with mandrake flowers. Shimon's tribe had a green flag showing buildings of the city of Shechem in the Judean Hills. Levi's flag of red, white and black displayed the High Priest's breastplate. Joseph's black flag depicting Egypt became two flags. Moses divided this tribe for Joseph's two sons to honor him because Joseph saved the Children of Israel during a great famine. Ephraim's flag depicting Egypt had a bull. Menashe's black flag depicting Egypt had a wild ox.[369]

A bluish-black flag with a sun and moon represented Issachar. The tribe of Issachar formed a partnership with the tribe of

Zebulon. The merchants of Zebulon agreed to support the Torah scholars of Issachar. The tribe of Zebulon had a white flag with a ship. Also seafaring merchants, the tribe of Dan had a blue flag with a snake.[370]

The tribe of Naphtali had a deep wine-colored flag with a deer. When Moses blessed the tribes he said the Naphtalites were satiated with favor. A pearlescent-colored flag with an olive tree became Asher's. Moses gave a multicolored flag with a wolf to the tribe of Benjamin. A black and white flag with a tent camp represented the tribe of Gad.[371]

During those four decades in the wilderness the Israelites developed their nation's legal, judiciary, and economic systems. They also adapted their writing system into a twenty-two letter alphabet after they left Egypt. Almost all modern phonetic alphabets, including Greek and Latin, derive from the Hebrew system. The first two letters of the Hebrew alphabet are *aleph* and *bet*, so the Hebrew writing system was, and still is, called the Aleph-Bet.[372]

At the end of the Exodus, Moses blessed the entire nation and each of the tribes. The line of Abraham and Sarah, through Jacob's descendants, had become a nation. They stood ready to enter their homeland as a tribal confederacy. The Children of Israel, after 430 years in Egypt and 40 years of preparation in the wilderness, were finally returning to the land of their ancestors.

They entered Israel with the tribe of Judah leading the way around 1400 BCE (Jewish calendar: 2360). Hoshe'a ben Nun from the tribe of Ephraim gathered the tribes together in Shechem, where the Children of Israel reaffirmed their observance of the Torah. Each of the tribes had a designated section of land except the tribe of Levi.

The tribes of Reuben and Gad wanted to settle outside the perimeters of the Promised Land. Moses had blessed both tribes and had granted their request. The Midianites who lived in the Jordan Valley opposed them. So the Reubenites joined with the Gadites to battle them. Following a successful battle the Reubenites lived in the Jordan Valley bordering the northern half of the Dead Sea.[373]

Archaeological evidence does not support a military conquest by the Israelites upon entering the Land of Israel, though some battles were fought with local tribes.[374] The tribal confederacy of Israel, represented by a new generation of Jews born in the wilderness, settled into abandoned towns and cities and built new ones, except for the pastoral tribes of Reuben and Shimon. They continued their semi-nomadic lifestyle as sheep herders on their allotted lands.[375]

The land settled by the tribe of Gad included a vast eastern border along the Jordan River from the south tip of Lake Kinneret (Sea of Galilee) to the north tip of the Dead Sea. With its strong military nature the Gadites would hold off some of Israel's future enemies.[376]

Judah's large portion bordered the west shore of the Dead Sea and stretched all the way to Dan's southern coastal land (now known as the Gaza Strip). Caleb received the area of Hebron in the Judean Hills, which he had scouted thirty-nine years earlier.

Because of their ongoing involvement with the Tabernacle/ Temple and Jewish education the Levites were not to receive land. Instead, they would receive a tithe of 10% donated from all agricultural produce of Israel. The Levites resided near Mount Moriah where the Temple would eventually stand. The tribe of Shimon lived in the Negev.[377]

The tribe of Benjamin settled a small portion of land west of the Dead Sea in the hills north of Jerusalem between Ephraim and Judah. The Benjaminite land included Jericho.

The tribe of Ephraim settled a vast tract of land north of the tribe of Benjamin. Bethel and Shiloh, where the Tent of Meetings housed the Ark of the Covenant, belonged to the Ephraimites. The Tent of Meetings was open to all the tribes.

Shechem, in the Judean Hills, became the capital—or center—for the tribe of Menashe. The Menashites settled north of Ephraim. Half the tribe settled west of the Jordan River including Mount Carmel and the fortified city of Megiddo. The other half lived east of the Jordan River next to the tribes of Reuben and Gad.

Issachar inherited a pleasant and fruitful small circular section of land from the western tip of Lake Kinneret into the Jezreel Valley next to the tribe of Zebulon. In the Galilee, sharing a border with the tribe of Asher, the tribe of Naphtali settled in the fertile mountains north and west of Lake Kinneret. The tribe of Asher settled into a fertile territory with olive trees near the coastline from Mt. Carmel to past the Hamite town of Tyre. The Asherites allowed their Hamite cousins to live among them.[378]

Three small independent towns, Tyre, Sidon, and Gebal (also called Byblos), were situated on Israel's northern coast when the Israelites entered the Promised Land. The Israelites knew the people in these three towns as Hamites. To the north of Israel were Hyksos towns Aleppo and Dammeseq. Former Sumerians not part of Abraham and Sarah's tribe in northern Mesopotamia were referred to as Hyksos.

The Israelite tribe of Zebulon settled north of Tyre and on the southern border of Sidon from the border of Issachar's land to Israel's northern coast. They became seacoast traders.[379]

The Danites built numerous cities, including the great port of Jaffa just south of Tyre. From Jaffa, Dan launched its commercial fleets mentioned by the prophetess Deborah in Judges 5:17. Some members of the tribe of Dan migrated far to the north in the territory of Naphtali in what is today the Golan Heights.[380] The Danites conquered or acquired a town in the Hula Valley near the source of the Jordan River named Laish (also called Leshem), which they renamed Dan.[381]

Monotheism and the essence of Sumerian knowledge that Abraham and Sarah left to their descendants changed the ancient world. His title, Abraham the Ivri (Monotheist), also became their legacy. The Children of Israel, the Israelites, were known for a long time as the Ivrim, the Hebrews. The name Ivri is found in numerous Biblical books, including Exodus, Kings, and Isaiah. The Jewish people eventually came to be known as Yehudim, Jews, but the name of the language remains Hebrew (Ivrit).

14

THE ANCIENT WORLD

TIMELINE

1225–1275 BCE ....**Bronze Age Collapse**
1000 BCE .... King David establishes Jerusalem as capital
722 BCE .... Assyrians attack Israel, exile Ten Tribes
586 BCE .... Babylonians destroy Temple, exile Judah
516 BCE .... Second Jerusalem Temple built
63 BCE .... Roman Republic annexes Israel
30 BCE .... Roman Republic annexes Egypt

Seven tribes of Canaan had originally inhabited the land of Canaan after the Great Flood. The tribes mentioned in the Torah were the Hittites, the Girgashites, the Amorites, the Canaanites, the Perizzites, the Hivvites, and the Jebusites. By the time the Israelite Nation returned from Egypt, the tribes of Canaan had been "scattered." Modern historians and scientists group various peoples living in ancient Israel as Canaanites, descendants of Noah's son Ham.

Different cultures resided in the Promised Land at the time

the Israelites arrived after the Exodus. Some were descendants of Noah and Na'ama's sons, Ham, and Yefet, who originally populated the area. Some were Sumerians who were not part of Abraham and Sarah's dynastic tribe, and some were Asians and North Africans who migrated into Israel during the great regional famines that began several hundred years earlier.

The Israelites may have inhabited some towns originally built by the Sumerians with Abraham and Sarah. The fortified Hyksos complex built near Tel Aviv in 1710 BCE (Jewish calendar: 2910) could have been designed and constructed by Jacob's grandchildren as a "safe town" in case of an emergency while they lived in Egypt.[382]

The monotheistic Israelite Nation may have influenced a pharaoh near the end of the Eighteenth Dynasty of Egypt. Pharaoh Akhenaten and his famous wife, Nefertiti, tried to persuade the Egyptian population to adopt monotheism. Akhenaten moved the capital of Egypt in 1350 BCE (Jewish calendar: 2410) from Thebes to Akhet-Aton (called Amarna in modern literature) to establish the new religion. The next Eighteenth Dynasty pharaoh continued the monotheistic practices. Thebans moved the capital back to Thebes thirty years later and polytheism gradually returned.[383]

Pharaoh Akhenaten had abandoned Egypt's former territories of Nubia, Syria, and Israel, and the Egyptians left the Israelites alone for the next 100 years.[384]

The Israelites are called the Twelve Tribes, even though the descendants of Joseph and his wife, Osnat, became two tribes. The tribal confederacy consisted of thirteen tribes living on twelve land sections. They built towns centered on an agricultural economy and remained independent of each other in many ways.

The tribes managed their lives with advice from their own elders, judges, and rabbis, and their leaders forbade intermarriage between tribes. Social classes didn't exist in the tribal society of ancient Israel. Widows and orphans were cared for by their tribes. Common laws and regulations protected workers, servants, poor people, and non-Jews.[385]

Every month in Jerusalem the chief rabbis declared the start of the New Moon. Signal fires on hilltops in the Judean Mountains were built throughout the Land of Israel so all tribes knew the correct day each month to observe Rosh Khodesh, the New Moon Celebration. Once a year the tribes came together in Jerusalem to celebrate and trade. The tribes joined forces to repel attackers if the nation became threatened by a foreign enemy.

In Egypt, an army general became Ramesses I and began the Nineteenth Dynasty. Pharaoh Ramesses I terrorized the region with the might of the Egyptian army. In 1260 BCE (Jewish calendar: 2500) his army battled against a kingdom to the north of Israel until the people living there agreed to pay tributes to Egypt. Ramesses I died, bickering relatives fought over the throne, and their military grip on the region ended. The nations around Egypt, such as the Hittites, the Mesopotamian Hyksos, and the Israelites, began to repel Egypt's predatory advances.[386]

Around 175 years after the Twelve Tribes entered Israel, the Mediterranean and Mesopotamian regions experienced the beginning of the Bronze Age Collapse, a time of widespread disaster. An earthquake storm is the likely cause for the destruction.[387]

Major earthquakes often occur in groups known as "sequences" or "storms" when one large earthquake on a weakened fault line is followed days, months, or years later by more earthquakes. Volcanic eruptions may cause a series of earthquakes. The earthquake storm began in 1225 BCE (Jewish calendar: 2560). For fifty years to seventy-five years, earthquakes in the Aegean and Eastern Mediterranean regions may have destroyed ancient civilizations. The epicenter of the earthquake "storm" may have been Thrace, comprising modern-day Greece, Macedonia, and Bulgaria.[388]

Also, pollen grains recovered from core samples under the Dead Sea and Red Sea dated to the Bronze Age Collapse reveal a reduction of water. The Israelites increased cultivation of dry-climate trees, such as olive trees, during this time because severe droughts in Canaan and in Mesopotamia followed or overlapped the earthquake storm.[389]

The earthquake storm that began around 1225 BCE (Jewish calendar: 2560) destroyed long-distance trade routes originally established by the Sumerians. Supplies such as tin to make bronze became scarce, and advanced metallurgy skills in the region declined. The Bronze Age that had started in the confederation of Sumeria ended. Iron ore replaced bronze and the more primitive Iron Age began.

Some researchers place the time of the Exodus during the Bronze Age Collapse because a few of the facts fit the narrative. A few others put the Exodus much earlier at the time of the Aegean Sea supervolcanic eruption of 1620 BCE (Jewish calendar: 2140).

It is possible that an earthquake or volcanic eruption happened at the time the Nation of Israel left Egypt. Or the Exodus story may be a compilation of events. The exact time of the Exodus isn't certain because the Torah doesn't name the reigning pharaoh.

Widespread devastation from earthquakes and severe drought in the Mediterranean and Mesopotamian regions drastically changed the political, economic, and ethnic landscape of the entire region. Refugees migrated to villages, towns, and cities still standing after an earthquake. Then another quake weeks, months, or years later could damage that place. This went on for over fifty years. Food shortages and the ensuing chaos of sudden, necessary migrations often gave rise to violent competition for resources.[390]

As in Thrace, major cities in Egypt were leveled. The drought intensified the suffering. Egyptians died of famine because their rulers lacked food reserves and couldn't provide for them. And desperate people from devastated areas arrived along the coastlines of Egypt and Israel in ships and makeshift boats. The Egyptians named these refugees Sea Peoples, and when they sought help the Egyptians built concentration camps and imprisoned them.[391] The refugees who arrived in Israel were not challenged; they were allowed to recover and establish themselves along parts of Israel's coastline.

Earthquakes in Israel destroyed towns and cities, including the great port city of Jaffe, also called Jaffa, or Yafo. The tribe of Dan spent thirty years rebuilding it.

Some of the Sea Peoples who escaped devastation in their homelands and fled to Israel were fierce warrior-types like the Philistines from Crete who settled Israel's Gaza region. Other refugees arriving in Israel during and after the Bronze Age Collapse were distant relations to the Israelites from Mycenae and Anatolia (Greece and Turkey).[392]

During the Bronze Age Collapse the Mycenaeans, now simply called "Sea People," escaped from different locations along the Aegean coastline to the northern coastline of Israel. The Mycenaeans-turned-Sea People naturally sought help from their former Sumerian cousins, now Israelites in Israel.[393]

Civilizations throughout the Aegean mainland, Anatolia, Egypt, and Mesopotamia became isolated for hundreds of years after the Bronze Age Collapse. Many civilizations disappeared. Thrace crumbled in ruins and went into 400 years of dark ages.[394]

The Hittite Empire, also distant cousins to the Israelite Hebrews, left ruined Anatolian towns and villages and ceased to function as an independent nation after the Bronze Age Collapse. City-states throughout the Mesopotamian and Mediterranean regions, including the famous city of Troy on the west coast of Anatolia, fell into ruin.[395]

Mesopotamian Hyksos survivors from the north, also cousins to the Israelites, migrated to refugee areas and merged with other populations. The three Hamite towns of Tyre, Sidon, and Gebal became large, thriving, independent city-states after the earthquake storm, perhaps due to help from the Israelites and from an influx of migrating Mesopotamian refugees and Sea Peoples.[396]

The Aramaeans, an ancient Mesopotamian people, migrated into territory north of Israel and rebuilt damaged city-states Aleppo and Dammeseq. The Aramaean Kingdom at times clashed with Israel, but the two cultures generally helped one another and traded with each other.[397]

When the earthquake storm subsided and the Danites rebuilt their port city they used their commercial fleet to trade various Israelite goods including rare purple dye from the murex snail and other Israelite goods to Egypt and to city-states around the Mediterranean coastline.

The later cultures of Macedonia and Rome referred to the Israelite seafaring merchants as "traders in purple" because the Israelites knew a complicated process to obtain the dye from the rare mollusk and were the only traders to have the purple dye. The Israelites used it in the fringe of their prayer shawls. A distinctive, dark "royal" blue color is still used by some modern Jews in prayer shawls.

The Israelites helped the region recover economically, established long-distance trade routes, and stimulated trade among the emerging or recovering nations. City-states around the Mediterranean coastline had contact with their commercial fleet, and the spread of the Hebrew Aleph-Bet by Israelite merchants became a major development in Western culture.

The Egyptians of the New Kingdom period after the Bronze Age Collapse referred to the residents of Gebal, Tyre, and Sidon as "Canaanite Sea People" because they were experienced seafarers.[398] A thousand years later, Greek historians named them, along with Aramaeans in Dammeseq, "Phoenicians." These four city-states operated independently of each other. However, Greek historians have lumped Gebal, Tyre, Sidon, and Dammeseq together into a fictional "Phoenicia." Phoenicia never existed as a place; nor did Phoenicians ever exist as a people.

The confederacy of Israel had set up a justice system with the elders of each tribe, and judges represented each tribe in the Great Sanhedrin, the Jewish high court in Jerusalem. This system, formalized during the Exodus, served the Israelites well.[399]

Israel prospered after the Bronze Age Collapse. The acquisition of material wealth by some families, and the desire to acquire more, may have caused pressure to change the political structure from a balanced tribalistic organization of resources to a new form of government—a constitutional monarchy.

The Nation of Israel had always kept their tribal family lines intact in twelve distinct tribes. Now, under a new form of centralized government, that was about to change.

Israel functioned as a tribal confederacy for nearly 400 years, including during the Exodus from Egypt, the settlement of Israel, the devastating Bronze Age Collapse, and subsequent rebuilding of Israelite towns and cities. However, with the influx of Sea Peoples refugees into the region, expanding populations, and occasional droughts, Israel's neighbors grew increasingly violent and hostile.

A number of Jewish leaders decided they needed a military leader and a unified defense of their borders. Certain influential families supported the change to a central government because they wanted the opportunity to acquire unlimited power and wealth. The common laws of the confederacy made taking advantage of others to acquire material possessions difficult.

Their dim memories of the golden age of Sumeria and the wealth combined with prestige surrounding their dynastic rule in Egypt before the enslavement may have grown into an overwhelming desire to re-create the glory days of past eras.

In 1032 BCE (Jewish calendar: 2750) the tribes agreed to appoint Saul ben Kish from the tribe of Benjamin as the first Jewish monarch of Israel. The prophet Samuel anointed Saul's head with oil at a ring of twelve stones in a field in Gilgal in the Judean Hills, and he became King Saul.

Jewish kings, unlike kings in most neighboring cultures, were subject to laws the same as any other citizen. A constitutional monarchy as a form of government was unique when the Jewish Nation conceived it. Jewish kings did not enact or decree laws; they adhered to the legal system of the Sanhedrin judges.[400]

King Saul and an army of Israelites successfully defended Israel's northern and eastern borders against neighboring tribes during his twenty-two-year reign. King Saul also fought the Philistines, the Semitic seafaring warrior people who sailed to Israel's Gaza region from Crete during the Bronze Age Collapse.

The Philistines marched their army through central Israel, defeated the Israelites, and killed King Saul in the Jezreel Valley. Philistine soldiers mutilated and displayed Saul's body as a trophy. The Philistines may have won the battle for the Jezreel Valley, but they would face the wrath of the next Israelite king from the fierce Tribe of Judah.[401]

Establishment of a central government caused competition for inheritance of the kingdom after Saul's death. His son Ishboshet claimed the throne, but the prophets and elders wanted David from the Tribe of Judah to be the next king. The elders turned to the Tribe of Naphtali, and an army of 38,000 Naphtalites marched into Jerusalem and announced their support for David. The prophet Samuel anointed David's head at the ring of stones in Gilgal, and he became the second king in 1010 BCE (Jewish calendar: 2750).[402]

King David established Jerusalem as the capital of Israel and is the most famous of all Jewish monarchs. As a boy he challenged a Philistine named Goliath the Giant. When David, the future king of Israel, struck down Goliath with a stone flung from a slingshot he became a hero to his nation.

A fierce warrior-king, he battled and finally vanquished the Philistines and they disappeared from the pages of history.[403] The gradual transition from an agricultural to an industrialized economy began under his leadership. King David extended Israel's borders by taking the lands of any tribe that attacked or threatened Israel. Adjacent nations respected him and generally left Israel alone during his reign.[404]

Israel at the time of his death extended well past Dammeseq all the way from the Euphrates River in Mesopotamia to the Gulf of Eilat at the northern tip of the Red Sea, including Petra, to the Sinai Peninsula.[405]

Solomon, David's son by his wife Bathsheba, became the third king in 967 BCE (Jewish calendar: 4727). He accepted his crown in Jerusalem before traveling to Shechem to be accepted as king by the northern tribes.

Solomon is most famous for building the Holy Temple, the Beit ha-Mikdash, in Jerusalem on Mount Moriah. Using forced labor, he also built an opulent palace nearby for his Egyptian wife, a daughter of the pharaoh. Solomon raised taxes to pay for the luxurious Temple project and palace-type house. He also traded twenty Jewish towns in the Galilee to the Hamite King of Tyre in exchange for cedar, fur, and gold.[406]

The monarchy under Solomon created a class of people

interested in the acquisition of wealth, people who ignored destitute widows and orphans. The change from common law to constitutional rule of law created a new class of rich, elite landowners. Judges often took bribes. High taxes and debtor's prisons terrorized poor people because debts owed by the poor were no longer forgiven in the seventh year as they had been under common law.[407]

The ruling class of Israel began buying, selling, and owning people who could not pay their debts. The elite ignored biblical laws regarding slavery.

The kings were granted extraordinary benefits and, as happens every time in history when extraordinary power combined with wealth is consolidated in the hands of a few, hardships on the common people soon followed. Israelites may have needed a strong central government because of threats from neighboring cultures, but the kingship system soon resulted in a few wealthy landholding families and a large population of homeless people.[408]

Big estates that the rich acquired left thousands of Jews unable to support themselves. Parents unable to pay their debts lost their sons and daughters into slavery. Some people sold themselves and/or their wives and children into indentured service, another form of slavery, to prevent starvation. Because the laws of Moses forbade the enslavement of one Jew by another, the prophets advised the rich to end the practice. But instead of following Mosaic Law, they passed laws for the fair treatment of slaves. Under the new rule of law, families could not be broken up and sold to satisfy debt.[409]

During the reigns of King Saul and King David, Israel still operated as a strong agricultural economy. The twelve landowning tribes taxed themselves and maintained armies. Solomon redistributed the Land of Israel into twelve taxable units that cut across established tribal lines.[410]

Heavy taxation forced people to move to new cities being built as national projects. In tribalistic, agricultural Israel, the family worked together as a unit. Under Solomon, individuals worked for employers, and families separated in order to work for different employers. The loss of tribal lands brought intermarriage between tribes, marriage with non-Jews, and the practice of polygamy. Saul had not practiced polygamy. David acquired many wives, including non-Jewish women. King Solomon kept hundreds of foreign wives and sex slaves. For Israelites trying to follow the Torah, the importance of allowing marriage only within each tribe became superseded by the importance of marriage within the Jewish Nation.[411]

King Solomon opened trade routes to foreign lands to acquire gold, silver, copper, turquoise, and ivory. A Jewish community started in Cochin, India, at this time when the king sent Jews there to acquire silver and ivory.[412]

The first three Jewish monarchs had been accepted by all twelve tribes as their kings. When Solomon died his son, Rehoboam, succeeded him and accepted the crown in Jerusalem. He went to Shechem, where the elders of the ten northern tribes refused to crown him as their king. Their spokesperson, Jeroboam, demanded relief from Solomon's heavy taxation.[413]

Rehoboam, representing the tribes of Judah and Benjamin, sent an army to force tax collection on the tribes of northern Israel. The ten tribes in central and northern Israel declared their independence in 933 BCE (Jewish calendar: 2827), became the Kingdom of Israel, and Jeroboam became their king. He built a temple in Bethel. Then fighting between the two kingdoms became a civil war lasting fifty years.[414]

King Omri united Israel and Judah by 866 BCE (Jewish calendar: 2894). Omri then led the Israelites against the armies of six hostile nations trying to invade Israel and Judah. The Israelites were fierce warriors. They defeated the six armies.[415]

King Omri moved the capital of the Kingdom of Israel from Shechem to Samaria. He built the city of Samaria, and then made it the property of the kings, not the tribes. He also reformed laws and encouraged trade. Nearby predatory cultures such as Assyria feared and respected Israel under his reign. A monument excavated from ancient Assyria refers to Israel as the Land of Omri. As King David had done, King Omri expanded the borders of Israel by battle.[416] He is famous for arranging the marriage of Princess Jezebel from the city-state Sidon to his son Ahab.

She became Queen Jezebel upon the death of Omri. Israelite civil rights were suspended under King Ahab and Queen Jezebel. Dissidents were executed. She tried unsuccessfully to introduce sacred prostitution and child sacrifice to the people of Israel, customs she had been taught as a child in Sidon. Sacred prostitution refers to temple prostitutes, young women trained to live inside various pagan temples and perform sex acts with wealthy patrons upon demand.[417]

The Torah records the walled city of Jericho in the Judean Hills as the first city acquired by the Israelites after the Exodus. Archaeological evidence indicates an earthquake may have destroyed Jericho. The prophets warned against rebuilding the crumbled city, and the earlier monarchs had heeded their advice. Ahab defied the prophets, rebuilt the city, and his son died.[418]

King Ahab, like his father, moved with force against enemies of Israel. An army from Judah joined Ahab's army from the northern tribes to fight an invasion from the Hamite city-states of Gebal, Sidon, Tyre, and the Aramaean city-state of Dammeseq. The Jews won the battle. The Hamites and their Aramaean allies retreated.[419]

The Assyrians, predatory Semitic nomads, subjugated Babylonia—former Sumeria—then attacked the Kingdom of Israel around 850 BCE (Jewish calendar: 2910). Israelite King Ahab had allied with twelve buffer states and arranged Jewish battalions on the front line. In a battle in northern Israel, Ahab and his allies defeated the much larger Assyrian army. An estimated 20,000 Jewish warriors, including King Ahab, died in the battle.[420]

Israeli archeologists discovered and excavated King Ahab's palace in Samaria. Items such as a beautifully carved ivory relief with the likeness of an angel were found and displayed at the Jewish Museum. The angel's profile in the relief is remarkably similar to a Minoan/Kaptaran face.[421]

The Israelites experienced fifty years of peace and prosperity before Tiglath-Pileser II seized the throne in Nineveh, capital of Assyria, and demanded tribute payments from Israel. The leaders of Israel refused. In 740 BCE (Jewish calendar: 3020) the Assyrian army invaded the Kingdom of Israel.

Israel won the war against Tiglath-Pileser II, the Assyrian army retreated, and Israel enjoyed another ten years of peace. Assyria then again demanded tribute payments. Most Israelite kings of that period paid the annual Assyrian tribute of several tons of silver to buy peace. The Jewish people were becoming enslaved as a silver-mining workforce for the Assyrians. In 722 BCE (Jewish calendar: 3038) Israel's king refused to pay the tributes.[422]

The Assyrians had a reputation for cruelty to their prisoners and that caused Jews to flee northern Israel to escape the expected invasion. Around 2,700 years ago, many Jews left the northern region for India (Hodu in Hebrew).

Some of the Israelites traveled to the Hindu Kush (formerly northern India) and may have joined a community started there around 5,000 years ago by a related tribe that settled Troy in Anatolia, Crete in the Mediterranean Sea, and Sumeria and

Akkadia in Mesopotamia. The true record of the Hindu Kush, now annexed to China, may never be revealed because of political power struggles among regional governments.

Israelites also left to settle in Morocco. Nomadic Jews lived independently in Morocco from the time of Sargon II, 2,700 years ago, until the Mohammedan conquest in the seventh century.

The Prophet Isaiah advised the Jews of Judah to pay the tributes demanded by Assyria and not join the military challenge against the giant Mesopotamian superpower. The Jews in Judah paid the tributes, and they were not harmed during the Assyrian attack on the northern tribes of Israel.[423]

Assyrian ruler Sargon II attacked and destroyed Samaria, capital of the Kingdom of Israel, in 722 BCE. The tribes of Naphtali and Reuben were the first tribes to be decimated and exiled by the Assyrians.[424] Some families escaped to Judah for refuge. Approximately 30,000 Jews were force-marched north to Assyria.[425]

The Assyrian attack on ancient Israel resulted in the first exile, the first time a subjugator forced Jews to leave their homes. The fate of the "Ten Lost Tribes" has fueled ideas and discussion for the last several hundred years and has resulted in fantastic speculation.

Jews and their ancestors have lived in northern Mesopotamia for thousands of years. Hebraic tribes originally built Aleppo, still operating in modern-day Syria, as part of the Akkadian empire. Aleppo, Ur, and Harran, in the time of Abraham and Sarah, were centers of astronomy. By the time of the Assyrian exile 2,700 years ago those towns were a blend of cultures.

Jews living in what used to be northern Mesopotamia, now parts of Turkey, Syria, Iraq, and Iran, share common Y-DNA haplotypes with Ashkenaz Jews, and Sephardic Jews from Italy. This common marker is also found in Iraqi, Iranian, Yemini, and Egyptian Mizrahi Jews.[426]

Until recently, communities of Mesopotamian Jews lived in the Kurdistan area consisting of parts of Turkey, Syria, Iraq, and Iran. Most Mesopotamian Jews believe they are the descendants of the Ten Tribes force-marched out of the Kingdom of Israel in 722 BCE. The Jewish Bible in II Kings 17:6 records the captured and exiled Ten Tribes as living in upper Mesopotamia.

Many Jews escaped Assyrian slavery. Some travelled to the Black Sea region, some returned to Israel, others traveled east to India. The tribes of the Bnei Menashe in Northeastern India trace their origin to the Israelite Tribe of Menashe. The Bnei Menashe oral history records the story of their escape 2,700 years ago from Assyrian captivity through Afghanistan, Tibet, and China before settling in India.[427]

The Judah monarchy made the enormous annual payments demanded by the King of Assyria for several years after the destruction of the Kingdom of Israel. Then the people from Judah, including survivors from the ravaged north, formed an alliance with Egypt to the south and Syria to the north to fight Assyria and end the tributes. When the Assyrian army marched west to forcibly collect the tributes, the Egyptians and Syrians immediately surrendered.[428]

The Jews of Judah chose to fight a battle they could not win rather than surrender. The following morning they found 185,000 Assyrian soldiers mysteriously dead and they watched the rest of the army flee. The Israelites celebrated the miracle. Later historians record that a typhus plague had infected the Assyrian army. The Jews of Judah resumed annual tribute payments the following year to avoid future wars.[429]

The Assyrian army in 650 BCE (Jewish calendar: 3110) marched on the Egyptian capital of Thebes. Assyrian soldiers plundered, murdered, destroyed the city, and left. In 605 BCE

(Jewish calendar: 3155), the Babylonians successfully revolted against the Assyrians. A tyrannical Babylonian king called Nebuchadnezzar II took control of the treasure plundered from Thebes and claimed former Assyrian territories, including the Kingdom of Judah.[430]

For nearly twenty years Jews successfully defended themselves against the predatory Babylonians. Then King Nebuchadnezzar II brought his soldiers to Judah.[431]

As the Babylonian soldiers surrounded Jerusalem, many people left Judah to escape the violence. Some Jews went to India to join the Jewish community living in northern India. More Jews traveled to the southwest coast of India to join the Jewish community in Cochin, established in King Solomon's time.[432]

Jews also traveled south through Egypt to join the Yebu Jews on their island near northern Nubia.[433]

Other Jews escaping the Babylonian invasion and massacres migrated northward around the Black Sea Caucasus region and into Crimea. Jews continued north to settle the land between the Black Sea and the Baltic Sea which would later become known as Poland.[434]

The three Hamite city-states on Israel's northern coastline, Tyre, Sidon, and Gebal, allied with the northern Israelite town of Megiddo to fight the invading army. The Babylonians attacked and destroyed Tyre, Sidon, Gebal, and Megiddo. After the war, the survivors abandoned those towns.

The Jews of Judah who stayed watched the Babylonian soldiers set up camps and build forts around the city of Jerusalem. The siege of Jerusalem had begun. The people trapped inside the city suffered through nearly two years of starvation, thirst, and disease. On the ninth of the Jewish month of Av in 586 BCE (Jewish calendar: 3174), Babylonian soldiers breached the walls of Jerusalem and the starving Jews surrendered.

Babylonian soldiers sacked the city, destroyed the Temple,

and force-marched most of the Jewish population back to Babylon, leaving the poorest Jews in Judah. King Nebuchadnezzar kept as trophies the gold items his soldiers looted from the Temple.[435]

The tenth of Tevet, the day the Babylonian siege began, became a day of fasting and reflection for the Jewish people. The ninth of Av, the day the city walls were breached, became one of the most important days of fasting and repentance for Jews. Modern Jews still observe the Tenth of Tevet and Tisha ba Av (ninth day of Av).

The Temple in Jerusalem lay in ruins after the Babylonian conquest and the forced Jewish exile. Then, King Cyrus of Persia conquered Babylon. Jewish communities enjoyed a good life under King Cyrus. A large population chose to stay in Babylon—former Sumeria—while others returned to their homeland to begin the Second Temple Period of Jewish history.

King Cyrus gave the former Jewish captives the gold vessels and items Nebuchadnezzar II had taken from their Temple. A descendant of King David, Zerubabel from the Tribe of Judah, with permission from King Cyrus, led 43,360 Jews, 7,337 Babylonian servants, and 200 singing men and women from Babylon back to Israel.[436]

Persian King Darius came to power following Cyrus. He exempted the Israelites from tribute payments and gave them gifts. Ezra, 58 years after Zerubabel and with the blessing of Darius, led another 1,800 returning exiles from Babylon back to Israel.[437]

Ezra and the exiles entered northern Israel. People living in northern Israel joined the exiles and followed Ezra to Jerusalem. They found the Temple destroyed and the land barren. Babylonian soldiers during the wars had cut down or uprooted trees and created a shortage of wood. The people built an altar with wood they could find, rejoiced, and celebrated the Feast of Tabernacles.[438]

A year later, they laid the foundation for the Second Temple on Mount Moriah, site of the original Temple. Ezra oversaw the rebuilding of the Temple and introduced a wood offering ceremony. The "wood offering" became a tradition and a great honor for anyone able to donate wood for the Temple fires.[439]

Ezra became the spiritual advisor to the Israelites, and he reestablished the common law of the tribal confederacy. Intermarriage became prohibited overnight, and Jews with foreign or non-Jewish wives who chose not to convert were pressured to send their wives away or leave with them.[440]

The Israelites generally organized themselves into three subgroups of belief called the Pharisees, the Essenes, and the Sadducees. The Pharisees became the forerunners of rabbinic Judaism that developed into today's Orthodox Judaism.

The Essenes called themselves Osay-hatorah, observers of Torah. They wore white clothing, practiced gender equality in their communities, and are famous for writing the Dead Sea Scrolls found in the ancient Qumran community in the Judean Hills. The Sadducees were mostly aristocrats. They represented a strict literal interpretation of the Torah and rejected rabbinic explanations based on Oral Law.[441]

Israelites flourished in their homeland for nearly 200 years after their return from Babylonian exile until a new military superpower, the Macedonians, began a chain of events that would destroy Israel's sovereignty.

The Aegean mainland had suffered through 400 years of dark ages after the earthquake storm, the severe drought, and social unrest destroyed the Thracian Empire during the Bronze Age Collapse. The area repopulated and became the Athenian Empire.

The first Olympic Games, known as the Games of Mount Olympus, were held in Athens in 776 BCE (Jewish calendar: 2984).[442]

Thracian and Athenian city-state kings fought over control of towns in the region for the next 400 years until the Macedonian culture rose to power. In 359 BCE (Jewish calendar: 3401) Philip II seized the Macedonian throne by murdering its rightful heir, his nephew.[443]

King Philip II raised an army, then he terrorized and conquered much of the Thracian and Athenian territories from the Aegean coastline to the edge of the Black Sea. Philip II used the wealth acquired from plundering and enslaving neighboring populations to create a new regional military superpower, including Anatolia, called the Empire of Macedonia.[444]

His son and heir, King Alexander III, also called Alexander the Macedon, expanded Macedonia's empire and influence. He then invaded and conquered Persia. Alexander and his armies also claimed Persia's vassal territories, including Israel.

Alexander's army marched in, abused, and subjugated Israel's neighbors. In 332 BCE (Jewish calendar: 3428) the high priest of Jerusalem, instead of preparing to fight the invaders, welcomed the king of Macedonia with a formal procession and a feast. Alexander, after his meeting with the high priest, guaranteed the Jews of Israel political and religious independence.

The Jews in Israel had escaped the viciousness and brutality Alexander and his soldiers used to subjugate peoples, including rape, or cruel torture such as burning people alive or dragging people to death. Entire towns were burned to the ground. Thousands were sold as slaves. Entire populations of "example" towns were slaughtered.

The peoples of North Africa did not escape the carnage. Alexander and his armies marched through the Nile Delta, destroying the Jewish population living there before conquering all of Egypt and Nubia. They even went to Yebu, the island on the Nile River, and plundered and razed the Jewish city-state, including the Yebu Temple that had thrived there for nearly a thousand years.[445]

While Alexander's military conquests created an expanded empire from the heel of Italy, the Aegean mainland (Macedonia, Thrace, and Athens), Anatolia, Syria, Mesopotamia, Persia (Iraq and Iran), northwest India (now Afghanistan and Pakistan), Egypt, and Nubia, Israel remained independent.[446]

Except for Israel, the conquered regions became known as Hellene around 325 BCE (Jewish calendar: 3435). The vast Mediterranean territory claimed by Alexander the Macedon in time became known as The Great, or simply as Greece. Later historians referred to him as Alexander of the Great, and Western historians call him Alexander the Great.

Alexander's officers and soldiers, ordered to intermarry with local, conquered populations to propagate Hellenic ideals including polytheism, founded cities and controlled towns and villages around the Mediterranean coastline. The Hellenic culture spread everywhere except in Israel because the Israelite Jews refused to intermarry.

The Hellenized Assyrian Semites were called Syrian Greeks or Seleucid Greeks, and they were particularly ruthless. Alexander died in 323 BCE (Jewish calendar: 3437), and his empire broke apart. The spawn of the Macedonians, the Syrian Greeks took control of Anatolia, Syria, and Persia. They claimed Judah as a vassal state, and they outlawed Rosh Chodesh and other Jewish holidays.[447] For the next 150 years they harassed Jews and desecrated their Temple.[448]

The Syrian Greeks tried to force their sex-oriented, decadent, self-indulgent customs and habits upon the Israelite population that stayed in Israel. The Jews fought back against infanticide, against raising their daughters to be temple prostitutes, and against displaying statues of naked people in their temples.

Syrian Greeks tortured people. Pederasty and infanticide were prevalent in their culture.[449]

In 164 BCE (Jewish calendar: 3596) a group of Jews in the Judean Hills organized a military resistance against the Syrian Greeks attempting to force polytheism upon the Jewish population.[450]

The Jews, led by the Maccabee family, fought for twenty-five years against a larger, well-equipped Syrian Greek army. The Jews won, immediately purged the Temple of pagan offerings, and reestablished the Kingdom of Judah in 143 BCE (Jewish calendar: 3617). The holiday that followed the Temple's first cleansing after the victory, still celebrated today, is named Chanukah. Unfortunately, the sons of the rulers of Israel then became engaged in a deadly power struggle resulting in collaboration with Romans and family assassinations.

In 125 BCE (Jewish calendar: 3635) the Judahites forced the neighboring Idumea tribe, living south of Judah, to convert to Judaism. The Idumea constantly harassed and initiated fights with the Israelites. The Tribe of Judah wanted to ensure their loyalty and stop the conflicts. The descendants of Jacob's brother, Esav, had originally settled Idumea, Edom in Hebrew.[451]

King Alexander Yannai, known as the Lion of Wrath, ruled Israel from 84 BCE until his death in 76 BCE (Jewish calendar: 3684-3676). During his reign he expanded the borders of Israel the way King David and King Omri had done before him; from Mt. Carmel and the Golan in the north to the Egyptian border, including Gaza, in the south. Israel's boundary in the east stretched across the Jordan Valley. King Yannai's military conquests angered the Pharisees, who initiated a civil war against him, and a neighboring tribe took control of the Jordan Valley. Before his death, he named his wife, Shlomtzion, as his heir.[452]

Then Israel had a peaceful, prosperous period during the reign of King Shlomtzion Alexandra. Her death in 67 BCE

(Jewish calendar: 3693) and a violent competition between her two sons opened the door to predatory Rome.[453]

The Roman Republic, a rising military superpower, had conquered Macedonia after several wars and claimed Greek (Macedonian) vassal states for Rome. Roman statesman and military general Gnaeus Pompey subdued Syria for annexation to Rome in 67 BCE while the sons of King Alexandra and their supporters were fighting a civil war in Judah over control of the kingdom. One of the brothers invited General Pompey to settle the conflict and choose the next ruler of Israel.[454]

Pompey chose himself. He entered Jerusalem with an army in 63 BCE (Jewish calendar: 3697). During a three-month siege on Mount Moriah where the Temple stood, Pompey and his soldiers killed several thousand defenders of the Temple, including Jewish priests, before defeating the Jews and entering the Temple.[455]

Self-determination for the Jews of Judah ended as Rome imposed heavy taxation on its new vassal state. The most vicious enemy that the Israelites faced, the superpower Roman Republic, wanted more than power, control, and wealth. They wanted the death of the Jewish Nation.

Thousands of Jews moved to the familiar Nile Delta region during the Roman invasion and conquest of Israel. They formed a community, established a Temple, and lived autonomously.[456]

By 48 BCE (Jewish calendar: 3712) Herod, grandson of one of the neighboring Idumea tribesmen forced to convert, rose to power within the Roman elite. They appointed him ruler of Jerusalem. The Jewish people did not accept him until he married Mariamne, sole survivor of the Maccabee family. He later murdered Mariamne, the last of the Hasmonean family line, along with their two sons.[457]

Rome annexed Egypt after the death of Cleopatra in 30 BCE (Jewish calendar: 3730). The Romans subjugated the Egyptians, the Macedonians, and the Syrian Greeks, and pursued aggressive policies of intermarriage in order to assimilate them.

The superpower Roman Republic suffered through a period of political conflicts, assassinations, and civil wars. The senate granted extraordinary powers to Octavian, adopted son of Julius Caesar. Octavian dissolved the republic and became emperor of the new empire.

Jews in Israel and throughout Europe, Anatolia, and North Africa remained loyal to Judaism and continued to resist Roman assimilation by refusing to intermarry or adopt the immoral Roman culture.[458] Romans, like the Syrian Greeks, tortured men, women, and children, practiced pederasty, and engaged in infanticide. Jews influenced by foreign cultures such as Rome fought against traditional Jews.[459]

Roman Empire lackey King Herod of Judea used murder and a ruthless secret police force to control and subjugate the Jewish population in Israel during his forty years as ruler. He used Jewish forced labor to complete national building projects.[460]

To redesign and expand the Temple, Herod used 10,000 laborers and 1,000 priests for nine years. Rome tried when he died in 4 BCE (Jewish calendar: 3756) to divide Judah into three kingdoms for Herod's three living sons, but the Jews successfully resisted the division.[461]

The Common Era began around two thousand years ago with the Romans flexing their regional power and the Israelites struggling to keep their sovereignty.

15

COMMON ERA

The two great military superpowers at the beginning of the Common Era were the Roman Empire in the west of Eurasia and Han China in the east.[462] Philo, a Hellenized Jewish philosopher from Alexandria, Egypt, recorded around the time of Herod's death in 4 BCE (Jewish calendar: 3756) that seven million Jews lived in the Roman Empire.[463]

Over a million Jews lived in Egypt and two million to three million Jews lived in Rome, Greece, Syria, Cyrene, and Libya. Several million lived in Israel. The Jewish population accounted for ten percent of the seventy million people living in the Roman Empire at the start of the Common Era.[464]

A million Jews also lived in Persia, another million resided in India, and Jews had migrated from Israel to parts of Europe since the Assyrian wars of 722 BCE (Jewish calendar: 3038). Another uncounted population of Jews lived throughout the Arabian Peninsula and Morocco at the beginning of the Common Era.[465]

In Israel, one of King Herod's sons built Tiberias overlooking

Lake Kinneret in 20 CE (Jewish calendar: 3780). Tiberias became one of Israel's four holiest cities, attracted Jews from all over the Roman Empire, and became a major center for Jewish spiritual life.[466]

Jews remaining in Israel lived with oppression, atrocities, and heavy taxation, which led to a confrontation in Judah in 66 CE (Jewish calendar: 3826). When the Roman procurator assigned to Judah stole silver from the Temple, Jewish crowds killed all the soldiers stationed in Jerusalem. Rome sent troops from Syria, but the Jews defeated them. The war that followed is the Great Revolt of 66–70 CE. Roman Emperor Titus Flavius Caesar Vespasianus Augustus, known as Titus Vespasian, sent 60,000 soldiers to the Galilee to murder, rape, take slaves, and to destroy one town after another. They captured an estimated 100,000 Jews for slavery. Survivors of the massacres fled to Jerusalem, the last stronghold.[467]

Vespasian then dispatched a large military force to Jerusalem to loot the Second Temple for the gold it contained. Roman soldiers crucified tens of thousands of Jewish defenders during the Great Revolt.[468]

The sadistic soldiers raped, maimed, and murdered inhabitants of Jerusalem. On the ninth of Av, the same date on which the Babylonians had breached the first Temple, Roman soldiers threw torches at the Temple and burned it. The Temple, which had stood for 420 years, fell by order of Emperor Vespasian in the summer of 70 CE (Jewish calendar: 3830).[469] The four-year assault ended with the plundering and destruction of the city.

An estimated one million Jews died and tens of thousands were maimed in the Great Revolt. One outer wall on the western side of the Temple courtyard is all that survived the conflagration. Known to this day as the Western Wall, in Hebrew the ha-kotel ha-Ma'aravi, it is an important site.[470]

The attack on the Jews in their capital enabled Emperor

Vespasian and the twelve ruling families living on the exclusive Palatine Hill of Rome, who controlled the political direction of the empire, to acquire enough gold to finance construction of the greatest amphitheater in ancient history.

To complete the project, 95,000 Jewish men were enslaved and forced to design, engineer, and build the "pride of Rome." Construction began in 70 CE. They completed the Coliseum ten years later. Vespasian died, leaving the empire to his son, Titus, during the last year of construction.

The pillaged gold and silver sacred vessels, the giant gold menorah, other objects, and stored gold from the Temple being carried away by smiling soldiers is depicted on the famous Arch of Titus, built in Rome after destruction of the Temple. It is still a popular tourist attraction.

After the Great Revolt the Roman Empire claimed territorial rights to Israel, but the Jewish story in the Promised Land was far from over. For the spiritual leaders of Israel, the business of defending the homeland became the business of preserving the Jewish tradition.

The beloved Rabbi Yochanan ben Zakkai escaped the Siege of Jerusalem and established a seminary in the nearby town of Yavneh in 70 CE. In Jerusalem, the Second Temple lay smashed, much of the city burned and torn down. The Great Sanhedrin, the Jewish high court that had seventy-one judges and ultimate legal and religious authority in Israel, moved from Jerusalem to Yavneh (also called Jabneh or Jabneel), and later, to Betar.

Jews visited the ruins of the Temple on Mount Moriah following the Great Revolt. Large crowds led by rabbis gathered regularly for prayer.[471] For fifty years the Israelites lived under Roman laws, paid taxes, and tried to appease the various governors placed over them, including Emperor Aelius Hadrian, who came to power in 118 CE (Jewish calendar: 3878). Called one of the five good Roman emperors by Western historians, Hadrian built beautiful Hellenic cities and the famous Hadrian Wall in England. But the "good emperor" also massacred Jews in Judah, indigenous peoples in North Africa, and used plunder to finance his building projects throughout the empire.[472]

Initially, Hadrian promised the Jews they could rebuild the Temple in Jerusalem, then heartlessly withdrew his commitment and began deporting Jews to North Africa. Jews throughout Israel began forming clandestine paramilitary forces and constructing shelters in caves.[473]

In 123 CE (Jewish calendar: 3883) Emperor Hadrian visited Jerusalem and decided to rebuild the damaged city into a palatial Roman city, like the luxurious Palatine Hill of Rome. Hadrian's engineers designed an extravagant pagan temple to cover the site of the former Jewish Temple.[474] Hadrian renamed Jerusalem Aelia Capitolina to honor himself and the Roman god Jupiter Capitolinus. He appointed a cruel, merciless governor, Titus Rufus, over the Roman province of Judea.

Rufus regularly raped Jewish women, ordered the deaths of Jews for minor infractions, and publicly challenged Judaism's greatest rabbis, including the famous Rabbi Akiva. For the next eight years, Zionist Jews conducted covert attacks against the Romans. Led by Shimon Bar Kokhba, the Jews declared a war of independence against their oppressors in 132 CE (Jewish calendar: 3892) when Rufus, on Tisha B' Av, ordered the sacred Temple site be ploughed over.[475]

Jews and even a few Gentile supporters from nearby countries arrived to join the war. The Jews managed to defeat the Romans in Jerusalem. Jews fought their way across Israel, defeating the battalions trying to stop them. They then took the coastal region away from Roman control. In the initial fighting, Jews defeated the Roman soldiers, including reinforcements Hadrian brought in from Egypt and Syria. In the first two years the Jewish warriors had taken back almost 1,000 towns and had set up 50 strongholds.[476]

With almost limitless military resources at his disposal, Hadrian called for attacks from the Mediterranean Sea against Israel. Next he sent for two brutal, sadistic generals, Julius Severus and his legions from Britannia, and Hadrianus Quintus Lollius Urbicus from Germania. Hadrian and his generals had twelve legions under their command. They surrounded the 50 Jewish fortresses, starved them until they were too weak to fight, and then massacred them. Roman soldiers, known for cruelty and for raping their victims, murdered and rampaged through the Galilee, Jerusalem, and the Negev.[477]

The fighting spread to northern Israel. Jews fought back and there were heavy losses on both sides. Thousands of Jewish towns and cities were leveled. Jews by the thousands fled to Betar, the last stronghold in the Judean Hills, the command center for Bar Kokhba, and location of the Sanhedrin, the Jewish high court. In 135 CE (Jewish calendar: 3895) the Romans fought their way into Betar where they slaughtered every man, woman, and child. Some accounts of the massacre recorded that the blood from Betar ran all the way to the Mediterranean Sea.[478]

Much of Israel lay in ruins, Jewish political infrastructure collapsed, and Roman authorities forbade Jews to live in Jerusalem or to gather on Mount Moriah. No other foreign power in Israel's history had prevented Jews from ascending the Temple Mount.

Several million Jews stayed in and around their homeland. Jews resettled outside their spiritual center and began gathering for prayer on the Mount of Olives from where they could see the ruined Second Temple. Jews had only the Torah and each other.[479]

The Jews of Tiberias did not join the war against the Romans. The cities and towns refraining from fighting in the war, such as

Tiberias, became a refuge for Jews escaping the violence. Tiberias after the revolt emerged intact as a major spiritual center of life for Jews.

Emperor Hadrian died in 138 CE (Jewish calendar: 3898). The name of his prized city Aelia Capitolina was changed back to Jerusalem. In ancient times countries with established borders did not exist. Land belonged to the group holding political/military control as a nation, kingdom, empire, or group of city states. Jews continued to refer to their homeland as the Land of Israel. But, for the Romans, once the Jews were subjugated and the Jewish capital destroyed, the Jewish "country" no longer existed. The Romans simply referred to the Land of Israel as the eastern part of the Roman Empire.

During the next 1,800 years of the Common Era, living conditions for Jews in the Land of Israel from the suppression by the Romans in the Bar Kokhba Revolt until establishment of modern Israel depended upon which superpower government or other foreign entity claimed territorial rights to their homeland.

A substantial number of Jews moved into the world of the Diaspora following the Bar Kokhba Revolt. They started communities and brought the concept of Judaism to the Americas, Pacific islands, China, Mongolia, Africa, the Middle East, India, Europe, Scandinavia, and Russia.

Entire communities traveled east into the Arabian Peninsula among nomadic Bedouins living in the desert and Quraish Arabs living along the coast. Jews built towns throughout desolate, undeveloped Arabia.[480]

Jews living throughout the empire (parts of southern Europe, the Middle East, and North Africa) had been taken as slaves by Roman citizens after the loss of self-determination following the Bar Kohkba Revolt. Jewish slaves suffered horrible abuse, and often death, at the hands of their masters.

Therefore, Rabbis in Yavneh announced new obligations

for Jewish communities to redeem (purchase) any Jew slaves owned by Romans within seven years of capture. Jewish communities were also required to provide a wedding dowry for poor brides. Rabbi Zakkai encouraged Jews to perform acts of loving kindness in the Diaspora. The Jewish leaders in Yavneh reaffirmed the ban on intermarriage, and declared that anyone outside the Jewish Nation who wanted to convert to Judaism had to receive rabbinical permission.[481]

Being under the control of the politically unstable Roman government left Jews still living in their homeland subject to the whims of the powerful ruling families in their palaces on the Palatine Hill of Rome. To ensure the survival of the Jewish Nation, Israel's leaders and Rabbis gathered in Yavneh and agreed to refrain from supporting revolts or other attempts to forcibly regain sovereignty during the Diaspora.

All Jews living in the Roman Empire in 212 CE (Jewish calendar: 3972) became citizens by decree. Within a few decades, the constitutional government of Rome collapsed. The army gained control of the empire, and Jews were free to live in Jerusalem again. Jews in great numbers resettled in their capital and began building new communities.[482]

Some rulers of the Roman superpower looked favorably toward Jewish self-determination. Others were merciless and despotic. Constantine, born in Serbia as Flavius Valerius Aurelius Constantinus Augustus, took control of the empire in the fourth century. He organized and introduced Christianity as the political-religious structure of the empire.

Constantine, a repressive tyrant, prohibited intermarriage between Jews and Christians. His new state-sponsored church declared him a saint.[483]

Pagan Julian became the emperor in 360 CE (Jewish calendar: 4120). He reversed the pro-Christian, anti-Jew laws his uncle Constantine had initiated. Julian abolished special taxes on Jews and encouraged the rebuilding of the Temple.[484]

Jews cleared the ground and made ready to rebuild their beloved Temple, but a strong earthquake in 363 CE (Jewish calendar: 4123) in the Galilee devastated the area. Then, Persians killed Julian the same year when he invaded Persia, and his successor did not allow the rebuilding of the Temple.[485]

By 388 CE (Jewish calendar: 4148) Jew-hating Emperor Theodosius I passed laws designed to prevent contact between Jews and Christians in the Roman Empire. The laws restricted Jews from trading or studying with Christians. Intermarriage carried the death penalty.[486]

Under Empress Eudocia, wife of Theodosius II, in 438 CE (Jewish calendar: 4198) Jews again gathered regularly on Mount Moriah until the European Christian population living in Jerusalem protested. Jewish rights were suspended to appease the Christians. Jews were once again forbidden to live in Jerusalem or visit their Temple ruins.[487]

In Samaria during the reign of Emperor Justin I, Jews built a synagogue in 520 CE (Jewish calendar: 4280) near Beit She'an. On one of the walls inside the synagogue Jewish artisans created a mosaic honoring Emperor Justin I.[488]

For the next hundred years the Christian Byzantines (the Christian Eastern half of the Roman Empire) and the Sassanid Empire (the last of the Persian kings before the rise of Islam) battled each other for control of Israel. More Jews again immigrated east into Arabia.

During the wars, the academy of Jewish learning, which had been moved back to Yavneh from Betar, closed and opened again in Babylon. As the intellectual centers of Judaism in Israel closed, new ones opened in Babylon to accommodate the growing population of Jews now living in Abraham and Sarah's former Sumerian homeland.[489]

The central government of the Christian Roman Empire fell, and the Ostrogoths founded Italy, the Visigoths established Spain, and the Franks and Burgundians claimed France. The Visigoth government of Spain began forcibly converting Jews to Catholicism in 586 CE (Jewish calendar: 4346). Most Spanish Jews moved to Italy, France, or Germany, where they joined existing Jewish communities and started the European textile industry.[490]

European Christians by 600 CE (Jewish calendar: 4360) occupied and controlled Jerusalem. The King of Persia in 613 CE (Jewish calendar: 4373) brought his army and 30,000 volunteer Babylonian Jew soldiers to Jerusalem to help Jews of Judah secure rights to the Temple Mount. After a fierce battle, his victory against the European Christians soon filled Jerusalem with Jewish communities.[491]

The rulers of the Eastern Roman Empire, or the Christian Empire, could not tolerate losing Jerusalem. Military forces swept out of the Christian capital, Constantinople in Anatolia (now Istanbul in Turkey), and took Jerusalem back from the Persians in 629 CE (Jewish calendar: 4389). Christian authorities tried to ban Jews from Jerusalem but their victory proved short-lived.

Islam formed in the seventh century, and shortly thereafter its followers, the Mohammedans, conquered the Arabian Peninsula. Jews, Arabs, and others were murdered throughout Arabia because they would not convert to Islam. Many more were forcibly expelled or managed to escape. Most of the Jewish population left the towns and cities they had built throughout the Arabian Peninsula rather than convert to Islam. Jews in great numbers moved back to Israel.

Arab Mohammedans arrived in Jerusalem in 638 CE

(Jewish calendar: 4398) to subjugate the population and claim the city as their territory. Unlike the Christians, the Mohammedan authorities allowed Jews to live in Jerusalem.[492] The Mohammedans gave the Jewish population in Israel the choice of living as second-class citizens under Islamic rule or leaving their homeland. Many stayed. Many left.

Some Jews, including several rabbis, moved during and after the Islamic conquest of Jerusalem to other parts of the (Eastern Roman) Christian Empire, especially to Alexandria, Egypt's capital city. Three years after conquering Israel the Mohammedan army crossed the Sinai to invade and ransack Egypt, Nubia, and North Africa. The Arabs seized the region from the Christian Europeans, plundered towns, decimated the populations, and began a Muslim occupation of North Africa.

The Arabs added the North African plundered treasure to their growing Islamic Empire. They settled in Egypt, built mosques throughout the country, and ruled the native Coptic and the resident Roman (European) populations in Egypt harshly from their new Islamic capital built in Fustat (near Cairo). Many Europeans converted to Islam or left Egypt after the Arab invasion.[493]

Most Jews living in Egypt's capital Alexandria fled back to Israel and other refuges. Jews in Israel built a synagogue on the Temple Mount near the ruins of their former Temple, and large crowds of Jews gathered regularly in the courtyard of the Temple site for prayer services. Some Mohammedan rulers allowed Jews access only to the Temple Mount gates leading to the site.[494]

Mohammedan Arabs ten years later attacked and conquered Persia, ending the Sassanid Empire in 651 CE (Jewish calendar: 4411). Islam spread to Morocco, and under Berber Mohammedans, Jews lived as second-class citizens.[495]

Many Jews entered the Diaspora while Mohammedan Arabs occupied their homeland. One group of Jews traveled together to the Black Sea region now called Ukraine and Crimea. Khazaria, with a population of blond, brown, and red-haired, blue-eyed, fair-skinned Ashkenaz Jews, started as a Jewish enclave around 650 CE (Jewish calendar: 4410) and then became a kingdom for several hundred years.[496]

The people who originally settled the Black Sea (Caucasus) region, according to the Torah, are descendants of Yefet, firstborn son of Noah and Na'ama, through Yefet's grandson, Ashkenaz, son of Gomer.[497]

The Silk Road provided Islam with access into China in the seventh century. Constant fighting left Mohammedans in charge of large areas of China for the next 300 years until the beginning of the Song Dynasty. For unknown reasons around 960 CE (Jewish calendar: 4720) a group of at least 200 Persian Jews migrated to Kaifeng, the capital of China during the Song Dynasty. China experienced a golden age during the Song Dynasty.[498]

In Europe in 936 CE (Jewish calendar: 4696), Otto I, a German king, unified the German tribes and then crowned himself emperor. Some historians refer to this event as the beginning of the Holy Roman Empire.

The Rus, a violent predatory Slavic tribe, settled north and west of Khazaria. In 969 CE (Jewish calendar: 4729) Rus warriors attacked, plundered, and conquered the Khazar Kingdom. The Rus annexed Khazaria to the Kievan Rus Empire. The Rus became Russians, Ukrainians, and Belarusians.[499] The 30,000 Khazars became Ashkenaz Jews and joined the 8,000 Jews already living in the Kievan Rus Empire.

This began a long history of violence to control land between the Baltic Sea and Black Sea. The same territory at different times would be called Russia, Poland, Prussia, or Germany.[500]

Berber Mohammedans from Morocco formed the Fatimid

Dynasty, raised an army, and attacked the Arabs controlling Israel in 970 CE (Jewish calendar: 4730). The Berber Mohammedans occupied the Jewish homeland for the next hundred years. Jews enjoyed limited prosperity and tolerance under Berber rule.[501]

As the first 1,000 years of the Common Era came to a close, populations had increased on every continent. Tribes throughout sub-Saharan Africa had grown, moved around, clashed with each other, and formed autonomous city states and kingdoms.

India's growing population had developed a caste system and had organized into regional kingdoms based on agricultural production. Warlords controlled individual states in China. Some tribes in the North American and South American continents retained a nomadic way of life while others developed empires, such as the Anasazi of North America and the Maya of the Yucatán Peninsula.

Diaspora Jews in Europe shared knowledge of the continent through Jewish merchants who traversed back and forth through various kingdoms, empires, and regions. On the Jewish map of Europe, Ashkenaz (Germany and France), Sephard (the Iberian Peninsula, Italy, and North Africa), and Rus (Slavic lands east of Ashkenaz) comprised the continent.[502]

Jews in Eretz Israel (Land of Israel) lived in their homeland through the first thousand years of the Common Era under the rule of Roman emperors, Christian Europeans, and various Islamic dynasties.

Mohammedan Turks from the Turkmenistan area north of Iran raided and plundered their way across Mesopotamia and entered Israel in 1071 (Jewish calendar: 4831). The Turks successfully fought the Berbers in Jerusalem. Jews in Jerusalem avoided contact with the Turks.[503]

Europe was in an economic depression by 1095 (Jewish calendar: 4855) from years of crop failure, and the Crusader armies of the Holy Roman Empire were restless and violent. The Roman pope while visiting in France organized a mission for them to march to the Holy Land. Representing the kingdoms of France, Flanders, and southern Italy, under an edict from Pope Urban II (Ortho de Lagery), the medieval Christian Crusaders ransacked Jewish towns, murdering and raping across Europe on their way toward Israel.[504]

They arrived in the Jewish homeland in 1099 (Jewish calendar: 4859) to raid Jerusalem and take control of the city from the Mohammedan Turks. The Crusaders broke through the city walls and defeated the Mohammedans.

Crusaders burned the main mosque, filled with Muslim women, children, and men. Then they attacked the Jews. They tortured, raped, and slaughtered the city's Jewish men, women, and children. Jews hiding in Jerusalem were burned to death or sold into slavery.[505]

Christians converted the two mosques (the former synagogues) on the Temple Mount into churches and banned non-Christians from the site. Jews then prayed at the gates leading to the former Temple and on the Mount of Olives.

After this atrocity, called the First Crusade, European Crusaders opened travel routes from Europe into Israel for Christians to make pilgrimages. Jews also used the travel routes to return to the Land of Israel. In one group, 300 rabbis from France and England traveled together to Israel. They settled in Jerusalem and Acro (Acre).[506]

Jewish warriors helped Saladin, a Kurdish Mohammedan with a fierce army, attack the Crusaders in 1187 (Jewish calendar: 4947). The Jews and Kurdish fighters regained control of Jerusalem. Some Kurdish Mohammedans allowed Jews access to the Temple Mount; others revoked the privilege. They sometimes mistreated Jews but generally encouraged them to live in Israel as second-class citizens. The Jewish population increased under Kurdish rule.

The Crusaders were a Teutonic (German) order of Catholic knights. After losing Jerusalem to the Kurdish Mohammedan warriors they took their army to Poland and destroyed part of the country. The knights took over the territory they conquered and renamed it Prussia.

Many Diaspora Jews stayed in Europe. Jewish fortunes increased throughout Europe between 900 CE and 1300 CE (Jewish calendar: 4660-5060). Trade increased, and the European economy began to prosper. Jews opened trade routes to the southwest coast of India along the Arabian Sea. The Jewish community in Cochin became an important spice trading partner.[507]

Jews living in Gaul-turned-France had enjoyed a good life from 135 CE until 1180 (Jewish calendar: 3895-4940) when Catholic King Philip Augustus suddenly turned on the Jewish communities. He confiscated their land and personal property. French brutality toward Jews continued and intensified.[508]

Jew-hating King Louis XI came up with a scheme to force French Jews to convert to Christianity around 1242 (Jewish calendar: 5002). The conversion attempt, of course, failed. Using as an excuse that the Talmud, a collection of Jewish writings, insulted Christianity, he recommended to Catholic theologians that all existing copies of the Talmud be collected and destroyed. Historians estimate that Catholics burned 24 cartloads with 12,000 volumes of priceless Hebrew manuscripts handwritten on parchments. King Louis XI then cancelled all Christian debts owed to Jews, and expelled them from France.[509]

Most French Jews moved to Austria. Duke Frederick of Austria and Syria offered in 1244 (Jewish calendar: 5004) to make a favorable treaty with Jews to attract Jewish commerce.

Jews moved to Vienna and other Austrian cities and became an influential part of the developing Austrian intelligentsia.[510]

Jews had lived in the "Great Poland" region for centuries before the "Polanie" (field people) clans joined together to form a nation in the tenth century. Jews and Poles had a long history of mutual trade and cooperation by the time Prince Boleslaw the Pious passed legislation in 1264 (Jewish calendar: 5024) guaranteeing Jewish rights and privileges in his kingdom. For instance, Jews appearing in court could make an oath using the Torah instead of the customary Bible.[511]

Large debts owed to Jews from England's elite were suddenly canceled when the Monarch Edward I, supported by England's nobles, issued a Jew-expulsion edict in 1290 (Jewish calendar: 5050). They had the order to leave delivered on Tisha B'Av, the day Jews mourn the destruction of both Temples. The royals and nobles then confiscated abandoned Jewish property throughout the kingdom.[512]

Christian Crusaders, the army of the Holy Roman Empire, targeted Jews and began raiding throughout Europe, plundering Jewish wealth and destroying Jewish communities.[513]

Violent territorial disputes also swept through most of China for hundreds of years. Warlords battled for control until Kublai Khan, grandson of Genghis Khan, unified the country in 1271 (Jewish calendar: 5031).[514]

Europe's population had exploded in the warm stable climate period from 1000 to 1300 (Jewish calendar: 4760-5060). Then heavy rains started in northern Europe before the onset of the Little Ice Age. Famine in parts of Europe followed crop failures. Europeans became violent as resources became scarce.

For instance, incited by church leaders, angry Jew-hating Germans razed the Ratisbon synagogue in the town of Deggendorf on the Danube in 1337 (Jewish calendar: 5107), erected a Christian church in its place, and confiscated Jewish property.[515]

The Dutch city of Amsterdam, first settled around 1300 (Jewish calendar: 5060), became a refuge for Jews and others escaping violence in other European countries.

Jews also migrated to Poland for protection. Kazimierz III the Great (also called Casimir) organized Poland into a sovereign kingdom during his reign of 1333 to 1370 (Jewish calendar: 5093-5130). He protected Jews living in his realm, and he invited Jewish refugees escaping violence in Europe to join their brethren in Poland.[516]

Jewish communities thrived in Bulgarian kingdoms for decades. Bulgaria even had a Jewish queen, Theodora (Sarah) from 1335 to 1355 (Jewish calendar: 5095-5115).[517]

Islamic Mongols from Central Asia had attacked and raided a wide territory, and in 1348 (Jewish calendar: 5108), after raiding throughout China and spreading a highly fatal plague, they attacked Italians trading in Crimea. The Mongols unknowingly brought with them rats infested with parasites carrying the plague. The Italians escaped to their homeland in ships carrying some of the plague-ridden rats. Once the plague hit, it spread from port to port, town to town.[518]

The Black Death, also called the "Terrible Death," swept across the Middle East, Europe, Russia, and the Balkans. Unsanitary, crowded living conditions contributed to the deaths.

In German cities, as well as in other European cities, church leaders promoted Jew hatred to angry, superstitious Christian populations and blamed Jews as the source of plague deaths. Christians burned thousands of Jews alive in wooden pens while political and religious leaders confiscated Jewish possessions.[519]

In Bulgaria during the height of the pandemic Czar Ivan Alexander, on advice from his council, issued a Jew expulsion order in 1352 (Jewish calendar: 5112) for allegedly influencing Christians.[520]

Jewish communities fared better in Croatia. A Sephardic

community in Dubrovnik built a large, beautiful synagogue in 1352.

Poland escaped the ravages of the plague pandemic that swept across Europe and became a refuge for Jews leaving disease-ridden towns and cities; also for Jews fleeing Christian hysteria or expulsion edicts.[521]

The plague killed an estimated 50 million to 100 million people, 60% of the population of Europe, the Middle East, Mesopotamia, and Asia. By 1355 (Jewish calendar: 5115) the plague had subsided in all but a few places, such as England. The plague would continue to appear in England until the 19th century. Poor diets and unsanitary, crowded living conditions among the common people caused death and disease outbreaks for hundreds of years.[522]

Powerful Ottoman Turks, originally from Turkmenistan in Central Asia, formed a Middle Eastern empire based in Anatolia (Turkey). They took control of the Balkan states by 1389 (Jewish calendar: 5149), and in 1453 (Jewish calendar: 5213) they captured the (Eastern Roman) Christian Empire capital of Constantinople and renamed it Istanbul.[523] A flood of scholars, with their ancient texts, fled Constantinople to Florence, Italy. The influx of scholars and an interest in the arts by the powerful Medici family, the bankers of Italy, started what is known as the Renaissance.

As trade, ideas, and art of the Renaissance took hold throughout Europe, the Catholic Church expanded its power, especially in Poland. While much of Europe gradually became hostile under the influence of Jew-hating clergy, Polish kings and princes continued to invite Jews to live safely in Poland. Jewish communities increased during and after the Renaissance in Poland. Wealthy Jews became part of the Polish aristocracy.[524]

Jews had settled throughout Europe after the plague and helped rebuild devastated economies. Then the pattern of royal robbery began again. French royals confiscated Jewish property and banned Jews from living in France around 1400 (Jewish calendar: 5160).

China had remained isolated during this time of turmoil in Europe. Then they built a fleet and traveled the oceans of the world in 1421. The Ming dynasty built larger sailing ships than the ships later sailed by Columbus. Chinese documents record that Zheng He made seven voyages to the western ocean from 1421 to 1434 (Jewish calendar: 5181-5184).[525]

Researchers have found evidence suggesting a Ming dynasty emperor in 1421 sent a fleet with colonizers from China to the American Southwest, and that the colony became isolated when the next emperor cut off contact in 1434. Most scientists reject the evidence as inconclusive.[526]

The first victims of the Tribunal of the Holy Office of the Inquisition—the Spanish Inquisition—initiated in 1478 (Jewish calendar: 5238) by Catholic monarchs Ferdinand II of Aragon and Isabella I of Castile were "insincere Catholics."[527] Only fourteen years later, the rulers of Spain in 1492 (Jewish calendar: 5252) also burned to death or exiled their Jewish citizens, again during Tisha B'Av, and again the elite confiscated Jewish property.[528]

Columbus in 1492 recruited his sailing crew from a prison of condemned Jews (who had refused to convert) for his famous voyage to the New World.[529]

A large population of Jews fled the bloodshed in Spain by moving to neighboring Portugal where King Joao II initially welcomed them. The king immediately ordered the removal of an estimated 2,000 children from Jewish parents. The children were exiled to a remote West African island called Sao Tome, where most of them died.[530]

King Joao II gave approval only to Jews with science or training in weapons manufacture to remain in Portugal. The rest were given deportation notices to leave. Some Jews paid a fee to remain. Others who could not afford to pay the fee or the travel expense were enslaved. At least 20,000 Jews became slaves.[531]

King Manuel I assumed the Portuguese throne two years later and married the daughter of Ferdinand and Isabella of Spain. The marriage contract contained a provision requiring the expulsion of Portugal's Jews by 1497 (Jewish calendar: 5257). Not wanting to lose part of his skilled workforce, King Manuel seized Jewish children for forced conversions. When 20,000 Jews arrived in Lisbon for scheduled transport out of Portugal, the king instead had them forcibly converted as "New Christians."[532]

Sephardic Jews in great numbers fled Spain and Portugal. Families traveled across Europe to Israel. Some stayed in Turkey where they joined existing Jewish communities. With so many new arrivals in Israel, places such as Safed became thriving centers of spiritual life and Kabbalah. Sephardic Jews also settled in Tiberius, Jerusalem, and other cities. Some Sephardic Jews kept traveling east to India and some joined the Jews of Cochin (now Kochi).[533]

Other Jews escaped Spain and Portugal by moving to Germany. Church reformers in Germany violently broke in the early 1500s from the Roman Catholic Church to form Protestant sects of Christianity. The new Protestants were initially friendly to Jews.

When German Jews failed to leave Judaism and join the new religious movement, Protestants under the order of Martin Luther became as vicious as their Catholic counterparts. Most of northern Europe joined the Protestants and most of southern Europe remained under the control of the Roman Catholics. The Teutonic Order grand master, ruler of Prussia, converted to the new Protestant religion in 1525 (Jewish calendar: 5285), and the Prussian population changed from Catholic to Protestant.

In this time of political upheaval the Earth was about to enter the Little Ice Age.

16

THE LITTLE ICE AGE

A freeing cold period called the Little Ice Age chilled Earth between 1550 and 1850 (Jewish calendar: 5310-5610). Sea levels lowered as glaciers advanced worldwide. An intense, freezing cold snap began around 1650 and lasted to after 1700 (Jewish calendar: 5410-5460).

China's leaders for a hundred years after the Zheng He voyages had isolated their country from Europe and Russia. But, news spread quickly throughout the known world when the deadliest earthquake in human history occurred in 1556 (Jewish calendar: 5316) in Shaanxi Province, the heart of China. An estimated 830,000 people died in the earthquake.[534]

As China tried to recover from the effects of the Shaanxi earthquake, resources dwindled in China, Europe, and Russia as crops failed at the beginning of the Little Ice Age. For the next 300 years populations around the world had to adapt their lifestyles to compensate during this cold stadial.

The Ottoman Turks annexed Kurdistan, Egypt, and Israel, including the Jordan Valley, in 1550 (Jewish calendar: 5310). The

Turkish Mohammedans called Israel "Southern Syria," and were generally open to Jewish settlement. Some Turkish rulers were hostile to Jews. But the Turks could not successfully police the Jewish population, and Jews from all over the world returned to their homeland during Turkish occupation.[535] Jewish scholars and rabbis settled in Safed and other northern towns in Eretz Israel.

Jews rebuilt Tiberias in 1558 (Jewish calendar: 5318). The Jewish population increased dramatically, and the city began to thrive with a majority Jewish population.[536]

People in Europe and Russia again turned violent as economies declined and populations increased. Beginning in the 1600s the Holy Roman Empire, centered in Germany, began to humiliate, intimidate, and torture their Jewish populations in order to confiscate their wealth. Authorities in parts of the Holy Roman Empire and in Romania forced much of European Jewry into ghettos.

Ukrainian peasants and Cossack warriors, both Russian Orthodox, formed an army in 1648 (Jewish calendar: 5408) and revolted against oppressive Polish feudal rule. The sadistic Cossacks and Ukrainians targeted the Jews and the Catholic Polish nobility for excessive and brutal torture. Cossacks confiscated property and possessions belonging to nobility or Jews. For the next year and a half the aggressors mutilated and murdered Jews and Poles. Cossacks desecrated synagogues and burned people alive. Historians estimate the number of Jews the Ukrainian Cossacks massacred to be between 200,000 and 400,000.[537] The Cossacks and Ukrainians also murdered hundreds of thousands of Poles and destroyed large sections of Poland.[538]

A few years later, Swedes crossed a narrow section of the Baltic Sea to invade the Polish region of Byelorussia in 1654 (Jewish calendar: 5414). For two years the Swedes destroyed parts of Poland. Jews remained neutral, but the Poles blamed them for collaborating with the Swedes against the Belarusians. In a rare display of violence against Jews, Polish citizens began attacking their Jewish neighbors in frenzied rampages.[539] Poles tortured Jews for their possessions and property before annihilating 700 Jewish communities across Poland.[540]

People moved to North America from freezing cold northern countries, including England, Poland, Germany, Scandinavia, and Russia. Migrations began in earnest during the intense cold snap of 1650 to 1700 (Jewish calendar: 5410-5460). Waves of Russian Jews also immigrated to Israel.

Sea levels lowered enough during the cold snap to expose the Azores Platform on the Mid-Atlantic Ridge. A Portuguese sailor in the North Atlantic drew a map of the exposed Azores landmass during the cold snap, and a German Jesuit scholar published it in 1678 (Jewish calendar: 5440). The map identified the landmass directly west from the Strait of Gibraltar as the continent of Atlantis. A Berlin cartographer published a similar map showing the Azores Platform as Atlantis. The cartographer's map also detailed the British Isles connecting to the European mainland by the landmass called Doggerland, now long submerged under the North Sea.[541]

The scholar and the mapmaker probably identified the Azores Platform as Atlantis on the two maps because the newly exposed landmass so closely matched Plato's description of a small, mountainous continent west of Gibraltar and the size of Anatolia (Asia Minor) and Libya combined.

The first Jews arrived in New Amsterdam, later called New York, from Brazil in 1654. They had fled their homes, fearing the Spanish Inquisition when Portugal conquered Brazil. The Dutch East India Company, owners of the American colony, allowed the twenty-three Sephardic men, women, and children to stay.

Thus began the migration of Jews to America and the beginning of the New York Jewish community.[542]

Europe in the 1700s became a time of turmoil as kingdoms with territories became governments of countries with borders.

The powerful military society of Prussia expanded their territory by force and emerged as a sovereign kingdom within the Holy Roman Empire in 1701 (Jewish calendar: 5461) with the coronation of Frederick I. The new king moved the capital of Prussia to Berlin.[543] Prussia included what are now Germany and parts of Poland, Russia, Lithuania, Denmark, Belgium, Switzerland, and the Czech Republic.

Flexing their power, European governments entered a time of territorial expansion causing numerous regional conflicts and wars.[544] The European and Russian populations continued to expand, and more Europeans and Russians moved to America as violence continued to erupt in their homelands.[545]

In 1700 (Jewish calendar: 5460) American colonists totaled 250,000. Jews were among the citizens in the colonial towns of New York, Newport, Philadelphia, and Charle's Town, later called Charleston.[546] By 1750 (Jewish calendar: 5510) American colonists totaled well over a million.[547]

An extended conflict called the Colonial War from 1689 to 1764 (Jewish calendar: 5449-5524) was really the first "world war," with military engagements involving Prussia, France, Great Britain, Austria, and Sweden fighting over territory in Europe, India, and the Caribbean. When the war between Great Britain and France spread to North America in 1756 (Jewish calendar: 5516), the Americans called it The French and Indian War (against the British). The French and British called it The Seven Years War.[548]

Like the Israelites of ancient Israel, Jews became "Traders in Purple" in the American colony. Wealthy Jewish families from London moved to Charle's Town in the 1750s. Among them, an English Jew named Moses Lindo left London to become an indigo planter in Carolina. Six years later Lindo and other Jews in his community had made indigo a major export of Charle's Town. Lindo was appointed surveyor and inspector general of indigo, drugs, and dye for South Carolina in 1756.[549]

Most European and Russian Christians flocking to America during the Little Ice Age brought their hatred and resentment of Jews, causing Jews to suffer exclusion from time to time from certain areas and from working in certain professions. But overall, Jews prospered in America while Jews in Europe and Russia suffered severe anti-Semitism.[550]

During the Colonial War the English fought France for control of the colonies in America and the Caribbean, and for control of India. England won the French and Indian War in 1764. Spain lost Florida to England and gained New France, also called French Louisiana, from France.[551]

The war nearly bankrupted England. In an effort to regain their financial losses in the American colonies and in India, England began to increase taxes on the American colonists. The Americans rebelled, and in 1776 (Jewish calendar: 5536) the English colony in America declared its independence. It was a time of unrest and divided allegiances. Some Americans were Loyalists who supported England; some were Colonists encouraging secession from England. Jews fought in the war on both sides. Loyalist Jews stayed in British-controlled New York. Colonist Jews from New York fled to Philadelphia.[552]

Backed by France, the Americans fought the English and won. The Revolutionary War ended in 1783 (Jewish calendar: 5543) with the signing of the Treaty of Paris. America immediately became a refuge for people oppressed in Europe and Russia. The victorious Colonists signed the United States Constitution in 1787 (Jewish calendar: 5547) and adopted it the following year.[553]

As England lost control of its American colony it claimed the continent of Australia in 1770 (Jewish calendar: 5530) and began a penal colony there.

Poland became a country with central leadership in 1764 with a constitutional monarchy. The centuries old Council of Four Lands, which had provided autonomy to Jews in Poland, was dissolved, the economy worsened, and a long Jewish and Polish Golden Age ended.[554]

Empress Catherine II of Russia, also called Catherine the Great, in collusion with Austria and Prussia, sent her army to attack and occupy Poland in 1791 (Jewish calendar: 5551). Russia, Austria, and Prussia agreed to divide Poland into three parts for their respective kingdoms. Austria acquired a southwestern section, Prussia absorbed a smaller Duchy of Prussia bordering the Baltic Sea, and Russia took the huge eastern portion including Ukraine, Crimea, and Lithuania.[555]

The new Russian territory came with a majority of Catholics and a large population of Jews, also called White Jews. Beginning in 1791, except for doctors, artists, engineers and others with university educations, Russian Jews were confined to towns in the newly partitioned geographic area known as the Jewish Pale of Settlement and needed government permits to travel outside the Pale.[556]

Russian Orthodox Church officials and the Russian government colluded to murder the Jews and the Catholics in the Pale to clear the way for Russian settlement. The Pale bordered Russia in the north and east. Prussia lay to the west and the Black Sea provided a natural southern border.

Inside Pale towns, Jews had permanent residency. With an exception for the Jewish intelligentsia, Jews were not permitted to live outside the Pale. All Jews, even the professional class, were barred from living in Moscow or Siberia or Finland.[557]

France faced a constant shortage of food and supplies after

the wars with England and the tremendous costs expended to back the American Revolution. Napoleon Bonaparte came to power in 1799 (Jewish calendar: 5559) during the bloody French Revolution. Napoleon invaded and plundered other European countries to provide needed funds to the government of France. The French also invaded and occupied Egypt for three years, breaking the hold the Ottoman Turks had held over the Egyptians for two hundred years.[558]

Napoleon regained control of French Louisiana in 1800 (Jewish calendar: 5560) through a secret treaty with Spain. Three years later, to raise additional funds for France, Napoleon sold French Louisiana to the United States for cash and debt relief totaling $15,000,000. This 828,000-square-mile (2,144,510 km^2) territory stretching from Canada to Mexico doubled the size of the United States.[559]

The Napoleonic Wars fragmented the Holy Roman Empire. Austria, the private estate of the emperor, became the Austrian Empire in 1804 (Jewish calendar: 5564).

Napoleon tried to preempt a Russian invasion of France and French territories by invading Russia in 1812 (Jewish calendar: 5572). However, Russian winters during the Little Ice Age were deadly. The Russian population, before leaving to stay with relatives in other parts of Russia, burned Moscow to the ground to deny shelter for the arriving French soldiers. Most of the French army died of exposure, causing a defeated Emperor Napoleon to return to France to be deposed and exiled.[560]

During his reign, Jewish ghettos had been abolished and many other reforms adopted in France, Italy, and other European countries he influenced.[561]

Especially during the Little Ice Age, Russia faced a constant shortage of food and supplies. Jew hatred, encouraged by Russian Orthodox clergy, intensified under the Tsarist rule of Catherine's grandson, Alexander Pavlovich Romanov, crowned

Emperor (Tsar) Alexander I. The first Pogrom, sponsored by the Tsar and the Russian Orthodox Church, happened in 1821 (Jewish calendar: 5581) in the Black Sea port town of Odessa.

The Russian Pogroms were state-sponsored terror-and-murder rampages organized by the Russian government in cooperation with the Russian Orthodox Church.[562]

Because of Russia's partition of Poland, one-half of world Jewry lived under Tsarist rule in Russia at the time of the Pogroms.[563] The Tsarist monarchies and the Orthodox Church harassed Jews to encourage them to leave Russia. As a result Jew hatred in the Russian Empire became common and often resulted in the torture and murder of Jews. Russians generally wanted to be not just the dominant ethnic group, but the only ethnic group in lands they claimed.[564]

By the time of the Pogroms, most Jews in Tsarist Russia were impoverished after living for nearly a hundred years in the Pale of Settlement (now Ukraine, Crimea, and Belarus). There, Jews endured lives of poverty by forming close-knit communities and working together.[565]

Oppression of Jews continued under the reign of Catherine's great-grandson, Nicholas I. From 1833 to 1854 (Jewish calendar: 5593-5614), the Russian army policed the country for Nicholas I. In an effort to fill its recruitment quotas, soldiers regularly entered the Pale and kidnapped Jewish boys under the bar mitzvah age of 13 to serve for 25 years.[566]

Separating Jewish boys from their families for a quarter-century made them vulnerable to Russian Orthodox conversion. An estimated 21,050 Jewish boys were snatched. Only a few of those kidnapped Jews returned to their families after their military service.[567]

As conditions for Jews deteriorated in Russia, American Jews prospered. Russian Jews fleeing to Eretz Israel needed help, and American Jews responded. New York Jews organized a relief agency in 1833 called Tarumat ha-Kodesh to send aid for several decades to Jews moving to Israel.[568]

The Spanish Inquisition, 350 years of torture and murder, ended in 1834 (Jewish calendar: 5594). However, anti-Semitism remained high in Spain, Portugal, and other European countries, and continued to affect Jews in America.[569]

As the Little Ice Age drew to a close, the Great Powers of Europe continued to compete for power and control.

Queen Alexandrina Victoria became monarch of Great Britain in 1837 (Jewish calendar: 5597). The Ottoman Turks in 1840 (Jewish calendar: 5600) called on England to decide its civil war with the Egyptians over the territory of Israel. Britain helped the Turks and then began to make secret plans to acquire Ottoman Empire Middle Eastern lands. To appease the French, France was included in the plan.[570]

Irish immigration to America surpassed all others as the Great Famine devastated Ireland beginning in 1845 (Jewish calendar: 5605). A potato blight and starvation policies by the ruling British government started the famine, also called the Great Hunger. Over a million Irish peasants starved to death in less than a decade.[571] A million more fled to America.

Jews in America, faced with religious discrimination, especially after the influx of over a million Irish Catholics, opened Jewish hospitals in most major cities. In New York, where city officials barred Jews from certain professions, the Jews' Hospital of New York, later named Mount Sinai Hospital, opened in 1855 (Jewish calendar: 5615) with Jewish doctors and kosher food for its patients.[572]

After China's bitter defeat by the British in the First Opium War in 1842 (Jewish calendar: 5602) the Chinese suffered from crop failures and increased internal unrest leading to the Taiping Rebellion, which started in 1851 (Jewish calendar: 5611). The rebellion evolved into a civil war costing 20 million to 30 million lives.[573]

Jews in Eretz Israel experienced a sort of guarded autonomy under the rule of the Ottoman Empire. Jews lived in relative prosperity in over fifty cities and towns including a vibrant, growing population in Jerusalem.[574] Jews in 1858 (Jewish calendar: 5618) constructed the Hurva Synagogue in the Jewish quarter of Jerusalem.

17

POWER AND CONTROL

Actions leading to the First World War began decades before the declaration of war. Along with other European kingdoms, the French and British ruling elite had displayed territorial greed for hundreds of years. The Rus tribe-turned-Russian had used brutal force to expand its territories.[575]

In America, political battles for power and control of the country had culminated in the savage Civil War of 1861 to 1865 (Jewish calendar: 5621-5625).

Countries throughout Europe, the Balkans, and Russia were generally ruled by relatives of the House of Hanover, the same German-English royal family related to Queen Victoria, monarch of Great Britain from 1837 to 1901 (Jewish calendar: 5597-5661). Family feuds, jealousies, betrayals, and competition sometimes broke out into trade hostilities and regional wars, caused assassinations, and created hardship on the local populations subjected to their disagreements.[576]

In Europe, the German Empire, the Second Reich, formed in 1871 (Jewish calendar: 5631) under Prussian Chancellor Otto von Bismarck as a Protestant country next to Catholic Austria. In the same year, William H. Seward, former President Abraham Lincoln's secretary of state, visited Jerusalem (under Ottoman control at this time). Seward recorded in his journal that the Jewish community was larger than any other community in Jerusalem. He observed Jews praying at the Western Wall, and he attended a Friday night service at the Hurva Synagogue.[577] As Seward traveled through Eretz Israel, another Pogrom happened in Odessa during the reign of Tsar Alexander II.

To beat the Russians in a race to influence the Balkans, Austrian Emperor Franz Joseph I, with the approval of Bismarck in an agreement called the 1878 Treaty of Berlin, or Congress of Berlin, sent 200,000 to 300,000 troops to the Balkan region of the Ottoman Empire to occupy Bosnia.[578]

With Austrian soldiers moving into Bosnia, Christian-versus-Muslim conflicts broke out, causing Muslims to move to other parts of the Ottoman Empire still under Islamic control. Thousands of Slavic Muslims from Bosnia and Croatia migrated to Eretz Israel (called Southern Syria by the Muslims) in the 1880s.[579] Some moved into old abandoned Crusader houses along the coast.

The 1878 Treaty of Berlin also granted autonomy to Bulgaria, and the Bulgarian government quickly declared its Jewish population to be stateless refugees, not allowed to work or attend schools.[580] Most Bulgarian Jews moved to Eretz Israel, and a few immigrated to the United States and Europe.

So many Jews came to Eretz Israel in 1880 (Jewish calendar: 5640) from Bulgaria that the mass migration is called the First Aliyah, the first wave of Jews returning to their homeland.

Russian Jews formed a nonsectarian organization called ORT, Society for Handicrafts and Agricultural Work, in St. Petersburg in 1880 to provide education and skilled-labor training for Jewish communities. ORT helped Jews become self-sufficient by teaching employable skills so Russian Jews could try to obtain permits to work outside the Pale. To help Jews in repressive Russia, ORT also held classes for Jews to gain knowledge and understanding of Judaism.[581]

Unfortunately, the Russian royal family had murderous intent for their country's population of Ashkenaz Jews. In 1881 (Jewish calendar: 5641) a widespread Pogrom swept across Russia, including Ukraine and Belarus, and continued for three years.[582]

On May 3, 1882 (Jewish calendar: 5642), the Russian government passed the "May Laws" intended to be a legal national Pogrom. Tsar Alexander III planned to eliminate millions of Russian Jews by forced conversion to the Orthodox Church, expulsion, and starvation. When Russian, Polish, and Lithuanian Jews learned of the May Laws, over a million Jews fled. They had to abandon their property and possessions because they lacked time to sell them. Government officials at border crossings confiscated anything of value that Jewish families carried.[583]

Serbia, adjacent to Bosnia-Herzegovina, became a center of conflict because the French and the Austrians wanted a Catholic-friendly king, the Russians wanted the monarch to be Russian Orthodox, the Serbian Christians wanted a Serbian Orthodox king, and the Serbian Muslims wanted an Islamic government.

The Austrians crowned a Serbian Orthodox prince to create the Kingdom of Serbia in 1882, and the Russians arranged his marriage to a Russian princess. Their son, Nicolas I, became tsar of Russia.[584]

An arms race began in Europe among the major powers, France, Britain, Russia, and Germany. Engaged in a power struggle for regional supremacy, they made plans to grab land in the Balkans and the Middle East before invading China and Africa.[585] Britain invaded and occupied Egypt in 1882. France in 1885 (Jewish calendar: 5645) declared Indochina a protectorate (a country or region controlled and defended by another country). French troops invaded and occupied Vietnam, Laos, and Cambodia. French government officials and French businessmen began building a European style infrastructure such as schools, hospitals, and government buildings throughout Indochina.

The 1885 Treaty of Berlin, called the Congo Conference, introduced a plan for the systematic invasion and occupation of Africa by the United Kingdom, France, Belgium, Germany, Portugal, Italy, and Spain. The United Kingdom and France took the lion's share of the continent, with Germany moving into four territories in Southwest Africa.

Under Chancellor Otto von Bismarck, Germany's philosophy of racial supremacy (later called "Nazism") took hold in Africa.

World population doubled after the Little Ice Age cold snap. It increased from an estimate of 700 million to 1.7 billion by 1900. Germany's population explosion in the mid to late 1800's created the need for more living space and Africa provided the opportunity for almost unlimited expansion. German settlers guarded by German soldiers moved into Southwest Africa. The soldiers began an organized annihilation of the native populations by hard labor with little food, deplorable living conditions in work camps, rape, murder, and forced marches to concentration camps built to house and murder native Africans.[586]

The racial supremacy philosophy continued under Kaiser Wilhelm II. In 1904 (Jewish calendar: 5664) he issued to his African command an extermination order of the remaining natives still living in "German territory." After poisoning watering holes in the Kalahari Desert, German troops surrounded African villages, murdered many, and forced marched the rest into the lifeless desert by firing rifles over their heads to make them run. Those who couldn't escape were stacked up in piles with the already dead, and burned.[587]

By 1905 (Jewish calendar: 5665) Second Reich Germany had created a major battleship fleet. Germany's fleet and economy had finally grown bigger than Britain's, and England's leaders had begun to fear Germany's power.[588]

The rulers of Britain, France, and Russia made a military pact, the Triple Entente, which when joined by other countries became known as the Allied Powers, also called the Allies. In response, Germany and Austria-Hungary formed the Triple Alliance, which became known as the Central Powers or the Axis.

Germany's Kaiser Wilhelm II did not promote a European war, but his advisors and his generals did. German political and military elite feared being overrun by Russian Slavs. Germans wanted a final, "great war" between the Teutonic German peoples and the Slavic peoples of Russian, European, and Balkan countries. Terror and murder campaigns continued under Nicholas II, the last Tsar of the Russian Empire. Six hundred Pogroms were conducted in three years across Russia from 1903 to 1906 (Jewish calendar: 5663-5666). During the Pogroms the Revolution of 1905 left a tsarist constitutional monarchy still eager to control the working masses of central and east Europe.[589]

In the first year of the massacres conducted under Nicholas II, Theodor Herzl, a Hungarian Jewish journalist, playwright, author, and one of the founders of the World Zionist Organization, met with Pope Pius X (Giuseppe Sarto) to try to negotiate safe passage for threatened Jews from Russia to Eretz Israel, still under Ottoman control. The Pope threatened Herzl with forced conversions to Catholicism for any Jew trying to enter "Palestine."[590]

Despite the Pope's empty threats, hundreds of thousands of Jews fled Russia and sought passage to America and to Eretz Israel during and after the massacres.

The waves of Jews entering Eretz Israel after the 1903-to-1906 Pogroms became known as the Second Aliyah, the second wave of Jews returning to their homeland. Again, Jews were stripped of their property and possessions before they could leave. News of the violence horrified people worldwide.[591] The American Jewish Committee formed in 1906 to fight anti-Semitism.

Chaim Nachman Bialik, born January 9, 1873 (Jewish calendar: 5633), is recognized as one of Israel's greatest national poets. Bialik wrote the poem "City of Slaughter" after the Jewish Historical Society commissioned him to report on the Kishinev massacre. "City of Slaughter" describes the 1903 Easter Sunday Pogrom and shames the sons of the Maccabees—the Jews—for not fighting back.[592]

Jews in communities around the world reacted to the viciousness of the Pogroms, and especially to the atrocities committed against pregnant women and small children. Jews formed self-defense units throughout Russia, and worldwide membership in Zionist organizations increased.[593]

Muslim hostility intensified during the Second Aliyah when thousands of escaping Russian Jews immigrated to the Land of Israel, still under Ottoman Turk control. Jews had to form a volunteer national guard called Ha-Shomer to protect settlements from Islamic violence. In 1909 (Jewish calendar: 5669), Ha-Shomer protected Jews camped near the Mediterranean Sea while they built Tel Aviv.[594]

The anxious Austrians had annexed Bosnia-Herzegovina into their empire in 1908 (Jewish calendar: 5668) to formalize their position in the Balkans as European and Russian arms production escalated. The annexation of Bosnia by a Christian government caused hundreds of thousands of Slavic Muslims to move from the Balkans to Turkey. The incoming Muslims were poor and resented the success of the estimated two million Christian Armenians living in Turkey.[595]

In 1909 newly arrived Slavic Muslims from Bosnia and resident Turk Muslims massacred hundreds of thousands of

Armenians living in Turkey, Syria, and Eretz Israel in order to confiscate their property. The Turkish government passed laws authorizing the genocide and the property confiscation. The Turk Muslims and the Bosnian Muslims force-marched thousands of Armenian men, women, and children into the Syrian Desert without water or food. Some were gassed to death, and others were put on barges to be taken out to sea and thrown overboard. Kurds also took part in the rape, torture, and murder of Christian Armenians.[596]

The Great Powers of Europe did not declare war on or even protest to the Turkish government to stop the slaughter of Armenian Christians. The Vatican did nothing. The mass murder of Armenians along with the confiscation of their property continued for the next five years.[597]

18

THE FIRST GREAT WAR

In 1913 (Jewish calendar: 5673) the Balkan Wars ousted the Ottoman Empire from the Balkans and established independent Christian governments in Bosnia and Albania.

A year after the Balkan Wars, a member of a Serbian armed-resistance group shot and killed Archduke Franz Ferdinand, heir to the Austro-Hungarian throne, and his wife, Sophie, during their visit to Sarajevo, Bosnia. Austria mobilized to invade Serbia.

Austria's ally Germany demanded that Russia and Russia's close ally, France, remain neutral. When they refused, the Germans declared war on both. German soldiers then entered Belgium to invade France. Belgium refused to cooperate, and on August 4, 1914 (Jewish calendar: 5674), the Kaiser declared war against Belgium. Britain then immediately declared war against Germany to protect France. World War I had begun.

During the arms race among France, Britain, Russia, and Germany, the Ottoman Empire had ordered and paid for two enormous battleships to be built by Britain. The ships were intended to defend the Turkish coastline while the Ottoman

Empire remained neutral in WWI. In 1914 the British government confiscated the two completed battleships instead of delivering them. As a result, the Ottoman Empire joined with Germany for protection.

Believing that their nation had altruistic reasons to go to war, British citizens turned out in great numbers to enlist. So many British Jews volunteered to fight for their country that Zionist leader Zeev Jabotinsky helped organize special all-Jew units, the Jewish Legion, within the British military.[598]

A year later Bulgaria joined the Germany and Austria-Hungary Central Power alliance, and declared war against Italy, an Allied country.

Before the war only Germany produced a chemical compound, cordite, needed for ammunition. Germany cut off supplies of the critical explosive material to Britain early in WWI. Dr. Chaim Weizmann, a Jewish biochemist living in London, invented a method for the British military to synthetically produce the essential ingredient. Because his invention helped the British war effort, Weizmann gained national attention and made influential contacts.[599]

Throughout WWI representatives of the British government and Jewish leaders met regularly in London to discuss a Jewish homeland in "Palestine." The Great Powers called the ancient Jewish homeland Palestine (Land of the Palaces), Ottoman Turks called it Southern Syria, and Jews called it Eretz Israel (Land of Israel). "Palestine" refers to the glory of the Palatine Hill of ancient Rome where the ruling elite lived in opulent palaces.[600]

Baron Walter Rothschild, Sir Herbert Samuel, Chief Rabbi of the United Kingdom Joseph Hertz, and other Zionist leaders represented the Jewish Nation at the meetings. Prime Minister David Lloyd George and Foreign Secretary Arthur James

Balfour attended, representing the British government. After his invention, Weizmann, who would become Israel's first president, joined the negotiations leading to the Balfour Declaration.[601]

Rumors spread throughout the Middle East at the beginning of WWI of a planned mass execution of Jews by the Ottoman Empire. The Ottoman government in Turkey isolated Eretz Israel and fear of death by starvation spread among the 60,000 Jews living there.[602] Friends and relatives in New York founded a Jewish relief organization, the Joint Distribution Committee, JDC, in 1914 (Jewish calendar: 5674) to send aid to Jews in danger of starving under Turkish rule.[603]

Witnessing the mass murder of Christian Armenians by Ottoman Muslims in Jerusalem and the starvation policy of the Ottoman government in Eretz Israel convinced Jewish scientist Aaron Aaronsohn, his younger sister Sara, and a few other Jews from Zichron Ya'akov, a small agriculture village in northern Israel, to form a sophisticated espionage ring called the Nili Spies. The British government expressed support for a Jewish homeland if the Turks could be defeated, so Aaron and Sara felt they had to help the British when WWI broke out.[604]

The Nili Spies collected information about the Turkish Mujahaddin stationed along the Mediterranean Coast. Aaron Aaronsohn, at great personal risk, traveled outside the Ottoman Empire borders to contact the British military command in Egypt. Aaronsohn delivered detailed maps and deployment schedules to the British in 1916 (Jewish calendar: 5676). Turkish Mujahaddin captured, tortured, and murdered Sara Aaronsohn in October 1917 (Jewish calendar: 5677) after they discovered a carrier pigeon transporting sensitive Nili Spy information.[605]

A month later, with American financial support, Aaron Aaronsohn's information, and the help of the Jewish Legion fighting alongside British soldiers, British General Edmund Allenby captured Jerusalem in the November 1917 Battle of Jerusalem against Ottoman Empire Turks. Few knew that Allenby wrested Eretz Israel including the Jordan Valley from the Ottomans with the help of the Jewish Legion and the Nili Spies.[606] British military commanders and troops after the Battle of Jerusalem stayed in Eretz Israel with no intention of leaving.

Also in November 1917, Balfour, representing the British Foreign Office, signed and delivered to Lord Walter Rothschild, representing the Zionist Federation of Britain and Ireland, a letter promising a Jewish homeland. Arabs throughout the Middle East violently protested the Balfour agreement. (See Appendix: Balfour Declaration)

America, Japan, and others entered the war as Allies during the last year of fighting in Europe.

The Allied Powers won WWI in 1918 (Jewish calendar: 5678). Of the nearly two million Armenians living in the Ottoman Empire before the outbreak of WWI, only around 200,000 survivors could be accounted for after the war.[607]

When the war ended, Jewish theoretical physicist Albert Einstein founded The Hebrew University in Jerusalem in 1918.

Ukraine briefly became an independent republic as Russia disintegrated into civil war after Bolshevik revolutionaries murdered Tsar Nicolas II, his wife, and their children in 1918.

Poland gained independence in 1919 (Jewish calendar: 5679), ending the 125-year occupation and partition by Russia, Germany, and Austria.

Weizmann's invention, the Jewish Legion, and Aaron and Sara Aaronsohn and the other Nili Spies helped Britain in WWI. Winston Churchill, when praising Allenby's successful Jerusalem campaign, failed to mention the Jewish Legion but did credit Aaron Aaronsohn's contributions.[608]

Aaron Aaronsohn became a Jewish representative at the

1919 Paris Peace Conference by invitation of Chaim Weizmann. The Allies agreed at the conference in the Treaty of Versailles to impose reparations designed to punish Germany. While on assignment for the treaty committee, Aaronsohn died under suspicious circumstances in May 1919 (Jewish calendar: 5679) in an RAF plane crash in the English Channel.[609]

In April 1920 (Jewish calendar: 5680) a well-planned "riot" led by Muslim terrorist Mohammad Amin al-Husayni took place in British occupied Jerusalem, and then spread to Hebron and other neighborhoods. The 1920 Jerusalem riot was a Pogrom, planned, financed, and facilitated by British military officials in Eretz Israel and their counterparts in the Colonial Office in London.[610] This extreme act of violence cost several Jews their lives and seriously injured two hundred more. British officials referred to al-Husayni as an ally.[611]

As a result of the violence of the rampage, and the refusal of the British troops to protect Jews during outbreaks of violence perpetrated by Arabs against Jews, Zeev Jabotinsky helped to form a defense organization called Haganah (Hebrew for Defense).[612] British officials arrested Jabotinsky and sentenced him to fifteen years hard labor. They released him a few months later.

British officials had arranged the riots to manufacture an excuse to withdraw their support for a Jewish homeland prior to the upcoming San Remo Convention. They claimed the riots were caused by Muslim hostility toward Jews and especially against a Jewish homeland. Muslim Arab leaders in Israel then issued a joint statement supporting Jewish right-of-return and Zionism, preferring Jewish control of Eretz Israel over that of the British.[613]

Representatives of the Allies gathered at the Italian resort town of San Remo in 1920 for the San Remo Convention to ratify into international law the Covenant of the League of Nations and the Balfour Declaration. The Ottoman Empire, except for

Turkey, had been claimed at the end of WWI by the League of Nations, precursor to the United Nations, under terms of the 1919 Paris Peace Conference. The San Remo Convention confirmed that a Jewish national homeland would be created within newly acquired Ottoman Empire lands.

At the same time as the San Remo Convention in 1920 the newly independent Ukrainians, under the rule of Simon Petlura, began a sadistic, state-sponsored Pogrom which went on for two years, murdering and terrorizing Ukrainian Jews.[614]

At San Remo, the League of Nations transferred to the Jewish people, under a mandate given to Britain as trustee, legal title to what the British called "Palestine," land east of the Mediterranean Sea extending beyond the Jordan Valley and approximating the area of ancient Israel and Judah.[615]

A mandate is an official command or instruction from an authority. The "authority" was the League of Nations and the "official command/instruction" was given to the British government to administer and then transfer Palestine to the Jewish people for their homeland.

But the British government did not honor the promise made under the Balfour Declaration nor obey the League of Nations mandate. Instead, the British began setting up a British controlled, Arab managed infrastructure headquartered in Jerusalem.

The British government had gratefully accepted Jewish help during WWI, signed the Balfour Declaration, and then acted in a shameful way because England's ruling elite wanted Jerusalem for British Christians, not for Jews.[616]

WWI may have resulted in the dissolution of the German Empire, but it did nothing to change the intent of governments willing to commit or encourage mass murder to gain domination.

19

NO PEACE IN OUR TIME

While the Allies were meeting in San Remo to congratulate themselves and to map out a new British-French controlled Middle East, German political and military elite, after their bitter loss in WWI, began planning for a new, grander empire.

The German Empire, dissolved at the end of WWI, had bordered Russia in the east, France in the west, and Austria-Hungary to the south. The new German government—changing from a monarchy to a republic—signed its constitution in the city of Weimar in 1919.

The German Reich government envisioned world domination. In Munich in 1920 German political elite officially started the National Socialist German Workers Party, known as the Nazi political party and adopted the swastika as their symbol. The party platform combined fanatical patriotism with totalitarian state-run socialism.[617]

The Treaty of Versailles ending WWI required the German elite to give up their empire territories, forbade any kind of

Austrian-German reunification, and required Germany to pay billions in reparations to Britain, France, Belgium, and America.

But the loss of their empire left the Germans resentful, economically depressed, and angry. And ready to return to war to regain their territory. German elite secretly planned to regain the territory they had once called the Holy Roman Empire.[618]

The British government, having failed to stop the confirmation of a Jewish homeland in "British-Palestine" by the League of Nations at the San Remo Conference, made their own secret plans to dominate Jerusalem and the entire Middle East. As part of their carefully planned, British managed infrastructure, officials in London invented an official position of Muslim authority called grand mufti of Jerusalem. In 1921 (Jewish calendar: 5681) British government officials appointed Mohammad Amin al-Husayni to the position.[619]

Some researchers and historians find it difficult to understand why British officials would appoint al-Husayni to such a position, especially considering his reputation as an Islamic radical and criminal. Others point to the appointment of al-Husayni as part of British subterfuge in trying to covertly change the purpose of the Mandate from helping to establish a Jewish homeland to the creation of a Jew free, British-controlled Arab vassal state.[620]

During British occupation multiple attacks and massacres of Jewish families by Arab, Bedouin, Turk, Balkan, and other Muslims, financed and facilitated by British officials and led by al-Husayni, occurred.[621] The Pogroms were acts of political vengefulness and sheer criminality.

In another blow to the Jewish Nation the British Parliament in 1921 decided to take 80% of the mandate land set aside for the future Jewish homeland to create in the Jordan Valley an exclusive (no Jews allowed) Arab/Slavic Muslim country.[622] Jews were legally barred from settling in the 35,000 square miles

(90,650 km²) of Arab-Palestine. Jews living east of the Jordan River had to leave immediately.⁶²³

The creation of Arab-Palestine by the British government, a clear violation of international law according to the terms of the League of Nations Mandate, was the first time in history that the eastern Jordan Valley was separated from Israel and the first time Jews were forbidden to live there.⁶²⁴ Jews living in the new British-created country were forced to leave with what they could carry.

The British government soon changed the name from Arab-Palestine to Transjordan and later, to Jordan. The League of Nations did not approve the separation, but reluctantly, a year and a half later, declared the territory of Transjordan as "ultimately determined," and exempted Transjordan from the establishment of a Jewish national homeland.⁶²⁵

Russia also harbored plans for world domination and in 1922 (Jewish calendar: 5682) became the Soviet Union by annexing Ukraine, Byelorussia, and a dozen countries in the West Asian Caucasus region. Two years later 67,000 Polish Jews fled from the annexed lands to Israel.⁶²⁶

During the annexation of Ukraine, Simon Petlura had fled to Paris. In 1926 (Jewish calendar: 5686), a survivor of the Ukrainian Pogrom, Sholem Schwartzbard, saw Petlura in Paris and assassinated him. A French court heard eyewitness testimony of the atrocities that Petlura, his Cossack soldiers, and Ukrainian masses had committed against the Jewish population and acquitted Schwartzbard.⁶²⁷

British officials and soldiers oppressed and harassed the Jews living in Eretz Israel. In an attempt to discourage and subjugate "Palestinian Jews," British officials had financed and facilitated another massacre of Jews in 1929 (Jewish calendar: 5689). This Pogrom targeted the rabbis and their families in the ancient Jewish town of Hebron in the Judean Hills.⁶²⁸

Many Jews were hidden and saved in Hebron by their Arab neighbors while Slavic Muslims from a nearby town, led by British operative Grand Mufti al-Husayni, publicly raped and murdered unprotected children, women, and men. Slavic Muslim women threw rocks at the victims. Many Jews were killed. Hundreds more were tortured, maimed, and burned. As part of the preplanned Pogrom, British soldiers did not interfere nor make arrests.[629] After the attack most Jewish families left. Some stayed in Hebron, one of the oldest continuously inhabited towns in the world, and the place where Abraham and Sarah, along with other Jewish patriarchs and matriarchs, are buried.

In Germany, the Second Reich's revived political leadership made secret plans with the Soviet Union's leaders to invade and divide Poland, restoring the prewar German-Russian border, but the onset of the Great Depression delayed their plans.[630]

The complicated Treaty of Versailles reparations agreement entwined the German and American economies through trade and investment. The Great Depression that started in 1929 with the American stock market crash collapsed the already inflationary economy of Germany the same year and spread worldwide the following year.[631]

In 1930 (Jewish calendar: 5690) on the advice of American industrialists, Germany, Belgium, France, the United Kingdom, Italy, Japan, the United States, and Switzerland set up the Bank for International Settlements, the BIS. Based in Basel, Switzerland, they established the BIS as a sovereign entity with international immunity, accountable only to its own board of directors, which included German military and business representatives.[632]

The collapse of the German economy left people rioting in the streets for food. Between 200,000 and 500,000 homeless men slept in streets and fields. The Nazi Party offered relief from the Great Depression by promising to create jobs, to give welfare to those in need, and to provide health care.[633]

The professional class of Germany did not support Adolf Hitler's political aspirations. The political and military elite of German society also rejected him. Foreigners supported Hitler. Initially, American and European industrialists, New York investment firms, and London bankers financed his rise to head the Nazi Party.[634] In 1932 (Jewish calendar: 5692) the Nazi Party won a seat in the German government with statements and promises of economic reforms.

Foreign and German industrialists supported Nazism after the election because it was anti-Communist. Both systems are totalitarian, but Communism supported workers' rights to strike, while Nazism supported complete employer control.[635]

Soviet Russia's Stalin enacted state-sponsored mass starvation policies in 1932 beginning with the Terror Famine in Ukraine, Crimea, and other parts of Russia, which left six million Russian "peasants" dead in two years. The starvation campaign took place in areas with high Jewish and Catholic rural populations.[636]

A British petroleum engineer discovered oil in newly created Saudi Arabia in 1932. To appease their new Islamic Arab best friends and strengthen British claims to Jerusalem, the British government began to restrict and then forbid Jews from entering Eretz Israel, even during the height of the Terror Famine.

The United States had refused to recognize the USSR since its inception in 1922, but under pressure from American and international businessmen, American President Franklin Delano Roosevelt welcomed Stalin's police state into the family of nations in 1933 (Jewish calendar: 5693) while the Terror Famine was in progress.[637]

Soviet genocidal policies continued after United States recognition. Stalin murdered by starvation, execution, or deportation to labor camps an estimated twenty million citizens in the 1930s, around one eighth of the Russian population.[638]

Representatives of America, Britain, France, Belgium, Italy, and Japan met in Berlin with Nazi Party Chair Hitler in 1933. The Allies agreed to support the German economy by cancelling most of the WWI reparations the Treaty of Versailles had imposed on the German Reich.[639]

German President Paul von Hindenburg appointed Hitler as chancellor in 1933, and the government built the first concentration camp in Dachau, southern Germany, for political prisoners.[640]

The president died the following year and Hitler made "head of state" his official title, while he went by the unofficial title of fuehrer (leader). The German Reich became the Greater German Reich (meaning the Greater German Realm) in 1933 and Nazism became the policy. The Greater German Reich was generally referred to as The Third Reich. The First Reich was the Holy Roman Empire that broke up in 1804. The Second Reich was the German Empire, or German Reich, under a monarchy from 1871 to 1918 and under a constitution from 1919 to 1932.

People who would not submit to Nazi tyranny had to be eliminated from influential positions, and Jews were at the top of the list, followed by clergy and German Catholics. To achieve complete domination, the Germans murdered or arrested the mostly Jewish professional class, the intelligentsia. The Nazi government also targeted Gypsies, Poles, people with mental or physical disabilities, and political or religious dissenters.

The first state to formally recognize the Third Reich, the Vatican, maintained diplomatic relations with the Nazi government throughout WWII until Germany's surrender. The Vatican issued a Concordat (official agreement) supporting the Nazis despite Hitler's targeting and murder of German Catholics.[641]

By the mid-1930s the reach of Nazi political propaganda stretched to America as well as Europe. Biased and distorted media coverage caused resentment, mistrust, and Jew hatred to grow.

Nazism in Germany included a religious component, a version of Christianity with Teutonic origins replacing Jewish origins.[642] Teutonic refers to German culture such as that in Germany, Austria, and Switzerland. The ancient Teutons were a Celtic people originating from Jutland, now Denmark. By 500 BCE (Jewish calendar: 3260) they became the Helveti Celts, who occupied what is now Switzerland. The Teutons migrated into the Rhine Valley around the time of the Roman Empire.[643] By inventing a Teutonic/Nordic "Christ" the Nazis tried to give themselves a noble heritage and the authority to rule the world.

The new state-sponsored religion featured an ancient Nordic (Teutonic) warrior as Christ, killed by Jews, and Adolf Hitler as a new (Teutonic) messiah to save the world from Jewish domination.[644] Upon implementation of the new religion the National Reich Church (also called the Protestant Reich Church) would have been the only church or religious institution allowed to operate in Germany. The German military uniform included a belt buckle inscribed "God is Great."[645]

Germany passed anti-Jew laws called the Nuremberg Laws in 1935 (Jewish calendar: 5695), which revoked Jewish citizenship, made marriage between Jews and Germans illegal, and restricted Jews from working or studying. Under the Nuremberg Laws, Jews became stateless refugees, no longer German citizens.[646]

Loss of German citizenship made acquiring visas or other official documents practically impossible. Jews without visas faced difficulty trying to immigrate to other countries. Thousands of Jews escaped Germany in 1935 and slipped into Eretz Israel without British permission.

The growing Jewish agricultural infrastructure inside Israel in 1935 meant jobs for Arab, Slavic, Turk, Bedouin, and other Muslims and they poured into Eretz Israel from all over the Middle East for the next two years.[647]

The League of Nations Mandate required the British to relinquish Israel to the Jewish people. By 1935 the Jewish population had reached a majority, built an infrastructure, created a governmental structure, had paramilitary organizations for defense, and stood ready to accept responsibility for the administration of their country. The British continued to discourage Jews from returning to their homeland while encouraging Muslims to move to British Palestine-Eretz Israel. By invitation of the British, around 200,000 Muslims workers entered Eretz Israel during British occupation, nearly doubling the Muslim population. Over seventy languages were spoken in British Palestine-Eretz Israel.[648]

In a sort of bizarre pact of cooperation from 1936 to 1939 (Jewish calendar: 5696-5699) Nazi Germany supplied weapons and funds to British operative Mufti al-Husayni to support a wave of deadly violence against Jews inside Eretz Israel. British officials did not interfere with the flow of arms or funds to al-Husayni. British soldiers did not arrest or interfere with Islamic massacres against Jews.[649] British soldiers, citing protection of Jews as the reason, forcibly removed the remaining Jewish families from Hebron in 1936 and "gave" Hebron, one of Israel's four holiest cities, to the Arabs.[650] [651]

In 1937 (Jewish calendar: 5697) the newly arrived Muslims joined forces with the resident Muslims into a British planned, nationalistic movement designed to eliminate the Jews from Eretz Israel. The Arabs and other Muslims, now armed by the British, decided to use the opportunity to oust both the Jews and the British.[652]

Again the British turned to the Jews for help, secretly allowing the Haganah to arm its members in order to join the British fight against armed Arabs for the next two years. Hundreds of Jews died. Thousands of Arabs and Slavic Muslims were killed, imprisoned, or deported.[653] The British then disarmed the

Haganah and continued to prevent Diaspora Jews from entering while promoting the narrative of an Arab-inspired national movement.

Austria, a German-speaking country, had been in a deep economic depression since the end of World War I with unemployed workers, people begging for food, and farmers declaring bankruptcy. In deadly competition for control, the Austrian Communists and the National Socialists fought each other, partially destroying Vienna and other cities.[654]

Regional and local media continually reported on the high lifestyle, satisfaction, and economic prosperity enjoyed by the German people. The Austrian media omitted any coverage critical to the Nazis. Relying on their media to inform them, in March 1938 (Jewish calendar: 5698) the desperate Austrians voted 98% for annexation of Austria to Germany and for Hitler as their ruler.[655]

People all over Austria upon annexation rushed to join the Nazi Party and military, or to form secret resistance groups to the Nazis. Austrians who opposed the annexation fled their country. The German government passed anti-Jew laws in Austria, and 192,000 Jews became stateless refugees.[656]

In June 1938, three months after Germany annexed Austria, representatives from Britain, France, the Soviet Union, America, and other countries met in France at Evian-les-Bains to discuss the stateless refugee Jews in Germany and Austria.

Churchill, representing Britain, reaffirmed that Jewish refugees were barred from entering Eretz Israel-British Palestine. Using the 1936-1939 Pogroms, which British officials had master-minded, Churchill reiterated the British desire for a pan-Arab Middle East.[657] American officials didn't want to upset their new Saudi friends by supporting Jewish immigration to

America.[658] In 1933 (Jewish calendar: 5693) the first joint American-Saudi Arabian oil company, ARAMCO, had formed, and in 1938 it opened gasoline stations in America.[659]

The Dominican Republic was the only country at the Evian Conference that opened its borders to the stateless refugees of Germany-Austria. That kindness saved approximately 100,000 Jews.[660] With the implicit support for Hitler's oppression of Jews expressed by world governments at Evian, especially by Great Britain and America, the escape window for Eastern Europe's Jews began closing rapidly.

Two months after the Evian Conference, Germany passed laws requiring Jewish women to add "Sara" to their last name and all Jewish men to add "Israel" to their last name. A month later representatives from Britain, France, and Italy met with Hitler in Munich, Germany, to sign the Munich Agreement in support of the planned German annexation of western Czechoslovakia, where the country's banks and industries operated.[661]

Czechs and Slovaks referred to the agreement as the Munich Betrayal. The major powers in Europe and the Nazi government referred to the agreement as promoting German self-determination. Western media, especially the *London Times*, reported how villainous Czechoslovakia attempted to impede peace-loving Adolf Hitler in his reasonable search for justice.[662] Radio Prague reported that 130,000 Czechs and Germans living in western Czechoslovakia fled because of the Munich Agreement.[663] Czechs and Germans also formed resistance groups.

The carefully planned, notorious Nazi rampage that occurred across Germany and Austria on November 9-10, 1938 (Jewish calendar: 5699), is called Kristallnacht (Night of Broken Glass). German storm troopers terrorized Jews for two days throughout

Germany and Austria, smashing windows and burning Jewish homes, businesses, synagogues, and orphanages.

In Vienna, as in major cities in Germany, almost all synagogues were burned. Nearly 100 Jews were murdered and thousands more were beaten, including children. German soldiers threw Jewish children through plate-glass windows into burning buildings. The soldiers tortured or arrested anyone who resisted or tried to put out the fires. During Kristallnacht, 30,000 Jews were arrested and sent to concentration camps. Signs went up on public buildings and park entryways forbidding entry of Jews or dogs.[664] Jews living in Germany-Austria tried to emigrate after this state-sponsored terror attack against a civilian population, but most countries refused their requests.

The Swiss government had terminated Jewish immigration to Switzerland one month before Kristallnacht. The US and England allowed a small number to enter, but the rest had nowhere to go because Britain controlled Eretz Israel-British Palestine and banned Jewish entry.[665] Within days after Kristallnacht, European Jews and righteous gentiles began planning rescue and relief operations for Jews in Germany-Austria and then expanded their efforts to rescue threatened Jews in other hostile European countries.

In Britain, Rabbi Solomon Schonfeld created the Chief Rabbi's Religious Emergency Council and immediately left for Vienna to begin his daring rescues of thousands of Jews in Germany-Austria and Eastern Europe between 1938 and 1948.

Righteous gentiles in Britain organized a government-funded Kindertransport program to rescue children of Jews. Civilians in Britain, Germany, Holland, Czechoslovakia, and Belgium worked together to immediately begin rescues out of Germany-Austria despite restrictions and limitations imposed by Britain.[666]

Rabbi Schonfeld managed to arrange, under the

Kindertransport program, transportation out of Germany for 300 Orthodox Jew children to the British Isles and into homes of Orthodox families. He could have rescued thousands more out of Germany through the program if the British government had been willing.[667]

German Kindertransport volunteers applied for the immediate removal of 10,000 threatened Jewish children to join families in Eretz Israel-British Palestine. British officials denied the request. Those children remained in Germany.[668] British officials, in accordance with their stated objectives at the Evian Conference, let those 10,000 children, some of them babies, be murdered rather than allow even one Jew child to join the 600,000 Jews already living there.

At least the British government allowed entry via the Kindertransport program of 9,500 German and Austrian children into the British Isles. A similar effort in the United States of America, the 1939 Wagner-Rogers bill, would have allowed 20,000 threatened children from Germany-Austria into America.

But President Franklin Delano Roosevelt acted against Jewish immigration. No Jewish children from Europe were rescued and allowed into America. Anne Frank, author of the famous published diary, was one of the children from Germany turned down by America in 1939.[669]

Germany-Austria stripped Jews of their property rights within a month following Kristallnacht and then ordered them to turn in all gold and silver to the Reich. No Western governments protested or imposed sanctions on Germany.[670]

In the spring of 1939, only a few months after Kristallnacht, a ship with nearly a thousand desperate Jews left Germany. The passengers on the SS *St. Louis* held valid Cuban visas, but Cuba refused them entry. The US Coast Guard fired on the vessel when it approached the Florida coastline, and US officials refused to allow it to dock. On the return voyage to Europe, England admitted a few of the passengers. The rest went to Belgium, Holland, and France, where most were killed by the Nazis.[671]

Newly passed laws in Nazi Germany diverted to the Reich government, instead of to the policyholders, insurance claim money for damaged Jewish properties. Five months after Kristallnacht, with a war chest of international insurance money, Germany invaded Czechoslovakia in March 1939 (Jewish calendar: 5699).

Hitler claimed territorial rights to western Czechoslovakia, which Germany called Sudetenland (the districts of German Bohemia, Moravia, and parts of Silesia) and took possession, through the Bank of International Settlements, of over 220 tons of Czech gold stored in the banks of London.[672]

Using the Arab "riots" in Jerusalem and Hebron as the justification, England's political leadership stunned Jews worldwide by issuing the White Paper of 1939 saying: "His Majesty's Government now declare unequivocally that it is not part of their policy that Palestine should become a Jewish state."[673] The so-called MacDonald White Paper prevented Jews from entering Eretz Israel-British Palestine.

England's main newspaper, the *Manchester Guardian*, called the White Paper a death sentence for Jews. British Colonial Secretary Malcolm MacDonald presented the White Paper of 1939 to the British Parliament. British Prime Minister Neville Chamberlain supported the "death sentence" policy.[674] Winston Churchill, as a Parliament member, voted against it, but it passed with a large majority. The League of Nations opposed the White Paper.

The US State Department generated a plan in 1939, called the Atlantic Charter, to supersede the League of Nations. The charter supported the White Paper policy.[675]

The Shoah, Hebrew for catastrophe, was well under way.

In the run-up to the second Great War "to end all wars," European, Balkan, Russian, Moroccan, and Middle Eastern Jews faced a deadly enemy. The Jewish Nation would have to come together with one goal: survival. Diaspora Jews throughout the world prayed during Passover each year, as their ancestors had done, that they would return to Jerusalem. But before that could happen, European and Russian Jewry would be decimated by World War II and the Nazi death camps.

20

THE SECOND GREAT WAR

In accordance with a secret agreement Hitler had with Soviet ruler Joseph Stalin, German and Austrian troops in September 1939 (Jewish calendar 5699) invaded Poland's western region while Russian troops invaded Poland from the east. Neither Germany nor Russia declared war on Poland.[676] The Poles could not fight two fronts and their government collapsed. France and Britain ignored the Soviet Union, declared war on Germany, and World War II began.

Germany and the Soviet Union split Poland into three sections with Stalin taking eastern Poland in 1939. Stalin sent a million Poles and Jews from the Soviet portion of partitioned Poland to Siberia. The intelligentsia, the aristocrats, and groups with arms training were deported first.[677] The Nazis and their supporters opened and operated euthanasia centers throughout Europe and in the Balkans. The 200,000 people killed at the euthanasia centers were disabled or sick or mentally ill.

High-ranking German officers were briefed on a secret ten-year plan for Poland. Central Poland would provide a source of slave labor for Germans. The northwest, with fertile agricultural land, would be cleared of (inferior) Poles and Jews, and the land would become part of the Greater German Reich.[678] Poland had been a major intellectual center of Jewish European Diaspora before the Shoah. Half of Polish doctors and a third of Polish lawyers were Jews. Jewish business owners employed 40% of Poland's workers.[679]

Nazis had used Jewish prisoners to build the Buchenwald concentration camp in 1937 (Jewish calendar: 5697) in eastern Germany. Buchenwald's 130 satellite camps held prisoners of war, POWs, following the German invasion of Poland in 1939. The first Buchenwald POWs were Polish soldiers, most of whom were Jews. The Geneva Convention required exchanges and releases of POWs. The prisoners brought there after the POW releases were not military and therefore not protected by the Geneva Protocols of 1925. They were Jews, political prisoners, and anyone who resisted Nazi occupation. The Buchenwald inmates were from Poland and other occupied countries.[680]

Officials in Britain underfunded the Kindertransport program and then declined to allocate enough to complete it. Once Britain declared war on Germany, lacking support, with no way to transport the remaining children, the volunteers had to leave to the Nazis hundreds of Jewish children waiting at ports in Holland and Belgium.[681]

The Finnish government allied with Germany during WWII for protection against the predatory Russian Soviet Union. The Finnish government and Finn citizens had refused to identify their Jewish citizens when Finland allied with Germany.[682]

In the winter of 1939 (Jewish calendar: 5699) Soviet troops invaded Finland, claiming it as lost Russian territory. During the "Winter War" Finns fought alongside German soldiers against

Russian troops. Jewish soldiers even set up a prayer tent in the middle of the camp where Nazi Germans and Finns, including Jews, came together to defend Finland against Russia.[683] The League of Nations in December 1939 expelled the Soviet Union for invading Finland. The war ended in the spring when Finland ceded land to Russia.

German-Austrian troops invaded France in 1940 (Jewish calendar: 5700). The French army held out for a short time before surrendering. Many in France became Nazis, as people had in Austria, Belgium, Poland, Slovakia, Sweden, Norway, and other countries. They joined the Nazi Party, proudly wore the Nazi military uniform, and in some cases, French Nazis comprised entire squadrons that fought the Allies. Of the 350,000 Jews living in France at the time of German occupation, tens of thousands of French Jews were shipped to concentration camps and an estimated 90,000 were murdered.[684]

That same year in Poland, Nazis established the Warsaw Ghetto and forced 500,000 Jews to live there. Jews inside the ghetto, without access to food ration coupons, died of starvation.[685]

Russian media censored any information of Nazi atrocities. In 1941 (Jewish calendar: 5701) Hitler sent German soldiers and Jew-hunting special forces into the Soviet Union. The German death squads required Jews to report to stations at major cities throughout Soviet Russia, Ukraine, Crimea, Belarus, and Soviet Balkan states.

Without media coverage to warn them, most Jews, unaware of Nazi atrocities occurring in neighboring countries, complied. Most were immediately murdered. The rest were shipped to camps. In the Ukraine town of Babi Yar the German death squads, with help from local Ukrainians, arrested 33,000 Jewish men, women, and children during the Rosh Hashanah holiday and murdered them in large pits. One and a half to two million Jews died in Russia during the German invasion.[686]

In France in 1941 Nazis destroyed synagogues throughout Paris and required Jews still living in the city to wear yellow stars on their clothing.

Nazi officials began a plan in 1941 to increase the number of Germans and decrease the Polish population by kidnapping from Polish parents an estimated 200,000 children, from babies to age twelve. Another 50,000 children were kidnapped in Romania and the Balkans. The children were given German names and adopted by German couples.[687]

As food supplies dwindled in Germany, Hitler imposed food rationing on occupied countries and transferred food to Germany. East Europe slowly began starving.

In contrast, the United States government through the Lend-Lease program sent billions of dollars worth of cash and supplies to Britain, Russia, France, and other Allied countries during the war.[688] After President Roosevelt, his personal aide Harry Hopkins, and Winston Churchill drafted the charter for the United Nations, the self described "Four Policemen," the United States, the United Kingdom, the Soviet Union, and mainland China, signed the UN charter in 1941 (Jewish calendar: 5701) with the stated intention to stop the spread of Nazism.[689]

On December 7, 1941 the Imperial Japanese naval fleet attacked the US naval base and headquarters of the US Pacific fleet at Pearl Harbor on Oahu, Hawaii. President Roosevelt immediately declared war on Germany and Japan.

British-appointed grand mufti, Mohammad Amin al-Husayni, saw his position cancelled by other Arab leaders. The ex-mufti arrived in Berlin in November 1941 to spend the remaining war years with Hitler, perhaps as a guest, perhaps an advisor.

Around 600,000 Jews had emigrated or fled from Nazi-occupied Europe. But the Nazi policy of forcing Jews to leave

Europe changed to a policy of extermination after Hitler met with al-Husayni. Following the meeting, Nazi strongman Heinrich Himmler announced an immediate prohibition of further Jewish emigration.[690]

Two months after al-Husayni met with Hitler, top Nazi officials met in Berlin at the Wannsee Conference to be briefed on the implementation of a plan, the Final Solution to the Jewish Question, to murder Europe's and Russia's remaining eleven million Jews.

Following the Wannsee Conference the Nazis built death camps in Germany, Poland, and Austria beginning in 1942 (Jewish calendar: 5702).[691] The man the British had appointed mufti, al-Husayni, advised infamous Nazi murderer Adolf Eichmann on implementation of the Final Solution.[692]

The most notorious camp, Auschwitz in annexed Poland, had a network of camps for concentration, forced labor, and mass murder of prisoners. The Nazis forced work crews of Jewish prisoners to dig for coal inside mountain tunnels and roughly constructed mines. Other prisoners labored at the Auschwitz oil factory where they converted the coal into synthetic gasoline. The majority of prisoners at this camp were Jews, although some Polish political prisoners were sent there.[693]

In northern Austria the Nazis constructed a massive camp complex using slave labor around the villages of Mauthausen and Gusen near the major city of Linz. The Mauthausen-Gusen system, classified by the Nazis as camps for extreme punishment, consisted of four main facilities with fifty satellite camps.[694]

The educated upper class of Austria, Jews and non-Jews, who were scholars, engineers, attorneys, teachers, rabbis, clergy, and other professionals were arrested and sent to Mauthausen-Gusen. The Austrian Nazis were known to be particularly sadistic and depraved, and those who ran Mauthausen-Gusen in Austria lived up to that reputation. Slave labor, with starvation rations of food and water, operated quarries, mines, arms-and-munitions factories, and a fighter-plane assembly plant. The camp guards often enjoyed the mass torture of their slaves, resulting in slow, painful deaths. The policy was murder through hard labor, with little food or water.[695] Over 100,000 other Austrian Jews were deported to Eastern Europe and held in deplorable conditions. Only 22,000 Austrian Jews managed to hide or escape.[696]

All Nazi camps were associated with death because Jews and other European prisoners died from abuse and inhumane conditions such as insufficient food. But the death camps, the most depraved of all, were designed to torture and mass murder European Jewry, Poles, and others.

Groups of Jews and groups of Poles fought back from hiding places throughout the forests of Eastern Europe and from inside Nazi death camps, concentration camps, and ghettos when they could. Mostly without guns, ammunition, or firearms training, they improvised.

Jews began an uprising in January 1943 (Jewish calendar: 5703) in the Warsaw Ghetto. Starting with only ten pistols, they shocked the Germans by fighting back for four days, forcing the Germans to pull back and reorganize. The Warsaw Jews managed to get from the Polish Home Army a few more working guns and supplies to manufacture Molotov cocktails. The Jews held out against the full force of the Nazi military, including tanks, longer than the French Army had fought during the Nazi invasion of France. By the end of April the Warsaw Jews were out of ammunition. The Germans moved in, burned the ghetto to the ground, and left no Jewish survivors. In May, the Nazis celebrated their mass murder of the exhausted, sick, starving Polish Jews of the Warsaw Ghetto by blowing up a beautiful 1877 Warsaw synagogue. The explosion could be felt throughout the city.[697]

The Vatican failed to condemn the persecution and murders of Jews, disabled people, and other minority ethnic groups throughout Europe. In 1943 during construction of the Nazi death camps, the Vatican restated formally and officially its longstanding policy that Christianity replaced Judaism and that the Christian Bible supplanted the abolished Jewish Bible.[698] Pope Pius XII (Eugenio Pacelli) issued his encyclical during the height of the genocide of European Jews.

By the end of 1943 the ex-Mufti al-Husayni, still advising or conferring with Hitler in Berlin, organized Bosnian Muslim "Black Legions" to fight the Allies in the Balkans.[699]

In the spring of 1944 (Jewish calendar: 5704) Germany invaded Hungary and began deportation of 750,000 Hungarian Jews by trains leaving from Budapest north through Slovakia to Auschwitz. Nazis murdered an estimated 450,000 to 600,000 Hungarian Jews.[700]

The Allies flew repeatedly over railroad tracks leading to Auschwitz at the same time the Hungarian Jews were being deported. Seeming indifferent to Jewish suffering, America and Britain bombed sites near Auschwitz for two years but never tried to destroy the gas chambers or crematoriums at any of the Nazi death camps nor bomb the train tracks used to transport millions of Jews to their deaths.

The camp buildings were large, and the camps were not well defended, making them easy targets. The oil factory made it a legitimate military target. The gas chambers and crematoriums should have been obvious targets for humanitarian reasons.

The Nazis became so efficient at transporting Jews to Auschwitz from all parts of their annexed and occupied territories that even with the gas chambers and crematoriums working constantly they could not keep up with the numbers of incoming families marked for death. Auschwitz guards began making their Jewish prisoners dig trenches. The Jews were forced to lie in them while guards poured gasoline over them and burned them alive. Witnesses have recorded several instances of Nazi atrocities, shockingly excessive cruel acts of violence such as burning to death large numbers of Jewish people in buildings, synagogues, and even warehouses in Germany and France.[701]

One bombing raid would have crippled one of the most sadistic of the Nazi death camps. Because the British Air Ministry, the British Foreign Office, and the US War Department sent bombing missions close to Auschwitz, Jewish representatives and supporters petitioned and pleaded with their government officials to destroy the death camp buildings. Bombing the gas chambers and the crematoriums would have slowed the Nazi extermination process. And crippling the train tracks would have seriously interfered with the large-scale genocide in progress.

The authorities of both countries denied those requests, saying air support could not be diverted and the military did not engage in the rescue of enemy prisoners. However, there is no justification for leaving intact the rail lines leading to Nazi death camps.

The refusal to destroy the camps or their transportation systems indirectly aided Hitler's genocide of European Jewry. Destroying the synthetic-oil factory at Auschwitz would have crippled Hitler's troops in the field.[702] Researchers for decades have sought reasons other than tacit support for the Nazi genocide of European Jewry to explain why officials in the governments of Britain and America refused to take any military or political actions to impede the genocide.

Occupied Norway had over 100 Nazi concentration and political prisoner camps, known for torture and cruelty. Norwegian Jews were shipped to Auschwitz. The camps in Norway, operated by sadistic Norwegian Nazis, held mostly non-Jewish political prisoners and Norway's intelligentsia.[703] In other countries including

Poland, Ukraine, and Russia, the locals aided the Nazis in massacring their Jewish populations. Some private citizens helped their Jewish friends and neighbors, while most Europeans were cruel to Jews.[704]

Jews survived in Italy and Bulgaria because, like the Danes and Finns, locals wouldn't identify them. Thousands of Bulgarian farmers threatened to block the railroad tracks to protest and prevent the deportation of Bulgarian Jews. The deportation orders were cancelled.[705] Only two European governments, those of Denmark and Finland, helped Jewish populations evade Nazi capture. Sweden did not have a Jewish population at that time but helped protect Danish Jews.

Germany occupied and annexed Denmark, then announced plans to deport Denmark's 8,000 Jews to concentration camps. Denmark's government secretly transported 7,600 Jews to Sweden with the cooperation of the Swedish government. In contrast to the situation in many other European countries, Denmark's Jewish communities returned after the war to find their properties intact.[706]

Nazis operated an estimated 27,000 Jewish ghettos and 15,000 camps and satellite camps in Germany-Austria, in occupied Europe, and in the Balkans. The camps were concentration camps, death camps, slave labor camps, or a combination. An estimated 15 million to 20 million prisoners were incarcerated in those horrible places, including approximately 34,000 female sex slaves. The camp brothel prostitutes were mostly young Jewish girls who arrived at the camps with their families. Usually between the ages of ten and eighteen, they were purchased for twenty-minute sessions with camp guards and administrators, visiting German soldiers, non-Jewish inmates, camp guests, and Reich officials.[707]

Many girls suffered forced abortions, sterilizations, and botched medical procedures without pain medication. Most died from abuse such as a combination of exhaustion, malnutrition, and internal injuries. They were murdered when they could no longer perform. Girls were shipped during the day by buses to a camp where they would work through the night.[708] Auschwitz officials operated differently. So many young girls, almost all Jewish, were brought to Auschwitz that other girls were not needed. Auschwitz sex slaves did not go to other camps.[709]

The Nazis counted and recorded their murders of six million European and Russian Jewish civilians. The Nazis did not keep records during the last six months of the war but are estimated to have murdered another one million to two million uncounted Jewish civilians in those final months.

The Nazis also murdered an estimated three million non-Jewish Polish civilians, and four million other European citizens of many nationalities.[710] Three million Jews lived in Poland before WWII. Less than 10% survived.[711]

Nuremberg trial testimony after the war revealed ex-Mufti al-Husayni to be one of the originators of the systematic Nazi murder of European Jewry. The former British operative visited gas chambers, inspected Nazi troops, and communicated directly with government ministers of Hungary and Romania to instruct them to send their Jews to concentration camps in Poland.[712]

In the Land of Israel during WWII, most English soldiers and officers were vehemently anti-Semitic and were often cruel to Jews living in Eretz Israel-British Palestine, though Irish-descent soldiers were often sympathetic. A few soldiers stationed in the British controlled territory defied their superiors and with great courage risked their lives to protect Jews from Muslim attacks or from unfair arrest and punishment.

However, Britain remained relentless in nonsupport of Jews while offering unconditional support to Arab, Bedouin, Turk, and Balkan Muslim populations. Documented massacres of Jewish men, women, and children by Muslims occurred regularly inside Eretz Israel while Britain controlled it.

European, Balkan, and Moroccan Jews fled to Eretz Israel-British Palestine during the war, in spite of British policy. Many were stopped. For instance, 769 escaping Romanian Jews in a decrepit ship named the *Struma* attempted to cross the Black Sea toward the Jewish homeland. The ship broke down near the port city of Istanbul, and the Turkish government wouldn't allow the Jews to leave the vessel.

Desperate and starving in a leaking ship, the refugees begged the British government for two months to allow them passage to Eretz Israel-British Palestine. British officials refused. Finally, Turks towed the *Struma* out of their harbor and sank it. After several hours in the water, except for one survivor, 428 men, 269 women, and 70 children drowned.[713]

European Jewry was being massacred by Nazis and their supporters. The British government isolated and abused Middle Eastern Jewry. The American government ignored and marginalized American Jewry. If ever modern Jews needed a miracle, it was in the last, dark days of WWII.

The Allies destroyed major cities in Germany, Nazi troops ran out of fuel on the battlefields, and the German military, not the Nazi government, surrendered unconditionally in May 1945 (Jewish calendar: 5705).[714] The Soviet Union declared war against the Empire of Japan, and Soviet troops invaded Manchuria. The US dropped two atomic bombs on Japanese cities in August 1945. Japan surrendered a few days later and WWII ended.

Most people think Nazism ended because Germany lost the

war, but that is far from true. A year before the war ended German industrialists and Nazi Party leadership met in Strasbourg, France, to plan for a postwar extra-territorial Nazi state with the goal of an economic takeover of Europe, a European Union. Using escrow accounts opened in Basel at the Bank for International Settlements, Nazi leadership deposited a vast fortune into the New York Stock Exchange and into holding companies in Argentina and Indonesia. This large sum of money, estimated to be over a billion dollars, would fund the ongoing Nazi agenda and provide for the future support of Nazi elite.[715]

The Nazi SS, the true believers, formed an organization called Odessa, also called The Brotherhood, to plan escape routes (called Ratlines) for Nazi officials. Through Odessa, with help from the Vatican, and from officials in Switzerland, England, Spain, Argentina, and America, the Nazi elite moved personnel out of Germany as the war ended.[716]

Thousands of Nazi political and military personnel moved to the Middle East where they received new identities. For example, Egypt's President Nasser invited and absorbed over 2,000 Nazi officials who "converted" to Islam and took Arabic names. Several hundred Nazis were employed to develop Egypt's missile and aircraft industry. They also worked in Egypt's secret service, became directors of anti-Israeli propaganda, and even became journalists. Syria employed hundreds of Nazis to develop Syria's secret police force.[717]

They also moved to Europe and America, pretending to be reformed. Hard-core Odessa members, many wanted by the Allies for war crimes, escaped to South America with aid from Argentine President Juan Perón to live in an isolated, guarded German-style town, called San Carlos de Bariloche, surrounded by jungle outside Buenos Aires. Nazi officer Adolf Eichmann moved to Buenos Aires where he was later caught by Israeli undercover agents. The agents transported him back to Israel to stand trial. He was executed for war crimes.

Odessa would keep the anti-Communist Nazi belief system operating on every continent after WWII. Postwar "Nazi International," also called the Fourth Reich, operates out of centers in Bonn, Rome, Buenos Aires, and Barcelona.[718]

21

THE CAUSE FOR PEACE

Americans celebrated the victorious conclusion of WWII. A half million people in New York marked the occasion with a day of festivities in Times Square. Also jubilant, hundreds of thousands of people danced in the streets of Paris, London, and Moscow.

The fighting was over, but Europe and Asia were left in rubble. Twenty million Asians died in the war and millions more starved to death. People across Europe lived on the edge of starvation with entire cities ravaged and thirty million dead. Crime escalated and infrastructure collapsed in the ruins.

As the war ended, Soviet troops in Germany rampaged through the country seeking revenge. Russians brutally raped two million German women, causing injury and death.

Russian troops invaded Austria in 1945 after the war ended. As they had done to the Germans, they tormented, raped, and injured the Austrian people. Russian soldiers gang raped the female population, pre-teen to elderly, sometimes repeatedly.

Many girls and woman died, mostly from suicide, some from broken backs or internal injuries.[719]

Entire factories were dismantled and removed for transport to Russia as the soldiers looted their way across Austria. After having first been subjugated and looted by the Nazi regime, then the Soviet Union, the Austrian people were left with sawed-down orchards, burned fields and buildings, and a traumatized population.[720][721] The Austrian professional class was gone. An estimated 200,000 Austrians and 70,000 Austrian Jews were murdered in Nazi camps.[722]

In the months following the end of the war, the governments of the Soviet Union, Poland, Czechoslovakia, Hungary, and Romania expelled twelve million German residents, after confiscating their possessions, forcing them into Germany. When they reached Germany, they found a war-torn country with most of the population starving. Hundreds of thousands of German refugees died, mostly from starvation. Because most of the cities had been destroyed, eight million homeless Germans wandered around committing acts of violence in order to survive. Concentration camps reopened and brutal acts of anti-Semitism raged across Germany for the next ten years.[723]

Many European Jews couldn't return to their former properties after the war because their homes had been confiscated, often by government officials. The exceptions, countries protecting Jewish property rights, were in Italy, Denmark, and Finland.[724]

Even though Germany did not occupy the British Isles, title to some Jewish properties in England became held by non-Jews while the Jewish owners were absent during the war. Some of the properties, in an act reminiscent of the first English government seizure of Jewish properties a thousand years earlier by King Edward I, were given to British officers and staff during and after WWII.[725]

The populace in Britain, especially in England, had generally backed the issuance of the White Paper of 1939, and throughout the war most supported discrimination against Jews. But a segment of the British population remained humanitarian. Some of the same Kindertransport volunteers who had helped Jewish children escape the Nazis before the war now brought Jewish orphans from Eastern Europe into their homes to help rebuild their shattered lives.

After Germany's surrender, ex-Mufti al-Husayni led 20,000 Croatian Muslim Nazis through Croatia and Hungary, where they indiscriminately murdered Jewish children, women, and men until the French arrested al-Husayni a year later for war crimes. He escaped French detention and moved his deadly war against Jews into Eretz Israel-British Palestine for the next four years.[726]

The United States continued funding Britain through the Lend-Lease program for a year after the war ended with more than a billion American taxpayer dollars.[727]

The League of Nations Charter was dissolved in April 1946 (Jewish calendar: 5706) and its assets transferred to the United Nations by authority of the United States, the United Kingdom, the Soviet Union, and mainland China.[728] Three months later the Allies, represented by officials from the United States, the United Kingdom, France, and the Soviet Union, met at the 1946 Paris Peace Conference to impose war reparations and border adjustments on Germany and the other defeated Axis governments.[729]

This conference convened while Russian soldiers plundered, raped, and murdered their way across Austria and Eastern Europe as part of the Soviet territorial expansion. Western media did not report postwar Soviet atrocities.[730] At the conference the Allies did not discuss the plight of the stateless, homeless European Jews waiting in camps throughout Europe. The Paris treaties were signed a year later.

The close of WWII ended the gruesome Nazi death camps, but the British government's oppression of Jews continued. Even after the Shoah/Holocaust the British refused to relinquish control of Israel to the Jewish people.

Instead, some of the former Nazi concentration camp signs were changed to read "Displaced Persons Camp," where 250,000 Jews remained in shockingly deplorable conditions until friends, relatives, and organized groups could arrange to sponsor them. Most had to wait several years.[731] Families separated during the war migrated to DP camps, sometimes to find missing family members, sometimes because Nazis had confiscated their homes and they had nowhere else to go. The Red Cross helped reunite families at the camps when possible.

Jewish political leadership began to understand at the close of WWII that there would be a battle for Israel. They also understood that Jews would face that battle alone. It wasn't enough that a remnant of European Jewry had survived genocide, or that Jews in Eretz Israel had recovered enough to rebuild their lives and their country. Now they faced the superpower British Empire.

British soldiers remained deployed in the Middle East, in East Africa, and on Cyprus. They caught and arrested Europe's most destitute refugees, Jewish Shoah/Holocaust survivors, trying to enter Eretz Israel-British Palestine because they had nowhere else to go after the war.

British military had built nine concentration camps on Cyprus in the Eastern Mediterranean Sea during WWI when they intended to occupy Turkey. WWI ended before the camps could be used. British soldiers interned Jewish refugees in the deplorable concentration camps on Cyprus during and after WWII. Britain also detained Jews in North African concentration camps they operated in Sembal, Eritrea, on the coast of the Red Sea.[732]

They incarcerated over 50,000 Jewish refugees, including 6,000 orphaned children, in camps known for crowded conditions, poor sanitation, and lack of potable water.[733] Men, women, and children who had survived Nazi death camps lived once more behind barbed wire with soldiers guarding them. These soldiers were British. Jewish relief agencies such as JDC provided extra food rations, medical supplies, and clean drinking water to the Jews interned in the nine camps on Cyprus.

British soldiers prevented Jews living in their homeland from possessing defensive weapons, the same way Nazis had prevented European Jews from owning firearms. The Haganah, protecting Jews living in British occupied Eretz Israel since the end of WWI, had splintered in 1931 (Jewish calendar: 5691) to form the more militant organization called Irgun Tz'vai Le'umi (National Military Organization). Both Jewish defense organizations protected Jews in Eretz Israel and began to fight against British occupation.

Jewish leadership also realized that the British administrators of British-Palestine were arming Arabs inside the country and advising the surrounding Arab governments to invade and attack Israel if the Jews declared independence.

Under these circumstances, when the expected fight for Israeli independence came, it would be well-equipped soldiers on the ground supported by jet bombers and fighter planes against unarmed Jewish men and women standing in front of children.

It was time for American Jews to join the struggle for statehood. After Ben-Gurion visited a few prominent New York Jewish businessmen to explain the situation firsthand, American Jews began to organize a massive clandestine arms-smuggling operation.

American Jews had to secretly supply an illegal army for

the defense of the future State of Israel. Zionists administered the project out of a hotel in New York. They gathered thousands of pistols and rifles donated by returning American servicemen from the battlefields of Europe and the Pacific. American Jews operating businesses in the United States purchased fighter planes and large arms. But American officials began investigating when the New York operation grew.[734]

British soldiers in 1946 (Jewish calendar 5706) conducted raids on Jewish kibbutz communities, the Jewish Agency office buildings, and the homes of Zionist leaders.

British soldiers arrested leaders of Haganah to prevent it from announcing independent statehood. British soldiers also arrested Jewish Agency members and other Zionists. Following the raids, 2,700 Jews were sent to one of the British detention camps, similar to a large jail, in the Judean Hills.

Irgun leaders learned that during the raids, British soldiers had confiscated a list containing the names of Irgun paramilitary defense force members. Irgun leaders believed the British would imprison or execute everyone on the confiscated list.

British officials had taken over a section of the King David Hotel in Jerusalem for their headquarters. On July 22, 1946, the Irgun placed a bomb in a trashcan in the British headquarters wing containing the list. An Irgun member called the hotel to warn people to get out, and another Irgun member used a hand-held loudspeaker to warn people in the hotel lobby. The threat was ignored. Ninety-one people lost their lives and forty-six were injured.

The British continued to arrest and execute Jews for arming themselves or for defending themselves against Muslims. The Irgun leadership argued among itself for hours about the necessity for retaliation against the British to stop them from arresting and executing Jews trying to defend themselves. Finally, they decided on a policy of matching executions of Jews with the kidnapping and execution of British soldiers.

After the execution by hanging of three young men belonging to the Irgun (one was nineteen years old) two British sergeants met their fate, and the British immediately suspended their policy of executing Jews for carrying a pistol or fighting with Muslims.[735]

Defenders of the Irgun's activities believed Jews had to act or the British would never leave the Jewish homeland. Some Jews did not support the King David Hotel bombing because of the loss of life. However, Jews everywhere feared that Britain would not give up control of Jerusalem. Zionist organizations, the Jewish Agency, and Jewish paramilitary organizations were ready for statehood, along with a sizable Jewish population inside Israel. Jews wanted Britain to leave their homeland.

Tens of thousands of neglected European and Balkan Jews languished in displaced persons camps throughout Europe, and tens of thousands more waited for freedom in British concentration camps on Cyprus and in North Africa. Jews in Eretz Israel-British Palestine when possible smuggled in survivors of the Nazi death camps and escapees from the British concentration camps.

When the UN and other major world powers refused to intervene, the growing Jewish population inside Eretz Israel-British Palestine became frustrated with British policy toward Jews. Jews had organized their political structure during the mandate years while they waited for statehood.

Then, a year after the King David Hotel bombing, something happened that caught worldwide attention.

In early 1947 (Jewish calendar: 5706) a Zionist organization purchased a cargo ship and boarded 4,500 Jewish refugees, including children, at a French port. The refugees renamed the ship *Exodus—1947* on the way to British-occupied Eretz Israel. The passengers were European Jews whom Allied soldiers had rescued from Nazi concentration camps.

Six British destroyers surrounded the *Exodus* during her voyage across the Mediterranean Sea, and twelve miles from the coastline of Israel soldiers aboard the destroyers opened fire on the ship. The British didn't know that, as the fight occurred, the *Exodus* crew radioed details of it to the resistance organization Haganah in Tel Aviv. Haganah broadcast the reports around the world. The Jews defended themselves through a prolonged gunfight until they ran out of ammunition. The British threatened to sink the *Exodus*, and the refugees surrendered.[736]

Britain's foreign minister, Ernest Bevin, ordered all 4,500 Shoah/Holocaust survivors to be taken by force off the *Exodus* and put onto transports converted into floating prisons. Bevin would not allow them to go to the Cyprus concentration camps a short distance away to join relatives, or to return to their countries of origin.

Instead, he ordered them to Germany. Upon arrival, British soldiers pushed and carried the desperate, weeping Jews off the transports and took them to concentration camps near Lubeck, where they would stay for the next two years.[737]

Haganah broadcast their fate worldwide. For perhaps the first time in history, common people around the world witnessed, by radio transmissions, British brutality against helpless victims. Support for Zionism, the right of Jews to live in their homeland, soared worldwide after the Haganah broadcasts.

After the *Exodus-1947* tragedy the modern world seemed ready to accept and even support the rights of modern Jews. But even with international pressure mounting against Britain it refused to fulfill its obligation and transfer authority for Israel, including Jerusalem, to the Jewish people.

Instead, the British government, after holding on to the

Land of Israel for twenty-eight years, announced it would refer the "Palestine question" back to the United Nations and terminate its mandate. After relinquishing trusteeship of Israel, the British continued to occupy Israel and incarcerate Jews.

To support the British, US President Harry Truman imposed an extreme and wide-ranging embargo in 1947 on military aid to Israel.[738] The cost was enormous for Britain to maintain military units throughout Israel, Cyprus, and North Africa for four years after the end of the war. At least to some extent, the Americans, through the Lend Lease program and the strict arms embargo, supported Britain's oppression of Jews after WWII.

Jews were not the only people subjected to Britain's meddling. The British government, with UN approval, partitioned Pakistan out of India in 1947. The partition caused fourteen million Hindu and Moslem refugees to flee both sides. Millions died during the transfer.

The Soviet Union annexed parts of Finland to Russia in 1947 and expelled half a million Finns from the newly gained Soviet territory.

Tens of millions of European refugees were being absorbed inside Europe. Hundreds of thousands of Jewish refugees in Europe, the Balkans, and Middle Eastern lands could have been absorbed, indeed, would have been welcomed, into their natural homeland, Israel, except for the unwarranted interference of the British government.

Authorities in Britain investigated the reversal of government policy from the Balfour Agreement to issuance of the 1939 White Paper. At the hearing, former Prime Minister David Lloyd George admitted that he had wanted to acquire "Palestine" for Britain only, not for Jews.[739]

WWI had ended with the British, through mandates, in control of much of the Middle East. Certain English political elite dreamed of creating a British controlled Middle Eastern

Empire. They faced three obstacles to their plan. The French had been granted mandates next to the British in parts of the Middle East. Most Western governments opposed British hegemony in the region. Perhaps the biggest problem of all, the Jews had been promised a national homeland, and they actually expected Britain to keep its word and to follow international law.

Officials in the London Colonial Office and the British military authorities headquartered in Jerusalem made a plan to use the Jews to eliminate the French claims to British Palestine. Jewish officials convinced French government officials to drop out of Palestine to allow the British to set up the Jewish homeland. British officials also financed and instigated several Arab massacres of Jews and prevented Diaspora Jews from entering Eretz Israel. However, the Arabs failed to demand independence. People around the world began a cause for peace, and survivors of the Shoah/Holocaust prepared for statehood.

22

MODERN ISRAEL

Politicians in America passed even more restrictive laws about what could be shipped to Jews in "British Palestine" as an independent Jewish state became inevitable.

The New York Zionists and others smuggled the small and large arms and the aircraft out of America as the FBI began making arrests. Some people went to prison for the serious crime of breaking the embargo laws. Some died trying to hurriedly fly overloaded planes out of America before they could be confiscated.[740]

The surviving planes and some of the arms were flown to an isolated airstrip in Czechoslovakia to await British departure from Israel. A cargo ship with "machine parts" and "office equipment" from America stayed near the coastline of northern Israel.[741] American Jews and non-Jews secretly traveled to Israel to train soldiers, repair damaged weapons, and manufacture parts for weapons and airplanes. Many stayed to join the fight on the ground and in the air.[742]

Israelis who over the previous decade had built the

infrastructure for their state were ready for independence. Even without Jerusalem, even with indefensible borders, Jewish leadership accepted a United Nations partition plan in November, 1947. The plan recommended dividing the remaining territory mandated for the Jewish homeland into three states; an Arab state, a Jewish state, and an international zone surrounding and including Jerusalem under UN control with British administration.[743]

It was a bold decision to agree because the land designated for the Jewish state consisted of two small, noncontiguous areas mostly in the Negev Desert and surrounded by Muslim Arab-controlled land. The UN plan designated for Israel approximately 10% of the original territory approved by the League of Nations for a Jewish homeland.[744]

Arab leaders rejected the UN partition plan, rendering it irrelevant.

In the following months British soldiers blocked a main road to Jerusalem and turned over to the Transjordanian Armed Forces the detention camps and British police forts strategically located above the Jerusalem-Tel Aviv Road. The British government sent military supplies to Transjordan and to Egypt.[745]

British soldiers released 30,000 Jews, mostly pregnant or nursing women, small children, and the elderly, from Cyprus internment with permission to enter Israel. The British kept the 10,000 military-age men imprisoned on Cyprus so they could not aid in the defense of their country.[746]

Immediately before their early, unannounced departure from Israel the day before the declaration of independence, British soldiers disarmed Jewish kibbutz populations while leaving Arab villages fully armed. Jews were now left on their own. Irish-descent British soldiers, familiar with British oppression from their own struggle for independence, defected and joined with Jews to fight for Israel's survival.

The fighter planes waiting in Czechoslovakia were flown in across the Mediterranean Sea as the British left. The American cargo ship docked at Haifa and began unloading thousands of disassembled guns packed in barrels while Arab armies mobilized to attack the Jewish state.

On May 14, 1948 (Jewish calendar: 5708) United Nations members passed a resolution to recognize the tiny state of Israel. The future prime minister, David Ben-Gurion, announced the count of thirty-three votes for and fourteen against and Israel's declaration of sovereignty over a loudspeaker to a crowd gathered at the Tel Aviv Museum. Israel's new radio station, Kol Yisrael, broadcast Ben-Gurion's voice around the world.

While David Ben-Gurion read the Proclamation of Independence over the radio, citizens celebrated in the streets of Tel Aviv and other cities. Jews in Jerusalem were already under attack and without electricity. Islamic Arabs and the Transjordanian Army smashed the Hurva Synagogue along with over fifty other Jerusalem synagogues in a rage over Israel's existence.[747] This was the beginning of a British-backed war meant to murder innocent civilians.

Armed Arabs under German (former Nazi) commanders with orders from ex-Mufti al-Husayni began surrounding kibbutz communities. Israeli defense forces did not have time to supply arms to the outlying kibbutz communities before they were attacked.

Within hours of the declaration, with support from Saudi Arabia and Yemen, governments of Egypt, Transjordan, Lebanon, Syria, and Iraq sent their armies to attack Israel. British troops under Transjordan commands led by British officers joined the invasion. British warships maintained a naval blockade of Israel's coast, and English pilots flew RAF Spitfires to obtain surveillance data for Israel's enemies.[748]

At the time Jews declared Israeli independence they were

still recovering from the horrors of Nazi death camps. WWII had been over for only three years. The UN and freedom-loving countries around the world refused to become involved as the invading Arab armies, British troops, and the Muslim Brotherhood (originally funded by the Nazis) tried to wipe out the Jewish population.[749]

British soldiers had even disarmed isolated kibbutz communities with few adults and large numbers of children. Some of the initial casualties resulted at those kibbutzim where adults and teenagers armed with rocks and kitchen knives tried to defend hundreds of children. In those cases, among the defenders there were no survivors.

The United States had been the first country to recognize modern Israel, but during the War of Independence the US State Department strictly enforced the military aid embargo. Israelis needed steel plating from the United States to cover civilian buses, which were under constant attack. The US State Department refused to lift the embargo or make an exception for the plating. American officials classified the steel plating as military, not defensive. At the same time, the Russian government sent its military planes and personnel to Egypt. Russian fighter pilots in Egyptian Army uniforms bombed Tel Aviv and nearby towns. The Russian jets they flew were marked with Egyptian military insignias.[750]

In early 1949 (Jewish calendar: 5709), after a year of fighting, Israel defeated the Arab armies, including the British soldiers fighting under Transjordan commands, and expanded her borders into a more defensible country. The United Nations had ignored this unprovoked attack. Israel's War of Independence claimed the lives of 6,000 Jewish men, women, and children. Intended to be a quick Islamic victory, in fact a massacre of Jews in Israel, it had turned into a fierce, year-long war to survive another attempted genocide.

Britain released the 10,000 military-age men imprisoned on Cyprus after Israel won the War of Independence.[751]

The UN initially refused membership but later accepted Israel with her expanded borders as a member state in late 1949. Angry Muslims murdered Jews throughout the Middle East in reaction to the existence of a Jewish country.[752] Many Islamic governments forced Jews to leave communities their ancestors had established centuries ago.

Before Israel's independence, 850,000 Mizrahi Jews lived in Egypt, Morocco, Iraq, and Yemen in communities that existed for hundreds of years and in some cases, for over two thousand years. After Israel's War of Independence Jews were killed or forced to leave Islamic countries. Over 550,000 Mizrahi refugees arrived in Israel to become Israeli citizens. The other 290,000 Mizrahi Jews were killed or they escaped to Europe.[753]

The Jewish people, not the UN, and certainly not the British government, established modern Israel. The British had used most of the mandate land intended for the Jewish homeland to create the exclusive (no Jews allowed) Arab/Slavic Muslim state of Palestine-Transjordan-Jordan. Britain relinquished Israel to the UN instead of to the Jewish people, and then fought against the Jewish people in their War of Independence.

Ten years later, Leon Uris published the novel *Exodus*, a fictionalized account of the events leading to the War of Independence. His book became a famous international movie by the same name starring Paul Newman. The popularity of the book and the movie created another wave of worldwide support for Israel and for Zionists.

The war created a modern state of Israel established by Jews and supporters. But after the victorious War of Independence Israel did not include all of Jerusalem nor Samaria nor

Judah. Transjordan, with British help, had captured Samaria and Judah during the war. Following the war American and international media referred to Judah and Samaria as the western bank of Jordan. The illegal annexation by Jordan of Judah and Samaria was not recognized by the UN or any other country except the United Kingdom and Pakistan.

Israel fought two more major defensive wars after independence. Egypt in 1967 (Jewish calendar: 5727) expelled UN peacekeepers, massed its army on the border with Israel, and blocked Israeli access to the Red Sea.

It is called the Six Day War because in six days Israel successfully defended against attacks from Egypt, Lebanon, Syria, Jordan, and Iraq. From Egypt the Israelis took Gaza and the Sinai Peninsula, from Jordan Israel gained Judah and Samaria. Israel reclaimed from Syria the Golan Heights with its 2,500-year-old synagogue ruins. The 1967 Six Day War also united Jerusalem.

American and international media began calling Judah and Samaria the "West Bank" after the Six Day War. Egypt continued to harass Israel after the Six Day War.

After the Six Day War, some Arab, Turkic, and Slavic Muslims began to self-identify as "Palestinians" and began working with neo-Nazis to attack Jews in Israel and around the world. Palestinians and neo-Nazis from West Germany, members of terrorist gang Black September, orchestrated the 1972 (Jewish calendar: 5732) Summer Olympics massacre of eleven Israeli athletes in Munich, West Germany.

Egypt and Syria attacked Israel on the Yom Kippur holiday in 1973 (Jewish calendar: 5734). Israel successfully defended the attacks. The 1973 Yom Kippur War resulted in small gains for Israel in the Golan Heights.

State-sponsored Islamic terrorism against Israelis intensified after Israel's successful conclusion of the 1973 Yom Kippur War. Palestinians and neo-Nazi Germans in 1976 (Jewish calendar: 5736), calling themselves members of the Palestinian Liberation Organization, hijacked an Air France airplane with 306 passengers out of Tel Aviv bound for Paris with a stopover in Athens.

The terrorists diverted the plane in Athens, first to Benghazi, Libya, for fuel, then to the Entebbe National Airport in Uganda. The Palestinians and the Germans, joined in their operation by 100 Ugandan soldiers, released the non-Jewish passengers and threatened to murder the Jews.

Israeli Defense Force commandos flew transport planes to Uganda a week after the hijacking and rescued the hostages in what has been called the greatest raid in history. Tragically, a Ugandan soldier killed Lt. Col. Yonatan Netanyahu during the firefight that ensued while the Israelis were boarding the hostages onto the rescue planes.

After the daring rescue the UN considered a resolution to condemn Israel for violating the sovereign airspace of Uganda and the US State Department sent Henry Kissinger to Israel to chastise the Israelis. The tactics used in Operation Thunderbolt—renamed Operation Yonatan to honor the fallen hero—have been taught at US military schools.

Syria, like the Soviet Union, refused to release its Jewish population until the 1990s.[754] Then thousands of Mizrahi Jews from Syria and over a million Ashkenaz Jews from Russia arrived in Israel.

Israelis, over seven decades, developed their homeland into a thriving economy with a happy population. Israel's economy in the twenty-first century is booming while most European countries, and even America, suffer through periods of economic downturns. Israeli Jews have made their desert bloom, developed high-tech industries that benefit the world, and produced numerous award-winning scientists. Israel has produced many Nobel Prize laureates in science and economics.

A Sci-Tech schools network operates in over 200 educational institutions throughout the country, and their educational programs are implemented in 300 Israeli public schools. The Sci-Tech curriculum prepares pre-college youth for careers in robotics, biotechnology, aviation and space, nanotechnology, mechanical engineering, and biomedical engineering.

Israel is on the front line in the war against the Islamic terrorism that threatens Western values. This tiny country is the only functioning democracy in the Middle East.

The constant violent attacks by Muslims against Jews in Israel are part of an Islamic war with shocking displays of Jew hatred. The American and international media call the vicious attacks against Israel part of an Arab-Israeli conflict. But it may be more accurate to describe it as an Islamic attack on Western civilization, and especially on the progenitor of Western ideals, the culture of Judaism. This Islamic-Judaic "conflict" is clearly not limited to Arabs, but includes Muslims of many nationalities. For example, the Iranian Muslims are not Arab, and Iranian opposition to the existence of Israel is well known.

The fight in Israel is not about land. This is not a battle over a small territory; it is a genocidal war being fought to annihilate the millions of Jews living in Israel. Islamic anti-Zionism reveals a belief held through several centuries; that as long as Jews (and other non-Muslims) remain second-class citizens in Islamic controlled territories they may be tolerated. For Jews to claim sovereignty over land once part of an Islamic empire outrages Muslims.[755]

After each attack, however, Jews resume their work of building modern Israel into the only industrialized economy and the only country with a free press in the Middle East. The Arab, Slavic, Turkic, and Bedouin Muslims living inside Israel enjoy more rights and privileges than any Islamic population elsewhere in the Middle East.[756]

Jews and Arabs are not natural enemies. Jewish attorneys in Israel regularly defend Christian Arab terror victims and Palestinians threatened by terror.[757] Israel sent soldiers into Southern Lebanon in the 1980s to defend Israelis living near the northern border and the Lebanese Christian Arabs in Southern Lebanon under attack from Hezbollah.

Modern Israel, aligned with Western governments, has proven to be a reliable ally to the West. But European and American governments, again protecting oil interests, have refused to acknowledge Jerusalem as the capital of Israel and have not moved their embassies from Tel Aviv to Jerusalem.

Jerusalem has been the heart of the Jewish Nation since King David's reign 3,000 years ago. Historically, the only time Jerusalem has been divided occurred from 1948 through 1967 (Jewish calendar: 5708–5727) during the British-backed Jordanian occupation.

Congress passed the Jerusalem Embassy Act of 1995, US law 104-45, recognizing Jerusalem as Israel's undivided capital. The act mandated that the United States Embassy be moved there from Tel Aviv by May of 1999 (Jewish calendar: 5759). A presidential waiver provision added to the act by Senator Dianne Feinstein enables American presidents to consistently suspend congressional attempts to recognize Jerusalem as Israel's capital even though Congress has voted to do so.

Successive American presidents including Bill Clinton, George W. Bush, and Barack Obama have used the waiver provision to successfully oppose congressional attempts to implement the Jerusalem Embassy Act of 1995 and move the US Embassy to Jerusalem.[758] Use of the presidential waiver enabled the State Department to deny American parents of children born in Jerusalem the right to name Israel as the child's country of birth. Only Jerusalem can be listed on the birth certificates and passports of Americans born there.[759]

Jews have sacrificed a tremendous amount, but European and American governments continue to pressure Israel to concede part of Jerusalem and all of Judah and Samaria to Islam. Even a basic understanding of Judaism reveals the connection the Hebraic people have with a specific land. For Jews, the Temple Mount in Jerusalem, site of the ancient Temple, is the spiritual center. Dividing Jerusalem strikes at the heart of the Jewish Nation.

American President Donald J. Trump spoke of his intention to implement the Jerusalem Embassy Act of 1995 and move the US Embassy to Jerusalem during his election campaign. Jews around the world, and especially in Israel, will celebrate the move.

The legal, historical, and biblical claim to the Land of Israel made by the Israelites is now made by modern Jews worldwide. Jews are the genetic descendants of an ancient people, Israel is their time-honored homeland, and Jerusalem is their eternal capital. The G-d of Israel, the people Israel, and Eretz Israel form a trilogy serving as the foundation for Judaism.

The Jewish spiritual connection to the Land of Israel began at least as far back as the fall of Sumeria, when Abraham and Sarah led their people out of Sumeria around 4,000 years ago. The Hebraic connection to the land may go back to the end of the last glacial period 11,000 years ago when survivors of the extinction-level Younger Dryas stadial began to emerge from refuges and form nations.

Babylonian Jews returned to Jerusalem after their exile to rebuild the Temple and continue their lifestyle in their homeland. And now Diaspora Jews return to modern Israel to join Israeli Jews with hopes of continuing self-determination in their homeland.

The establishment of modern Israel allows the Jewish people to thrive in an environment designed to support a future where people can live in peace, prosperity, and happiness. The modern state of Israel represents the past, the present, and the future for the Jewish people.

23

HISTORY REPEATS

A true and complete account of history is important, and Hebraic history is an essential part of ancient history because Hebraic/Sumerian/Jewish history is a record of the ancient world recorded by a people whose culture reflects an affinity for the truth. It is the story of a people who look to the past to understand the future.

Ancient history reveals repetitive patterns of human activities. Predatory governments used military force against ancient Israel and other peaceful nations. Medieval European and Russian governments murdered and looted their own and each other's populations. Many modern historians and researchers agree that powerful European governments with goals of territorial expansion and financial gain orchestrated events leading to the First World War and to the Second World War. [760]

American and European support for Islamic countries known to have visions of world domination is eerily similar to the financial, insurance, and advisory support initially given to Nazi Germany's Third Reich, the brutal, totalitarian regime with its state-sponsored religion and intention to rid Europe of Jews. Islamic governments, with their state-sponsored religion, have openly declared their intentions for regional or world domination and the elimination of Israel and other Western cultures. Iran declared war on Israel.

Worldwide attacks by Muslims against Jews, Europeans, and Americans reveal a pattern of racist Islamic terrorism. The "death to America and to Israel" rhetoric coming out of Iran is clear evidence that Islam is a culture of determined aggressors who want to annihilate the Jewish state and other non-Muslim governments.[761]

The Islamic intolerance of non-Muslims mirrors the Nazi intolerance for non-Teutonic populations. The Nazi intention to eliminate Jews, Slavs, and others from territory controlled by the German government mirrors Tsarist Russia's plans fifty years earlier to eliminate Jews from Russia.[762]

Britain may be continuing their scheme to create a (Jew-free) pan-Arab empire in the Middle East. The British Parliament in October 2014 (Jewish calendar: 5774), by a vote of 274 to 12, decided to recognize a Jew-free "Palestine," a totalitarian dictatorship that combines fanatical patriotism and racism with state-run socialism and a state-sponsored religion. With a dependency on international funds and a stated intention to destroy Israel and rid the world of Jews, the Islamic PA, the Palestinian Authority, echoes the intentions of Nazism.[763]

This early, undeserved recognition of a "Palestinian" state, a state Israel has not approved, will result in more attacks against innocent Israeli citizens by Muslims dedicated to the destruction of Israel. In a New York press release on October 15, 2014, Morton A. Klein, Zionist Organization of America national president, said that this pro-Palestine vote in London is plainly wrong, dangerous, and naively absurd. Recognizing an unreconstructed terror-promoting organization like Abbas's PA and pretending it is a sovereign state does not assist the cause of peace.[764]

He called the PA a terrorist-supporting entity run by Fatah in Judah and Samaria and by Hamas in Gaza. "Fatah's Al Aqsa Martyrs Brigades is a deadly and proscribed terrorist organization which has murdered hundreds of Israeli civilians. It [Fatah] recently signed a unity government agreement with Hamas, which calls in its Charter for the destruction of Israel (Article 15) and the murder of Jews (Article 7)."[765]

Egyptian-born Yasser Arafat, a nephew of British-appointed Grand Mufti al-Husayni, assumed leadership of the Palestinian Authority in the same way Hitler took over the Nazi Party. With funding from Britain and others, Arafat conducted terrorist activities and called for the destruction of Israel before and after the signing of the so-called Oslo Peace Accords.[766]

The Vatican, the first to officially recognize the Nazi Third Reich, has expressed support for dividing modern Israel for decades. The Vatican in 2012 (Jewish calendar: 5772) announced recognition of a totalitarian, Jew-free fictional state of Palestine. Some see the move as a "disturbing return to a horrifying past" at a time when Middle Eastern Christians are being slaughtered by Islamic supporters of a "Palestine."[767] In contrast, it took the Vatican forty-five years after Israel declared sovereignty to officially recognize the modern state of Israel.

The Europeans and the Vatican who voted for this recognition of a terrorist state threaten Israel's existence as a sovereign country. The Palestinians are moving to destroy the State of Israel by first carving a fictional "Palestine" out of the heart of Israel. The charter of the PA calls for the destruction of Israel, not peacefully sharing a border with the Jewish state.

Since the 1957 Refugee Conference held in Homs, Syria, the

intent of the Arab states surrounding Israel has been clear: to introduce into Israel an army of Islamic militants labeled "refugees" to destroy the Jewish State from within.[768]

Many Europeans and Americans in 2016 (Jewish calendar: 5776) question the actions of the European Union and the American government in introducing several million Syrian so-called refugees, called by some an army of military-age males, into Europe and America since the beginning of the Syrian War in 2011 (Jewish calendar: 5771).

Why don't Israeli Jews give up and move to safer locations in friendly countries? This is a question that has been asked for well over two thousand years.

Before the fall of ancient Israel, the Temple in Jerusalem, center of the world for Jews, was razed twice. Since the fall of ancient Israel after the failed Bar Kokhba Revolt, Jews in Israel and in the Diaspora have been, at times, harassed and murdered by Christians and Muslims, usually supported by their governments.

The Roman Republic-turned-Empire represented the first European attempt to supplant the Jewish spiritual system. As the Roman Empire became the Christian Empire, the Holy Roman Empire, and then broke into the German Empire, France, England, and Italy, the Christian governments of Europe and the Vatican seemed to increase their desire to destroy Judaism. Since the rise of Islam, Islamics have tried many times to force conversion on their Jewish neighbors.

But Jews are not a nation of victims. Throughout the ages, all the Jewish people had to do to end the suffering was to renounce Judaism and accept conversion. The first offer to convert was to Roman paganism, next to Christianity, and finally to Islam. Circumstances vary, but most Jewish people have refused to convert. Some Jews, forced to convert to Christianity or die, secretly maintained their Jewish heritage through successive generations. To remain true to Judaism is the choice, not of victims, but of a tough, resilient people.

The Shoah, also called the Holocaust, followed a long history of European and Russian attempts to eradicate Judaism and assimilate Jews into their Christian cultures. The real underlying cause of this Jew hatred is the inability of tyrannical governments, fanatical religious leaders, or one-world-government socialists to force the Jewish people to give up Judaism and conform to a non-Jewish way of life.

Totalitarian regimes and other centralized government systems are opposed to any citizen group deciding, without government interference, how or when to express and celebrate their nationalism and religion. Jewish devotion to the laws of Judaism is perceived as a threat to the absolute power required by totalitarian and other centralized governments and as a threat to the "unity" of socialist governments. The offer to convert, when refused, is usually followed by expulsion or genocide.[769]

Christian anti-Semitism is capricious. A Jew friendly country can quickly turn unfriendly. Against the threat of genocide, a sovereign Jewish country is the only reliable safe haven for the Jewish Nation. Children of Jewish Shoah/Holocaust survivors say that "never again" is a call to action, not merely a slogan. A common phrase is: "We know how genocide ends—we must stop it from beginning."[770] The call to prevent genocide is not only for Jews, but for all people with a desire to remain free.

The steady militarization of Islam over the last two decades and its stated intention to destroy Jews and Israel resemble Germany's post-WWI massive arms buildup and its stated intention to rid Europe of Jews. The current silence of Western media on the totalitarianism of Islam while emphasizing peaceful aspects of Islamic teachings mirrors past media coverage initially highlighting positive details of Nazism and even Communism.[771]

Diana West, author and Washington correspondent, wrote, "Just as today's opinion-makers seek to divorce Islam from its impact — for example, brutal conquest, forced conversion, religiously sanctioned sex slavery, beheadings — past opinion-makers worked equally hard to divorce communism from its impact — for example, brutal conquest, forced collectivization, concentration camps (Gulags), mass murder."[772]

History seems to be repeating patterns occurring prior to both world wars. Russia and China are engaged in massive military increases—in fact, an arms race. Berlin has surpassed both New York and London as the world's financial capital.

Russia has moved troops into Ukraine to protect Russian interests while the United States and other Western governments continue to pour billions of taxpayer dollars into the small ruling group of oligarchs controlling the Ukrainian government. Western aid to Ukraine enables massive corruption at the top with little relief trickling down to the main population of long-suffering Ukrainians.[773]

China is building massive artificial islands in and claiming territorial rights to the entire South China Sea. Other nations ringing the South China Sea, and dependent on its rich fishing resources, are nervously watching China's rapid expansion.

Islam spreads over Europe like a scourge. Timid European government officials make statements of protest and wring their hands. European and American mainstream media play down the growing threat of Islam to Western culture in a similar manner to the European and American media minimizing the danger of Nazism before the outbreak of WWII.

The American government has made a compromising deal—called an appeasement policy by some—with militant Iran.

In response, in a televised, historic speech to a joint session of the American Congress in March 2015 (Jewish calendar: 5775), Israeli Prime Minister Benjamin Netanyahu urged America's leaders, along with all world leaders, not to repeat the mistakes of the past.

24

THE FUTURE

The past may be the best predictor of the future. If history does repeat, and if the past behavior of world leaders can predict future events, the consequence of ignoring the ongoing violence of totalitarian governments against the West could lead to another massive world war to "finally" end all wars.

Nostradamus, a Jewish Kabbalist and physician born Michel de Nostredame in 1503 (Jewish calendar: 5263), lived in France during the Dark Ages of the bubonic plague pandemic. He made predictions that some modern-day researchers interpret to indicate a third world war.[774]

Albert Einstein, the Jewish theoretical physicist who received the 1921 Nobel Prize in Physics for his services to Theoretical Physics, and especially for his discovery of the law of the photoelectric effect, escaped from Nazi Germany to America. He predicted a third world war so destructive that it would drive humankind back into a Stone Age and a fourth world war that would be fought with sticks and stones.[775]

The result of reprising past mistakes could lead to a

worldwide nuclear war. But even regional wars employing nuclear weapons could have devastating consequences on every continent. A cyber attack on a country's financial or energy infrastructure could be just as serious as a military attack.

Hostiles in the future could employ weather manipulation technology resulting in hurricanes, tsunamis, or earthquakes. The US, Russia, China, the European Union, and perhaps others have government programs to develop and test weather-manipulation systems.

The nature of world warfare will change dramatically in the next major confrontation. Winning a war has always been about superior technology—bigger, better firepower. Wars in the future will employ various types of unmanned technology engaged in colossal battles.

Powered exoskeleton super soldier androids will replace human troops. Driverless, crewless tanks and trucks will face off on future battlefields while pilotless fighter planes dogfight it out and artificial intelligence guided stealth bombers streak by in the skies above. Crewless submarines from competing sides will play cat-and-mouse in the oceans while trying to maneuver within range to deliver a nuclear weapon missile barrage into the fighting theatre.

Drone swarms may be used in the future for surveillance, to drive target populations from their homes, or for crowd control.

Russia is developing driverless tanks, Israel is developing an autonomous border control system, China is developing a supersonic air force, Iran is developing nuclear weapons, and the US is developing stealth planes and submarines.

A future war, or even a regional conflict, could involve deployment of an electromagnetic pulse weapon, an EMP. The catastrophic potential of an EMP to a society dependent on electric power grids has become a major concern to scientists and politicians.[776] An EMP can result from detonation of a high-altitude nuclear device (a nuclear bomb shot into space by a long-range missile) above a target country. The resulting disturbance moving through Earth's magnetic field can cause currents to surge in power lines.

A pulse strong enough to burn out wires and circuits throughout a country, such as America, can also be caused by a major solar storm. A powerful solar storm in 1859 (Jewish calendar: 5619), the Carrington Event, sent a CME, coronal mass ejection, crashing into Earth's magnetic field. The geomagnetic storm that followed blew out newly invented telegraph lines in America. A similar direct hit from a CME today would be a disaster because it could burn out the entire American electrical power grid.[777]

Without utility services the majority of people in the cities, towns, and suburbs of America would die from lack of food, water, and medicine. Even rural populations would suffer. Most residential and farm wells rely on electricity to pump water. Nuclear power plants, like the one at Fukishima, Japan, need electricity to remain cool. Once fuel for the emergency generators is exhausted, reactors across America would have to be taken off-line or experience catastrophic meltdowns.[778]

Whether from war or natural disasters, destruction of cities and major trade routes could result in violent struggles over dwindling resources.

Humankind could also experience another mass-extinction event. The Yellowstone Plateau volcanic field hotspot is one of only a few under North America. Another supervolcanic explosion from Yellowstone is not likely because the last supereruption 600,000 years ago destroyed the crust material needed to fuel another eruption.[779] But a supervolcanic eruption could occur somewhere else on the planet. The Old Faithful Geyser in Yellowstone National Park reminds us that Earth's formation is a continuing process.

If a supervolcanic eruption or a major impact from space darkened Earth's skies once again, it could plunge the planet into a period of glaciation as happened 74,000 years ago from the Toba supervolcanic eruption, or 12,000 years ago during what is called the thousand-year freezing cold "end of the last ice age" (the Younger Dryas stadial).

Some scientists and researchers point out that this current Holocene warm period may be an interglacial and that another freezing cold period could develop. Glaciers advancing again in the Northern Hemispheres would throw Earth back into another phase of the Quaternary Glaciation, the current ice age.

The sixth ice age, the Quaternary Glaciation, began 2.5 million years ago and, technically, continues to the present. It has included many stages of glacial and interglacial periods. The Holocene, the warm period that began 11,700 years ago, is sometimes called the end of the ice age, but ice sheets and glaciers still occupy Greenland, the Arctic region, Antarctica, and ice sheets cover vast regions of Siberia. Remnants of the last glaciers now occupy about 10% of Earth's land surface.

If the present warm trend continues and the remaining glaciers and ice sheets melt, then the end of the Younger Dryas will be referred to as the end of the last ice age. Or a freezing cold period could develop and begin another glacial advance. Then this current Holocene warm phase will be referred to as an interglacial of the continuing Quaternary Glaciation.

Any number of natural or human-caused future disasters could cause people to once again seek refuge in natural caverns, massive stone structures, or underground cities on every continent.

Or this current warm period may continue with a stable climate. Once coastal populations adjust to rising sea levels, a lush, paradisiacal environment may support happy, productive populations.

Friendly androids could soon replace elder care attendants, housekeepers, and gardeners so the humans could pursue enjoyable activities. Other friendly androids would prepare and serve food in restaurants. Driverless cars using concentrated solar power will soon deliver humans wherever they want to go. Artificial intelligence robot vacuum cleaners already operate in homes across America, Europe, and Asia.

Robot farming to produce and deliver the food supply may be the future of agriculture.

Life for humans living in developed countries will change rapidly as technology improves in the next decades. Living quarters may be built using light-transmitting "concrete" blocks. Homes may be independently powered using home fuel cells. People could use 3D printing to produce products, cars, electronics, furniture, and clothes.

Home entertainment might include phased-array optics producing three dimensional images on screenless displays. Or a virtual vacation headset could provide a person with an adventure or pure relaxation while resting in a vacation lounge chair with scents, vibrations, and warmth or coolness emanating from the cushions.

Home tricorders will allow individuals to self diagnose medical conditions. Online pharmacies will approve, dispense, and arrange delivery of medications. Android dentists might use bioglass fillings to fill cavities in the future. Bioglass filings dispense appropriate minerals into the affected tooth causing it to repair and heal. Longevity products and treatments in the future could double current life expectancy ages for men and women.

Space exploration or scientific discoveries on our home planet could deepen our understanding of the very nature of existence. The recent detection of gravitational waves is exciting scientists around the world. The gravitational waves, also called ripples in space-time, confirm part of Albert Einstein's 1915 Theory of General Relativity.[780]

Freedom to explore outer space and inner consciousness without the distractions of conflicts and the burdens of wars would give Earth's peoples an opportunity to develop Golden Age civilizations once again.

APPENDIX ~ EARTH TIMELINE

EARTH TIMELINE (Y.A. MEANS YEARS AGO)

4.6 billion y.a. .... Earth and solar system formed
3.8–2 billion y.a. .... Crust forms on Earth
3.5 billion y.a. .... Magnetic field forms around Earth
3.5 billion y.a. .... First anaerobic organisms emerge
3.1–2.8 billion y.a. .... Vaalbara supercontinent forms/breaks apart
Paleoproterozoic Era 2.5 billion to 1.6 billion y.a.
2.4–2.1 billion y.a. .... First ice age (Huronian)
2 billion y.a. .... Blue-green algae emerges
1.8–1.5 billion y.a. .... Columbia supercontinent forms/breaks apart
Mesoproterozoic Era 1.6 billion to 1 billion y.a.
1.5 billion y.a. .... Muticellular organisms emerge and develop
Neoproterozoic Era 1 billion–543 million y.a.
1 billion–720 million y.a. .... Rodinia supercontinent
720–660 million y.a. .... Second ice age (Sturtian)
660 million y.a. .... First animal life, sponges emerge and develop
650–635 million y.a. .... Third ice age (Marinoan)
Paleozoic Era 543 million to 250 million y.a.
543 million y.a. .... Sudden increase in plant life begins
460–430 million y.a. .... Fourth ice age (Andean-Saharan)
360–260 million y.a. .... Fifth ice age (Karoo)
Mesozoic Era 250 million to 65 million y.a.
250 million y.a. .... Pangaea supercontinent forms
220 million y.a. .... Mid-Atlantic Ridge forms and splits Pangaea
220 million y.a. .... Atlantic Ocean forms when Pangaea separates
85 million y.a. .... Primates emerge in Africa
Cenozoic Era 65 million to present
65 million y.a. .... Massive meteorite strikes Yucatán Peninsula
23 million y.a. .... La Garita supervolcano erupts in North America
23–5.3 million y.a. .... Mediterranean basin forms
5.3 million y.a. .... Megaflood creates Mediterranean Sea

2.6 million y.a. .... Isthmus of Panama separates Atlantic and Pacific
2.5 million y.a. .... Sixth (last) ice age (Quaternary) begins
600,000 y.a. .... Yellowstone supervolcano erupts in North America
94,000 y.a. .... Laurentide Ice Sheet forms over North America
74,000 y.a. .... Toba supervolcano erupts in Indonesia
12,800–11,700 y.a. .... Last ice age ends
11,700 y.a. .... Populations increase, civilizations develop worldwide

* * *

APPENDIX ~ CLIMATE CHANGES DURING THE LAST ICE AGE

Dates used for the climate change timeline are summarized from worldwide data of ice cores, deep ocean cores, and lakes and ocean sediments, compiled as a United States government funded project in 2012.

CLIMATE CHANGE TIMELINE (Y.A. MEANS YEARS AGO)

2.5 million y.a. .... Sixth (last) ice begins
2.5 million–1.6 million y.a. .... Long periods of glaciation
900,000–150,000 y.a. .... Climate oscillates between cold and warm
150,000–130,000 y.a. .... Severe cold, dry glacial period
130,000–110,000 y.a. .... Warm, moist period
110,000–105,000 y.a. .... Cool period
105,000–74,000 y.a. .... Climate oscillates between warm and cool
74,000 y.a. .... Toba supervolcanic eruption in Indonesia
74,000–60,000 y.a. .... Full glacial conditions worldwide
60,000–57,000 y.a. .... Glaciers and ice sheets recede worldwide
57,000–26,500 y.a. .... Oxygen Isotope Stage 3 warm period
26,500–22,000 y.a. .... Last Glacial Maximum cold period
22,000–19,000 y.a. .... Warming trend
19,000–18,000 y.a. .... Cool, dry period settles across Europe
18,000–14,500 y.a. .... Oldest Dryas cold period
14,500–14,140 y.a. .... Warming trend continues
14,140–14,000 y.a. .... Older Dryas cold period
14,000–12,800 y.a. .... Warming trend continues
12,800–11,700 y.a. .... Younger Dryas extinction-level events

Holocene warm period—11,700 y.a. to present
9,000–8,200 y.a. .... Warm and moist climate worldwide
8,200–8,000 y. a. ....Sudden cool, dry period
8,000–4,500 y.a. .... Warm and moist climate worldwide
4,500–2,600 y.a. ....Cooler and drier, similar to present climate
2,600–2,500 y.a. .... Sudden wet, cold period
2,500–365 y.a. .... Stable warm period
365–165 y.a. ....(1550 to 1850) Little Ice Age
165 y.a. to present.. Stable warm period

* * *

APPENDIX ~ CANAAN HISTORY AT A GLANCE

EARLY CANAAN

200,000–12,000 years ago
198,000 BCE–10,000 BCE

EARLY CANAAN TIMELINE (Y.A. MEANS YEARS AGO)

200,000–45,000 y.a. .... Neandertal cave sites
130,000–80,000 y.a. .... Early Cro-Magnon cave sites
74,000 y.a. .... Toba eruption reduces world population
55,000–20,000 y.a. ...... Cro-Magnons return, form Aurignacian culture
45,000 y.a. .... Neandertals leave/merge with Aurignacians
26,500–22,000 y.a. ....Last Glacial Maximum
20,000 y.a. .... Aurignacians leave Early Canaan
20,000–12,000 y.a. .... Kebaran Nomads occupy northern Israel
13,000–11,700 y.a. .... Natufians occupy southern Canaan
12,800–11,700 y.a. ....Younger Dryas (end of the ice age)

CANAAN

12,000–4,000 years ago
10,000 BCE–2,000 BCE

CANAAN TIMELINE (Y.A. MEANS YEARS AGO)

11,800–y.a. .... El Khiams occupy Canaan, make figurine amulets
11,000 y.a. ....Nomads settle in Jericho in Samaria
9,000 y.a. .... Settlements begin in Jezreel Valley
9,000 y.a. ....Jericho city is built
8,200 y.a. ....Laurentide Ice Sheet collapse raises sea levels

8,100 y.a. .... Proto-Hebrew spoken in Canaan
6,500–5,500 y.a. .... Megiddo becomes fortified city
5,900–4,900 y.a. .... Severe aridification period
5,600 y.a. .... Bronze Age begins
4,200–4,100 y.a. ....Severe regional droughts
4,000 y.a. .... Sumerians move to Canaan, build town of Schehem
4,000 y.a. .... Canaan becomes Promised Land/Israel

* * *

APPENDIX ~ ISRAEL HISTORY AT A GLANCE

TIME PERIODS OF ISRAEL

Ancient Israel .... 2000 BCE–135 CE
Eretz Israel .... 135 CE –1520
Eretz Israel–Southern Syria 1520–1920
Eretz Israel–British Palestine 1920–1948
Modern Israel .... 1948 to present

ANCIENT ISRAEL TIMELINE

2000 BCE .... Abraham, Sarah, and clan enter the Promised Land
1870 BCE .... Jacob (Yisrael) and family migrate to Egypt
1860 BCE .... Egyptian army attacks and plunders Shechem
1620 BCE .... Thera supervolcanic eruption in Aegean Sea
1440 BCE .... Exodus of the Twelve Tribes from Egypt to Israel
1400 BCE .... The Twelve Tribes establish Israel
1275–1225 BCE .... Bronze Age Collapse, Iron Age begins
1032 BCE .... Constitutional monarchy, first king Saul ben Kish
1000 BCE .... King David establishes Jerusalem as Israel's capital
960 BCE .... King Solomon builds Temple in Jerusalem
933 BCE .... Kingdoms of Israel and Judah separate
866 BCE .... King Omri reunites Israel and Judah
722 BCE .... Assyrians attack Israel, exile Ten Tribes
586 BCE .... Babylonians attack Judah, destroy Temple, exile Jews
516 BCE .... Babylonian exile ends, Second Temple built
198 BCE .... Syrian Greeks conquer Israel
167–142 BCE .... Maccabean War is waged against Syrian Greeks
142 BCE .... Kingdom of Judah reestablished by Maccabees
63 BCE .... Rome invades Kingdom of Judah
40 BCE .... Kingdom of Judah reestablished by Hasmoneans

37 BCE .... Rome annexes Kingdom of Judah
4 BCE .... Census counts seven million Jews in Roman Empire
20 CE .... Tiberias is built overlooking Lake Kinneret
66 CE–70 CE .... The Great Revolt, Jews battle the Roman army
70 CE .... Romans destroy Second Temple
70 CE .... Yavneh seminary established near Jerusalem
132–135 CE ...... Bar-Kokhba Revolt, Jews nearly defeat Roman army
135 CE .... Diaspora begins, Tiberias becomes Jewish center

Eretz Israel Timeline

135 CE .... Diaspora begins, many Jews leave Israel, many stay
150 CE .... Sanhedrin (Jewish high court) moves to Tiberias
613 CE .... Persia occupies Israel
638 CE–1099 .... Jews live under Mohammedan rule
1099 .... Catholic Crusaders destroy Jerusalem, occupy Israel
1187 .... Kurd Mohammedans defeat Christians, occupy Israel
1340 .... Bubonic plague spreads across Muslim-occupied Israel
1500 .... Spanish Jews arrive, Safed becomes Kabbalah center
1550 .... Ottoman Turks annex Israel, Jews settle in Tiberias
1880 .... First Aliyah, Bulgarian Jews arrive in Israel
1903–1906 .... Second Aliyah, Russian Jews arrive in Israel
1914–1918 .... WWI, Jews suffer in Israel under Ottomans
1914–1918 .... Jews witness Armenian genocide
1920 .... San Remo Conference ratifies Jewish homeland
1922 .... Britain confiscates 80% of Jewish homeland
1939 .... England restricts Jewish entry into "British Palestine"
1939–1945 .... WWII, the Shoah, Jews suffer in Israel under British
1945–1948 .... British soldiers incarcerate 50,000 Jews

Modern Israel Timeline

1948 .... Jews declare national independence
1948–1949 .... Arabs and British units attack Israel
1949 .... Jews win war, Israel accepted by UN as member state
1967 .... Six Day War, Israel defeats four Arab countries
1972 .... Munich Olympics massacre of eleven Israeli athletes

1973..........Egypt and Syria attack Israel, Israel wins Yom Kippur War
1976........................Air France airplane hijacked to Entebbe, Uganda
1995......... US Congress passes the Jerusalem Embassy Act of 1995
2000........................ Israel's Sci-Tech programs in 300 Israeli schools
2015........... International poll finds Israeli population world's happiest

* * *

APPENDIX ~ SUMERIAN HISTORY AT A GLANCE

SUMERIA AND AKKADIA

8,200–3,900 years ago
6200 BCE–1900 BCE (Jewish calendar begins 5,775 years ago)

SUMERIA/AKKADIA TIMELINE (Y.A. MEANS YEARS AGO)

8,200 y.a. .... **Laurentide Ice Sheet collapse raises ocean levels**
8,100 y.a. .... Settlements are built in Mesopotamia (Sumeria)
7,000 y.a. .... First palace built in Kish
6,900 y.a. .... City-state Mari built in Sumeria
5,900 y.a. .... **Severe worldwide aridification period**
5,800 y.a. .... Sumerian confederation of city-states begins
5,775 y.a. .... Jewish calendar begins (Calendar of Nineveh)
5,650 y.a. .... Bronze Age begins in Sumeria
5,650 y.a. .... Sumerian outpost established on Crete (Kaptara)
4,270–4215 y.a. .... Ur becomes Sumerian capital
4,200–4,100 y.a. .... **Severe droughts**
4,100 y.a. .... Akkad is overrun by desperate Syrian nomads
4,000 y.a. .... Abraham and Sarah move to Canaan
3,940 y.a. .... Sumeria falls to Syrian Amorites

* * *

APPENDIX ~ EGYPTIAN HISTORY AT A GLANCE

Pre-Dynastic Period: 6000 BCE to 3000 BCE

Natufians and Kebarans occupy part of Egypt, Naqada culture develops, bakes female figurines

Early Dynastic 3000–2575 BCE

1st Dynasty.................................Unknown first king is "King Memi"
2nd Dynasty ....City-states may have united at end of dynasty
3rd Dynasty ......Transition from wood to stone for building; turquoise mining begins in Sinai

Old Kingdom 2575–2150 BCE

4th Dynasty ....Egyptian military builds trade base in Nubia
5th Dynasty ...Solar religion is established, weak central government
6th Dynasty .... Nile River decreases flow; collapse of central government into city-states; Theban army attacks Bedouin raiders in Sinai and tribes living in Canaan
2200 BCE......................severe climate change causes worldwide droughts, regional migrations

1st Intermediate 2150–2040 BCE

7th/8th Dynasties .... City-states raise armies, compete for resources
9th/10th Dynasties .... Civil war between city-states
11th Dynasty ....Theban king reunites Upper-Lower Egypt, subdues Bedouins

Middle Kingdom 1991–1805 BCE

12th Dynasty .... Capital moves from Thebes to Itj-tawi; huge fortresses are built in Nubia; Egyptian army attacks Shechem in Judean Hills

HEQE-KHASE KINGDOM (2ND INTERMEDIATE) 1807–1521 BCE

13th Dynasty .... Thebans rule Upper Egypt, Lower Egypt is autonomous
14th Dynasty .... Hyksos kings rule Lower Egypt, build Avaris
1640 BCE .... Thera supervolcanic eruption devastates region
15th Dynasty ...... Hyksos kings rule Egypt; continue Egyptian culture
16th (minor) Dynasty....Hyksos vassal kings rule Thebes and Abydos
17th (minor) Dynasty .... Theban kings rule Thebes and Abydos

NEW KINGDOM 1540–1070 BCE

18th Dynasty .... Theban warrior-king Ahmose attacks Hyksos capital Avaris, conquers northern Sudan, Egypt, Israel, southeastern Turkey, and western Arabia, uses plunder to finance forced labor building projects throughout Egypt
1440 BCE.................................. Proposed date of Hebrew Exodus
Capital moved from Thebes to Akhet-Aton, capital moved back to Thebes
19th Dynasty .... General Paramesu becomes Ramesses I
1225–1175 BCE .... Bronze Age Collapse, Iron Age Begins
20th Dynasty ....Reign marked by corruption and social turmoil; Theban priests rule Upper Egypt while Pharaoh rules Lower Egypt, former Libyan prisoners now major part of Egyptian military; military campaigns in Israel, Syria, and Nubia rebuffed by local populations

LATE DYNASTIC 1070–332 BCE

21st Dynasty....... Libyan kings rule north, Theban priests ruled south
22nd–24th Dynasties....................... Kings and priests rule city-states
25th DynastyNubians occupy and rule (observed Egyptian customs), Assyrians attack, plunder, and destroy Thebes
26th Dynasty .... Egyptian king unites Egypt
27th Dynasty .... First Persian occupation and rule by Persian kings
28th–30th Dynasties Independent Egyptian rule, restoration of culture
31st Dynasty .... Persian occupation, Persian culture reintroduced

MACEDONIAN/PTOLEMAIC KINGDOMS 332–30 BCE

Alexander the Macedonian liberates Egypt from Persia and introduces Hellenistic culture; Macedonian troops given land grants and orders to intermarry with locals; Alexander's general begins new Ptolemaic Dynasties, last Ptolemaic king is Cleopatra VI who aligns with Rome, attempts to save Egyptian culture

ROMAN EMPIRE 30 BCE–641 CE

Rome annexes Egypt after death of Cleopatra VI, rules native Coptic population from their capital in Alexandria, introduces Hellenistic culture

ISLAMIC EMPIRES 641–1798
ARAB/COPTIC/PERSIAN/GREEK/SLAVIC/TURKISH

Arab Mohammedans rule from 641–969; Persians rule briefly before the Berber Islamic Empire (Afro-Asiatic-Algerian) annexes Egypt 909–1170; the Kurds defeat the Berbers and rule from 1170–1250; the Mamuks (Turkish/Balkan/Slavic/Greek) create a North African Empire and rule Egypt from 1250–1517; Black Death pandemic kills 40% of Egyptian population in 1350; Ottoman Turks form Anatolian empire, battle the Mamuks, and rule Egypt from 1571–1798

FRENCH OCCUPATION 1798–1801

Napoleon and the French army in 1798 conquer and occupy Egypt for three years ending Ottoman rule

ALI DYNASTY 1805–1882

An Albanian Ottoman army commander seizes control of Egypt and starts the Ali Dynasty; France and Britain construct the Suez Canal in 1867 and together control the Egyptian government

BRITISH OCCUPATION 1882–1953

The League of Nations makes Britain the protectorate of Egypt in 1914; Egyptians revolt and force Britain to declare Egyptian independence in 1922, but British troops continue to occupy Egypt until 1953

INDEPENDENT ISLAMIC REPUBLIC 1953–PRESENT

In 2014 the Egyptian government signs a new constitution stating Egypt is an Arab nation

* * *

APPENDIX
BALFOUR DECLARATION

A letter from Arthur James Balfour, former British prime minister and lord of the admiralty, to Jewish community leader Lord Walter Rothschild for the Zionist Federation of Great Britain and Ireland, is known as the Balfour Declaration.

> Foreign Office
> November 2nd, 1917
>
> Dear Lord Rothschild,
> I have much pleasure in conveying to you, on behalf of His Majesty's Government, the following declaration of sympathy with Jewish Zionist aspirations which has been submitted to, and approved by, the cabinet.
> "His Majesty's Government views with favour the establishment in Palestine of a national home for the Jewish people, and will use their best endeavours to facilitate the achievement of this object, it being clearly understood that nothing shall be done which may prejudice the civil and religious rights of existing non-Jewish communities in Palestine, or the rights and political status enjoyed by Jews in any other country."
> I should be grateful if you would bring this declaration to the knowledge of the Zionist Federation.
>
> Yours sincerely,
>
> Arthur James Balfour

ENDNOTES

1. Brian K. Hall of Dalhousie University, Benedikt Hallgrimsson of University of Calgary, *Strickberger's Evolution* (Sudbury: Jones & Bartlett, Fourth Edition, 2008).
2. G. W. Trompf, *The Idea of Historical Recurrence in Western Thought* (California: University of California Press, 1979).
3. Amnesty International, 2012 Report, accessed March 13, 2013, <http://www.amnestyusa.org/>.
4. For instance, UN Agenda 21 is a plan, created in 1996, to standardize the lifestyles of people worldwide to a single set of protocols, such as high density housing and limited vehicle use.
5. Bob Kobres, "Comets and the Bronze Age Collapse," *University of Georgia Libraries* (February 2010), accessed June 11, 2011, <http://abob.libs.uga.edu/bobk/bronze.html>.
6. Andrew Curry, "The Birth of Religion," *Smithsonian* (June 2011), accessed May 2, 2013, <http://www.smithsonianmag.com/history-archaeology/gobekli-tepe.html#ixzz2TImivFwK>.
7. Budge, *Babylonian Life and History*, 25, 87.
8. Budge, *Babylonian Life and History*, 104.
9. Michael S. Heiser, "The Myth of a Sumerian 12th Planet: Nibiru According to the Cuneiform Sources," *MichaelHeiser.com* (2012), accessed May 17, 2013, <http://www.michaelsheiser.com/nibirupage.htm>.
10. "Nimrod," *The unedited full-text of the 1906 Jewish Encyclopedia*, accessed March 11, 2014, <http://www.jewishencyclopedia.com/articles/11548-nimrod>.
11. British Museum, *The Babylonian Legends of the Creation* (Lenox: HardPress Publishing, 2010); J.A. Black et al, *The Electronic Text Corpus of Sumerian Literature (1998)*, accessed November 1, 2012, <http://etcsl.orinst.ox.ac.uk/>; J.A. Black et al, *The Electronic Text Corpus of Sumerian Literature (1998)*, accessed November 1, 2012, <http://etcsl.orinst.ox.ac.uk/>; Samuel Noah Kramer, *Sumerian Mythology* (Philadelphia: University of Pennsylvania Press, 1972), 30-75; C. Leonard Woolley, *The Sumerians* (New York: W. W. Norton & Company, Inc., 1965), 90-129; Zecharia Sitchin, *Twelfth Planet: Book I of the Earth Chronicles* (Vermont: Bear & Company, 1991), 187-322; Budge, *Babylonian Life and History*, 77-85.
12. "Astronomers Tweak Age of the Universe," *San Diego Union-Tribune*, March 22, 2013, sec A4.
13. The Reader's Digest Association, *How Did It Really Happen* (New York: Readers Digest Association, 2000), 12-14.

14 Alexander Abad-Santos, "Harvard-Smithsonian Scientists Have the First Direct Evidence of Cosmic Inflation," *The Atlantic* (March 17, 2014), accessed October 18, 2015, <http://news.yahoo.com/could-major-discovery-astrophysicists-planning-announce-today-135308336.html>.
15 Andrew Zimmerman Jones, "Evolution of General Relativity," *about education* (Dec 2014), accessed April 28, 2015, <http://physics.about.com/od/relativisticmechanics/a/relativity_4.htm>.
16 Don Lincoln, *The Large Hadron Collider* (Baltimore: John Hopkins University Press, 2014), 3.
17 Timothy Ferris, "Sun Struck," *National Geographic* (June 2012): 44.
18 G. Brent Dalrymple "The age of the Earth in the twentieth century: a problem (mostly) solved," *Geological Society, London, Special Publications* (January 2001): v. 190; 205-221.
19 Ker Than, "Mission to Study Earth's Gaping Open Wound," *Live Science* (March 2007), accessed March 18, 20013, <www.livescience.com/1317-mission-study-earth-gaping-open-wound.html>.
20 <http://etcsl.orinst.ox.ac.uk/>.
21 "The Archean Eon and the Hadean," *University of California Museum of Paleontology* (July 2011), accessed March 29, 2013, <http://www.ucmp.berkeley.edu/precambrian/archean_hadean.php>.
22 Nick Eyles, Andrew Miall, *Canada Rocks: The Geologic Journey* (Markham: Fitzhenry and Whiteside Limited, 2010), 79-81.
23 Gary A. Glatmaiers, Paul H. Roberts, "A three-dimensional self-consistent computer simulation of a geomagnetic field reversal," *Nature* (September 1995), accessed February 3, 2013, <http://adsabs.harvard.edu/abs/1995Natur.377..203G>.
24 Stuart Gary, "Survey finds not all meteors the same," *ABC Science Online* (December 2011), accessed November 10, 2012, <http://www.abc.net.au/science/articles/2011/12/22/3396756.htm>.
25 "Supercontinents," *eNotes* (2009), accessed January 18, 2013, <http://www.enotes.com/supercontinents-reference/supercontinents>.
26 Michel Pidwirny, "Proterozoic," *The Encyclopedia of Earth* (June 2012), accessed August 27, 2014, <http://www.eoearth.org/view/article/155427/>.
27 Phil Plait, "Poisoned Planet," *Bad Astronomy* (July 2014), accessed August 1, 2015, <http://www.slate.com/blogs/bad_astronomy/2014/07/28/the_great_oxygenation_event_the_earth_s_first_mass_extinction.html>.
28 Robert Grei, Claudio Gaucher, Simon W. Poulton, Don E. Canfield, "Fluctuations in Precambrian atmospheric oxygenation recorded by chromium isotopes," *Nature International Journal of Science* (September 2009), accessed March 15, 2014, <http://www.nature.com/search?journal=nature%2Cnews&q=Fluctuations%20in%20Precambrian%20atmospheric%20oxygenation>.
29 Wynne Parry, "Cold Water Tossed on 'Snowball Earth' Theory," *Live Science* (October 2011), accessed November 13, 2012, <http://www.livescience.com/16402-snowball-earth-carbon-dioxide.html />.

30 "Welcome to the Vredefort Dome," *Vredefort Dome.org* (2010), accessed November 11, 2012, <http://www.vredefortdome.org/index.html>.

31 "New Supercontinent Dubbed Columbia Once Ruled Earth," *Space Daily* (March 2002), accessed December 12, 2012, <www.spacedaily.com/news/tectonics-02b.html>.

32 Wei Wang, Mei-Fu Zhou "Provenance and tectonic setting of the Paleo to Mesoproterozoic Dongchuan Group in the southwestern Yangtze Block, South China: Implication for the breakup of the supercontinent Columbia," *Science Direct* (January 2014), accessed August 20, 2014, <http://www.sciencedirect.com/science/article/pii/S0040195113006537>.

33 "The Canadian Shield: Sudbury Basin, Ontario," *Geologic Journey News* (2012), Field Guide.

34 <http://www.enotes.com/supercontinents-reference/supercontinents>; Richard P. Tollo, Louise Corriveau, James M. McLelland, Mervin J. Bartholomew, "Proterozoic Tectonic Evolution of the Grenville Orogen in North America," *abstract-Geological Society of America Memoirs* (August 2003), accessed June 18, 2012, <http://memoirs.gsapubs.org/content/197/1.abstract>.

35 <http://www.enotes.com/supercontinents-reference/supercontinents>.

36 <http://www.enotes.com/supercontinents-reference/supercontinents>.

37 "Snowball Earth: New Evidence Hints at Global Glaciation 716.5 Million Years Ago," *Science Daily* (March 2010), accessed January 15, 2011, <http://www.sciencedaily.com/releases/2010/03/100304142228.htm>.

38 <http://www.sciencedaily.com/releases/2010/03/100304142228.htm>.

39 "Research evidence supports three major glaciation events in the distant past," *Virginia Tech News*, accessed January 18, 2011, <http://www.vtnews.vt.edu/articles/2004/04/2004-237.html>; G. A. Shields "Palaeoclimate: Marinoan meltdown," *nature geosciences* (2008), accessed March 7, 2013, <http://www.nature.com/ngeo/journal/v1/n6/abs/ngeo214.html>.

40 Mark A. S. McMenamin, Dianna L. Schulte McMenamin, *The Emergence of Animals: The Cambrian Breakthrough* (New York: Columbia University Press, 1990), 1-4; "Cambrian," *New World Encyclopedia* (April 2013), accessed September 17, 2015, <http://www.newworldencyclopedia.org/entry/Cambrian#Cambrian_explosion>.

41 "Researchers find direct evidence that acidic oceans caused Earth's worst mass extinction," *San Diego Union-Tribune*, April 11, 2015, Sec. In Brief.

42 <http://www.enotes.com/supercontinents-reference/supercontinents>; Marjorie Wilson, "Central Atlantic passive margins: continental break-up above a Mesozoic super-plume," *Geo Science World, Journal of the Geological Society* (June 1997): v. 154, no. 3, 491-495.

43 W.M. Ewing, H.J. Ericson, J.N. Heezen, B.C. Heezen, "Exploration of the northwest Atlantic mid-ocean canyon," *Bulletin of the Geological Society of America 64* (1953): 865-868, accessed January 13, 2012, <http://dx.doi.org/10.1130/0016-7606(1953)64[865:EOTNAM]2.0.CO;2>.

44 Helen J. Chatterjee, Simon Y.W. Ho, Ian Barnes, Colin Groves, "Estimating the phylogeny and divergence times of primates using a supermatrix

approach," *BMC Evol Biol* (April 2009), accessed May 20, 2014, <http://bmcevolbiol.biomedcentral.com/articles/10.1186/1471-2148-9-259>.

45 Edward F. Malkowski, *Ancient Egypt 39,000 BCE: The History, Technology, and Philosophy of Civilization X* (Vermont: Bear & Company, 2010), 2.

46 Malkowski, *Ancient Egypt 39,000 BCE*, 2.

47 "The Great Rift Valley," *National Geographic* (November 2011): map supplement.

48 John Hawks, *The Rise of Humans: Great Scientific Debates* (Virginia: The Great Courses, 2011), 122.

49 Robert Roy Britt, "Super Volcano Will Challenge Civilization, Geologists Warn," *Live Science* (March 2009), accessed May 22, 2010, <http://www.livescience.com/200-super-volcano-challenge-civilization-geologists-warn.html>.

50 "The Great Rift Valley," *National Geographic*, map supplement.

51 Georges Clauzon et al, "Alternate interpretation of the Messinian salinity crisis: Controversy resolved," *abstract-Geology* (April 1996), accessed January 27, 2013, <http://geology.gsapubs.org/content/24/4/363.abstract>.

52 "The Great Rift Valley," *National Geographic*, map supplement.

53 *California Academy of Sciences*, Press Release August 11, 2010, "Scientists Discover Oldest Evidence of Stone Tool Use and Meat-Eating Among Human ancestors: New finds from Ethiopia push tool use back by almost a million years," accessed June 12, 2012, <http://www.calacademy.org/newsroom/releases/2010/oldest_tool_use.php>.

54 Jenny Gross, "Fossil Discovery Clouds Human Origin Story," *The Wall Street Journal*, May 28, 2015, A9; Rachel Feltman, "Find Called Crucial to Human Evolution," *San Diego Union-Tribune*, March 5, 2015, A10.

55 Feltman, (Find Called Crucial)," *San Diego Union-Tribune*, A10.

56 Hawks, *The Rise of Humans*, 48.

57 Dave Lawrence, "Microfossil lineages support slushy snowball Earth," *Geotimes* (April 2003), accessed September 16, 2010, <http://www.geotimes.org/apr03/WebExtra041803.html>.

58 Robin McKie, "How a hobbit is rewriting the history of the human race," *The Observer* (February 2010), accessed July 16, 2013, <http://www.guardian.co.uk/science/2010/feb/21/hobbit-rewriting-history-human-race>.

59 <http://www.guardian.co.uk/science/2010/feb/21/hobbit-rewriting-history-human-race>.

60 Hawks, *The Rise of Humans*, 32.

61 Hawks, *The Rise of Humans*, 48.

62 Stephen J. Lycett, Christopher J. Bae, "The Movius Line controversy: the state of the debate," *Debates in World Archaeology* (2010), accessed July 5, 2011, <http://www.anthropology.hawaii.edu/People/Faculty/Bae/pdfs/2010_Lycett%20and%20Bae_WA.pdf>.

63 Ann Gibbons, "Ancient Island Tools Suggest Homo erectus Was a Seafarer," *Science* (March 1998), accessed October 14, 2011, <http://www.sciencemag.org/content/279/5357/1635>.

64. "Fire out of Africa: a key to the migration of prehistoric man," The Hebrew University of Jerusalem press release (Jerusalem, October 28, 2008), *Science Dailey*, accessed October 19, 2012, <http://www.sciencedaily.com/releases/2008/10/081027082314.htm>.
65. Hong Shang et al, "An early modern human from Tianyuan Cave, Zhoukoudian, China," abstract-*Proceedings of the National Academy Science* (April 2007), accessed July 21, 2015, <http://www.pnas.org/content/104/16/6573.abstract>.
66. <http://www.sciencedaily.com/releases/2008/10/081027082314.htm>.
67. Chip Walter, "First Artists," *National Geographic*, (January 2014): 45.
68. Walter, *National Geographic*, 45.
69. Walter, *National Geographic*, 45.
70. Charles Q. Choi, "Mysterious Chinese Fossils May Be New Human species," *Live Science* (March 2012), accessed November 24, 2015, <http://www.livescience.com/19039-human-species-china-cave.html>.
71. Hawks, *The Rise of Humans*, 72.
72. Hawks, *The Rise of Humans*, 117, 122.
73. Walter, *National Geographic*, 38-41.
74. Sarah Kaplan, "170,000 years before Stonehenge, Neanderthals built their own incredible structure," *Washington Post* (May 26, 2016), accessed July 10, 2016, <https://www.washingtonpost.com/news/speaking-of-science/wp/2016/05/26/170000-years-before-stonehenge-neanderthals-built-their-own-incredible-structure/?postshare=7051467949174664&tid=ss_tw>.
75. Sarah Kaplan, "Grisly evidence of Neanderthal cannibalism uncovered in a Belgian cave," *Washington Post* (July 8, 2016), accessed July 8, 2016, <https://www.washingtonpost.com/news/speaking-of-science/wp/2016/07/08/grisly-evidence-of-neanderthal-cannibalism-uncovered-in-a-belgian-cave/?wpisrc=nl_az_most>.
76. "The Neanderthal theory," abstract-*The Neanderthal theory of autism, Asperger, and ADHD* (April 2001), accessed September 25, 2012, <http://www.rdos.net/eng/asperger.htm>.
77. <http://www.rdos.net/eng/asperger.htm>.
78. Rachel Feltman, "Neanderthals Possible Inventors of Jewelry," *San Diego Union-Tribune*, March 12, 2015, A10.
79. <https://www.washingtonpost.com/news/speaking-of-science/wp/2016/05/26/170000-years-before-stonehenge-neanderthals-built-their-own-incredible-structure/?postshare=7051467949174664&tid=ss_tw>.
80. Nick Redfern, *Bloodlines of the Gods* (New Jersey: The Career Press, Inc., 2015), 42.
81. Rachel Feltman, "Human and Neanderthal love affair is traced back to Israel, 55,000 years ago," *Washington Post* (January 28, 2015), accessed January 21, 2016, <https://www.washingtonpost.com/news/speaking-of-science/wp/2015/01/28/

human-and-neanderthal-love-affair-is-traced-back-to-israel-55000-years-ago/>.
82 <http://www.rdos.net/eng/asperger.htm>.
83 Redfern, *Bloodlines of the Gods*, 15.
84 Robert Sanders, "160,000-year-old fossilized skulls uncovered in Ethiopia are oldest anatomically modern humans," *UC Berkeley News: Press Release (June 11, 2003)*, accessed May 22, 2013, <http://www.berkeley.edu/news/media/releases/2003/06/11_idaltu.shtml>.
85 C. Michael Hogan, "Eemian," *The Encyclopedia of Earth* (July 2012), accessed March 24, 2015, <http://www.eoearth.org/view/article/169588/>.
86 Charles Q. Choi, "Humans May Have Dispersed Out of Africa Earlier Than Thought," *Live Science* (April 2014), accessed January 27, 2015, <http://www.livescience.com/44988-humans-dispersed-earlier-than-thought.html>.
87 Paul Pettitt, *The Palaeolithic Origins of Human Burial* (New York: Routledge, 2010), 59.
88 John Noble Wilford, "On Crete, New Evidence of Very Ancient Mariners," *New York Times* February 16, 2010, sec. Science, D1.
89 Pettitt, *The Palaeolithic Origins of Human Burial*, 59.
90 Pettitt, *The Palaeolithic Origins of Human Burial*, 59.
91 "Field Project Jebel Irhoud," *Department of Human Evolution* (2007), accessed May 8, 2015, <http://www.eva.mpg.de/evolution/files/irhoud.htm>.
92 Walter, *National Geographic*, 40; Pettitt, *The Palaeolithic Origins of Human Burial*, 59.
93 Pettitt, *The Palaeolithic Origins of Human Burial*, 59.
94 T.M. Smith et al, "Earliest evidence of modern human life history in North African early Homo sapiens," *abstract-Proceedings of the National Academy Science* (March 2010), accessed May 2, 2012, <http://www.pnas.org/content/104/15/6128.full>.
95 Rachel Kaufman, "Oldest Modern Human Outside of Africa Found," *National Geographic News* (October 2010), accessed July 7, 2015, <http://news.nationalgeographic.com/news/2010/10/101025-oldest-human-fossil-china-out-of-africa-science/>.
96 Alfredo Coppa, et al, "Newly recognized Pleistocene human teeth from Tabun Cave, Israel," *Journal of Human Evolution* (September 2005): Volume 49, Issue 3, 301-315.
97 Coppa, et al, *Journal of Human Evolution*, 301-315.
98 Coppa, et al, *Journal of Human Evolution*, 301-315.
99 Pettitt, *The Palaeolithic Origins of Human Burial*, 59.
100 Pettitt, *The Palaeolithic Origins of Human Burial*, 59.
101 *A quick background to the last ice age*, accessed October 27, 2012, <http://www.esd.ornl.gov/projects/qen/nerc130k.html>.
102 <http://www.esd.ornl.gov/projects/qen/nerc130k.html>.
103 <http://www.esd.ornl.gov/projects/qen/nerc130k.html>.
104 Malkowski, *Ancient Egypt 39,000 BCE*, 4.

105 <http://www.esd.ornl.gov/projects/qen/nerc130k.html>.
106 <http://www.esd.ornl.gov/projects/qen/nerc130k.html>.
107 <http://www.rdos.net/eng/asperger.htm>.
108 "Preterm babies living longer," *New York Times*, May 7, 2015, front page, A-18.
109 Hawks, *The Rise of Humans*, 54.
110 <http://www.guardian.co.uk/science/2010/feb/21/hobbit-rewriting-history-human-race>.
111 Walter, *National Geographic*, 38-41.
112 Walter, *National Geographic*, 39.
113 "Africa Rock Art Archive," *Bradshaw Foundation*, accessed July 11, 2015, <http://www.bradshawfoundation.com/africa/oldest_art/>.
114 Walter, "First Artists," *National Geographic*, 39.
115 Dennis J. Stanford, Bruce A. Bradley, *Across Atlantic Ice: The Origins of America's Clovis Culture* (Berkeley: University of California Press, 2012), 186-187.
116 Walter, *National Geographic*, 40-41.
117 Jeff Tollefson, "Human evolution: Cultural roots," *Nature* (February 2012), accessed June 5, 2012, <http://www.nature.com/news/human-evolution-cultural-roots-1.10025>.
118 <http://www.esd.ornl.gov/projects/qen/nerc130k.html>.
119 Walter, *National Geographic*, 41.
120 ed. Michael D. Petraglia, Bridget Allchin, *The Evolution and History of Human Populations in South Asia* (Dordrecht: Springer, 2007), 6.
121 <http://www.esd.ornl.gov/projects/qen/nerc130k.html>.
122 <https://www.washingtonpost.com/news/speaking-of-science/wp/2015/01/28/human-and-neanderthal-love-affair-is-traced-back-to-israel-55000-years-ago/>.
123 <http://www.esd.ornl.gov/projects/qen/nerc130k.html>.
124 <http://news.nationalgeographic.com/news/2010/10/101025-oldest-human-fossil-china-out-of-africa-science/>.
125 Pettitt, *The Palaeolithic Origins of Human Burial*, 59.
126 Coppa, et al, *Journal of Human Evolution*, 301-315; <https://www.washingtonpost.com/news/speaking-of-science/wp/2015/01/28/human-and-neanderthal-love-affair-is-traced-back-to-israel-55000-years-ago/>.
127 <http://www.rdos.net/eng/asperger.htm>.
128 <https://www.washingtonpost.com/news/speaking-of-science/wp/2015/01/28/human-and-neanderthal-love-affair-is-traced-back-to-israel-55000-years-ago/>. Pettitt, *The Palaeolithic Origins of Human Burial*, 59.
129 Steven L. Kuhn, Mary C. Stiner, David S. Reese, Erksin Gulec, "Ornaments of the earliest Upper Paleolithic: New insights from the Levant," *Proceedings of the National Academy Science* (April 10, 2001), accessed March 2, 2013, <http://www.pnas.org/content/98/13/7641.full>.
130 <http://www.rdos.net/eng/asperger.htm>.

131 "Aurignacian Culture," *Encyclopeadia Britannica*, accessed December 6, 2013, <http://www.britannica.com/topic/Aurignacian-culture>.
132 <http://www.britannica.com/topic/Aurignacian-culture>.
133 <https://www.ncbi.nlm.nih.gov/pmc/articles/PMC1871827/>.
134 "Why Am I Denisovan," *National Geographic Genographic Project*, accessed June 8, 2015, <https://genographic.nationalgeographic.com/denisovan/>.
135 <https://genographic.nationalgeographic.com/denisovan/>.
136 <http://www.britannica.com/topic/Aurignacian-culture>.
137 <http://www.rdos.net/eng/asperger.htm>.
138 <http://www.rdos.net/eng/asperger.htm>.
139 <http://www.britannica.com/topic/Aurignacian-culture>.
140 <http://www.britannica.com/topic/Aurignacian-culture>.
141 Budge, *Babylonian Life and History*, 263.
142 Walter, *National Geographic*, 45.
143 Walter, *National Geographic*, 55.
144 Libor Balak, "The Culture of the Gravettian," *Anthropark* (2013), accessed February 10, 2014, <http://www.anthropark.wz.cz/gravettian.htm>.
145 <http://www.esd.ornl.gov/projects/qen/nerc130k.html>.
146 Walter, *National Geographic*, 55.
147 <http://www.britannica.com/topic/Aurignacian-culture>.
148 Libor Balak, "The Culture of the Gravettian," *Anthropark* (2013), accessed February 10, 2014, <http://www.anthropark.wz.cz/gravettian.htm>.
149 Elizabeth Wayland Barber, *Women's Work: The First 20,000 Years: Women, Cloth, and Society in Early Times* (New York: W.W. Norton and Company, 1994), 44.
150 <http://www.anthropark.wz.cz/gravettian.htm>.
151 <http://www.rdos.net/eng/asperger.htm>.
152 <http://www.eva.mpg.de/evolution/files/irhoud.htm>.
153 Stanford, Bradley, *Across Atlantic Ice*, 186-187.
154 Stanford, Bradley, *Across Atlantic Ice*, 186-187.
155 Stanford, Bradley, *Across Atlantic Ice*, 186-187.
156 "Balzi Rossi (Rochers Rouges) caves and the Ligurian Epigravettian," *Aggsbach's Paleolithic Blog* (January 2017), accessed March 6, 2016, <http://www.aggsbach.de/2016/01/balzi-rossi-rochers-rouges-caves-and-the-ligurian-epigravettian/>.
157 "Magdalenian Culture," *Encyclopaedia Britannica Online*, accessed February 21, 2011, <http://www.britannica.com/topic/Magdalenian-culture>.
158 <http://www.britannica.com/topic/Aurignacian-culture>.
159 "Ashkenazi Jews' roots tied to 330 ancestors," *Los Angeles Times*, 10 September 2014, sec. A1.
160 "After the big cold: Kebaran from Kebara Cave," *Aggsbach's Paleolithic Blog* (August 2010), accessed August 15, 2013, <http://www.aggsbach.de/2010/08/after-the-big-cold-kebaran-from-kebara-cave/>.

161 James Owen, "Cave Fossil Find: New Human Species or Nothing Extraordinary," *National Geographic News* (March 2012), accessed July 29, 2015, <http://news.nationalgeographic.com/news/2012/03/120314-new-human-species-chinese-plos-science-red-deer-cave/>.

162 Sion Morgan, "Missing Link to the Past Rises from the Depths; It Was an Ancient Land Once Home to Man...," *questa Trusted online research* (September 2015), accessed January 26, 2016, <https://www.questia.com/article/1G1-427943905/missing-link-to-the-past-rises-from-the-depths-it>.

163 Frank Urquhart, "Doggerland: The real Atlantis, just off Scotland," *The Scotsman*, March 7, 2012, front page.

164 Laura Spinney, "Archaeology: The lost world," *Nature454* (July 2008): 151-154.

165 Urquhart, *The Scotsman*, front page.

166 Stanford, Bradley, *Across Atlantic Ice*, 186-187.

167 James K. Feathers et al, "Luminescence Dating of Sand Deposits Related to Late Pleistocene Human Occupation at the Cactus Hill Site, Virginia, United States," *abstract-Science Direct Quaternary Geochronology* (August 2006), accessed June 10, 2012, <http://www.sciencedirect.com/science/article/pii/S1871101406000483>.

168 Stanford, Bradley, *Across Atlantic Ice*, 149-203.

169 <http://www.esd.ornl.gov/projects/qen/nerc130k.html>.

170 Stanford, Bradley, *Across Atlantic Ice*, 186-187.

171 "Artifacts in Texas predate Clovis culture by 2,500 years, new study shows," *Science Daily* (March 2011), accessed June 15, 2012, <http://www.sciencedaily.com/releases/2011/03/110324153013.htm>.

172 Glenn Hodges, "The first face of the first Americans," *National Geographic* (January 2015): 132-133.

173 "The Magdalenians," *Society for Nordish Physical Anthropology* (July 2006), accessed April 18, 2015, <http://www.theapricity.com/snpa/chapter-II10.htm>.

174 <http://www.livescience.com/19039-human-species-china-cave.html>; <http://news.nationalgeographic.com/news/2012/03/120314-new-human-species-chinese-plos-science-red-deer-cave/>.

175 "Cave Art Trove Discovered in Spain," *San Diego Union-Tribune*, May 29, 2016, A32.

176 <https://www.questia.com/article/1G1-427943905/missing-link-to-the-past-rises-from-the-depths-it>.

177 Malkowski, *Ancient Egypt 39,000 BCE*, 227-229.

178 <http://www.aggsbach.de/2016/01/balzi-rossi-rochers-rouges-caves-and-the-ligurian-epigravettian/>.

179 The Reader's Digest Association, *How Did It Really Happen*, 92.

180 Richard Firestone, Allen West, Simon Warwick-Smith, *The Cycle of Cosmic Catastrophes: How a Stone-Age Comet Changed the Course of World Culture* (Rochester: Bear & Company, 2006), 328.

181 "Atlas Mountains," *Encyclopedia.com* (2004), accessed March 8, 2014, <http://www.encyclopedia.com/topic/Atlas_Mountains.aspx>.
182 Malkowski, *Ancient Egypt 39,000 BCE*, 271.
183 Louis De Cordier, *Mataha Expedition Hawara 2008*, accessed March 13, 2015, <http://www.labyrinthofegypt.com/>.
184 Bertrand Russell, *History of Western Philosophy* (New York: Simon and Schuster, 1972), 165.
185 "Western Barbary; Morocco and the Canary Islands," *Society for Nordish Physical Anthropology* (July 2006), accessed April 18, 2015, <http://www.theapricity.com/snpa/index2.htm>.
186 The Reader's Digest Association, *How Did It Really Happen*, 92.
187 The Reader's Digest Association, *How Did It Really Happen*, 92.
188 The Reader's Digest Association, *How Did It Really Happen*, 47.
189 Jacques Kinnaer, "History," *Ancient Egypt* (June 2013), accessed December 20, 2013, <http://www.ancient-egypt.org/index.html>.
190 <http://www.esd.ornl.gov/projects/qen/nerc130k.html>.
191 The Reader's Digest Association, *How Did It Really Happen*, 47.
192 The Reader's Digest Association, *How Did It Really Happen*, 48.
193 Malkowski, *Ancient Egypt 39,000 BCE*, 12, Fig. 1.3.
194 Malkowski, *Ancient Egypt 39,000 BCE*, 41.
195 The Reader's Digest Association, *How Did It Really Happen*, 48.
196 Malkowski, *Ancient Egypt 39,000 BCE*, 41.
197 Malkowski, *Ancient Egypt 39,000 BCE*, 41.
198 Robert M. Schoch, *The Great Sphinx*, accessed April 23, 2013, <http://www.robertschoch.com>.
199 <http://www.robertschoch.com>.
200 "Edgar Cayce," *Encyclopaedia Britannica* (2016), accessed March 2, 2016, <http://www.britannica.com/biography/Edgar-Cayce>.
201 "Top 10 Edgar Cayce Predictions," *in5d Esoteric Metaphysical Spiritual Database*, accessed January 14, 2016, <http://in5d.com/top-10-edgar-cayce-predictions/>.
202 <http://www.robertschoch.com>.
203 Malkowski, *Ancient Egypt 39,000 BCE*, 41.
204 <http://in5d.com/top-10-edgar-cayce-predictions/>.
205 <http://www.smithsonianmag.com/history-archaeology/gobekli-tepe.html#ixzz2TImivFwK>.
206 <http://www.smithsonianmag.com/history-archaeology/gobekli-tepe.html#ixzz2TImivFwK>.
207 Charles Mann, "Göbekli Tepe," *National Geographic Magazine* (June 2011), accessed May 4, 2013, <http://ngm.nationalgeographic.com/2011/06/gobekli-tepe/mann-text>.
208 <http://ngm.nationalgeographic.com/2011/06/gobekli-tepe/mann-text>.
209 Hugh Newman, "Megalithic Origins: Ancient connections between Göbekli

Tepe and Peru," *Graham Hancock* (March 2014), accessed January 27, 2015, <https://grahamhancock.com/newmanh2/>.
210 <http://ngm.nationalgeographic.com/2011/06/gobekli-tepe/mann-text>.
211 <http://ngm.nationalgeographic.com/2011/06/gobekli-tepe/mann-text>.
212 Daisy Carrington, "Mysterious structure found at bottom of ancient lake," *CNN* (April 19, 2013), accessed April 23, 2013, <http://www.cnn.com/2013/04/19/world/meast/israel-ancient-structure-mystery/>.
213 <http://www.smithsonianmag.com/history-archaeology/gobekli-tepe.html#ixzz2TImivFwK>.
214 <http://www.cnn.com/2013/04/19/world/meast/israel-ancient-structure-mystery/>.
215 Semir Oswmanagich, *Pyramids Around the World* (Kindle edition: The New Era Times Press, 2012), introduction.
216 <http://www.smithsonianmag.com/history-archaeology/gobekli-tepe.html#ixzz2TImivFwK>.
217 As used by *Encyclopedia* Britannica and Turkey's First Geography Congress, Anatolia means Asia Minor, or Asian part of Turkey.
218 <http://www.esd.ornl.gov/projects/qen/nerc130k.html>.
219 Dr. Robert M. Schoch, *Plasma, Solar Outbursts, and the End of the Last Ice Age* (February 2010), accessed September 2, 2013, <http://robertschoch.com/plasma.html>.
220 <http://robertschoch.com/plasma.html>.
221 <http://www.esd.ornl.gov/projects/qen/nerc130k.html>.
222 Ian M. Lange, *Ice Age Mammals of North America* (Missoula: Mountain Press Publishing, 2002), 185.
223 <http://www.esd.ornl.gov/projects/qen/nerc130k.html>.
224 <http://news.nationalgeographic.com/news/2012/03/120314-new-human-species-chinese-plos-science-red-deer-cave/>.
225 Cauvin, *The Birth of the Gods and the Origins of Agriculture*, 26.
226 Jacques Cauvin, *The Birth of the Gods and the Origins of Agriculture* (New York: Cambridge University Press, 2000), 25.
227 <http://robertschoch.com/plasma.html>.
228 *Healing Crystals, Healing Stones* (2015), accessed June 3, 2015, <http://www.healing-crystals-healing-stones.com/#!t-stones-crystals/c1exs>.
229 <http://www.healing-crystals-healing-stones.com/#!t-stones-crystals/c1exs>.
230 "Libyan Desert Glass," *tekitites.com.uk* (2011), accessed June 4, 2014, <http://www.tektites.co.uk/libyan-desert-glass.html>.
231 "Ivory Coast Tektites," *tekitites.com.uk* (2011), accessed June 6, 2014, <http://www.tektites.co.uk/ivory-coast.html>.
232 "Nanodiamond Technologies: from soot to diamonds," *Ray Techniques Ltd* (2014), accessed June 14, 2014, <http://www.nanodiamond.co.il>.
233 "The History," *The Big Hole Kimberley* (2015), accessed November 25, 2015, <http://www.thebighole.co.za/thebighole.php>.

234 Stephen Haggerty, "Mystery Diamonds: Geoscientists Investigate Rare Carbon Formation," *Bonedigger* (August 2011), accessed June 1, 2012, <http://bonedigger.lefora.com/topic/4123499/Mystery-Diamonds-Geoscientists-Investigate-Rare-Carbon-Form#.VwHEamf2aP8>.
235 <http://www.nature.com/nature/journal/v447/n7142/full/447256a.html>.
236 Firestone, West, Warwick-Smith, *Cosmic Catastrophes*, 174-175.
237 < http://bonedigger.lefora.com/topic/4123499/Mystery-Diamonds-Geoscientists-Investigate-Rare-Carbon-Form#.VwHEamf2aP8 >.
238 Rex Dalton, "Archaeology: Blast in the Past," *nature.com* (May 2007), accessed June 15, 2014, <http://www.nature.com/nature/journal/v447/n7142/full/447256a.html>.
239 <http://www.nature.com/nature/journal/v447/n7142/full/447256a.html>.
240 Plato, *Timaeus and Critias*, ed. Thomas Kjeller Johansen (New York: Penguin Books, 1977), 34-38, 148-149.
241 <http://robertschoch.com/plasma.html>.
242 The Reader's Digest Association, *How Did It Really Happen*, 92
243 Plato, *The Timaeus and Critias or Atlanticus of Plato: The Thomas Taylor Translation*, ed. Thomas Taylor (New Jersey: Princeton University Press, 1968), 100-101.
244 <http://www.sciencedirect.com/science/article/pii/S0012821X11003177>.
245 "A Massive Star Explodes," *National Geographic* (March 2007): 92.
246 "Discovery of Most Recent Supernova in Our Galaxy," NASA News release May 2008, accessed January 10, 2014, <http://www.nasa.gov/home/hqnews/2008/may/HQ_08126_Chandra_Supernova.html>.
247 Firestone, West, Warwick-Smith, *Cosmic Catastrophes*, 174-175.
248 Firestone, West, Warwick-Smith, *Cosmic Catastrophes*, 174-175.
249 Firestone, West, Warwick-Smith, *Cosmic Catastrophes*, 174-175.
250 "Supernova Explosion May Have Caused Mammoth Extinction," *American Physical Society* (September 2005), accessed September 20, 2008, <http://phys.org/news/2005-09-supernova-explosion-mammoth-extinction.html>.
251 Firestone, West, Warwick-Smith, *Cosmic Catastrophes*, 174-175.
252 Firestone, West, Warwick-Smith, *Cosmic Catastrophes*, 174-175.
253 <http://robertschoch.com/plasma.html>.
254 "Bene Ha'elohim," *Sephardic Institute* (2009), accessed December 25, 2013, <http://judaicseminar.org/bible/beresheet5.pdf>.
255 "Nephilim," *Jewish Virtual Library*, accessed May 1, 2014, <http://www.jewishvirtuallibrary.org/jsource/judaica/ejud_0002_0015_0_14693.html>.
256 Rabbi Nosson Scherman, Artscroll series/Stone Edition, *commentary-The Chumash: The Torah: Haftaros and Five Megillos with a Commentary Anthologized from the Rabbinic Writings* (Brooklyn: Mesorah Publications, ltd, 1997), 27.
257 Joseph Telushkin, *Jewish Literacy: The Most Important Things to Know About*

the Jewish Religion, Its People, and Its History (New York: William Morrow and Company, Inc., 1991), 138.
258 Salo W. Baron, et al, *Great Ages and Ideas of the Jewish People*, ed. Leo W. Schwarz (New York: Random House, Inc., 1956), 112.
259 Baron, et al, *Great Ages and Ideas of the Jewish People*, 112.
260 Baron, et al, *Great Ages and Ideas of the Jewish People*, 112.
261 J.A. Blacket, et al, "Gilgamesh and Huwawa, version A: translation," *The Electronic Text Corpus of Sumerian Literature* (1998) accessed March 24, 2013, <http://etcsl.orinst.ox.ac.uk/section1/tr1815.htm>.
262 <http://etcsl.orinst.ox.ac.uk/section1/tr1815.htm>.
263 "The Flood," *The unedited full-text of the 1906 Jewish Encyclopedia*, accessed November 8, 2015, <http://www.jewishvirtuallibrary.org/jsource/judaica/ejud_0002_0007_0_06576.html>.
264 Dalley, *Myths from Mesopotamia*, 2-5.
265 The Reader's Digest Association, *How Did It Really Happen*, 59.
266 "Has Noah's ark been found in Turkey," *Reasons You Can Trust The Bible* (July 2011), accessed November 2, 2015, <www.trustbible.com/ark.htm>.
267 Scherman, *The Chumash*, xxiii.
268 Abraham Rabinovich, "Scholars decipher oldest Bible text," *Jerusalem Post International Edition*, June 28, 1986, sec. Word for Word.
269 Rabinovich, *Jerusalem Post International Edition*, sec. Word for Word.
270 Firestone, West, Warwick-Smith, *Cosmic Catastrophes*, 174.
271 Malkowski, *Ancient Egypt 39,000 BCE*, 227-229.
272 Everett Fox, *commentary-The Five Books of Moses* (New York: Schocken Books, Inc., 1995), 34.
273 "Shem ben Noah," *Jewish Treats* (October 2011), accessed October 26, 2011, <http://www.jewishtreats.org/2011/10/shem-ben-noah.html>.
274 <http://www.jewishtreats.org/2011/10/shem-ben-noah.html>.
275 Lange, *Ice Age Mammals of North America*, 181-182.
276 "As Old As...,"*Jewish Treats* (November 2011), accessed November 22, 2013, <http://www.jewishtreats.org/2011/11/asoldas>.
277 Scherman, *The Chumash*, 25.
278 Scherman, *The Chumash*, 25.
279 <http://robertschoch.com/plasma.html>.
280 <http://www.robertschoch.com>.
281 <http://www.esd.ornl.gov/projects/qen/nerc130k.html>.
282 "Middle East Oldest Village Found in Iran," *Iran Review* (May 2009), accessed June 22, 2014, <http://www.iranreview.org/content/Documents/Middle_East_Oldest_Village_Found_in_Iran.htm>.
283 Cauvin, *The Birth of the Gods and the Origins of Agriculture*, 26.
284 Cauvin, *The Birth of the Gods and the Origins of Agriculture*, 54.
285 "Nevali Cori," *Ancient Wisdom* (April 2012), accessed March 31, 2015, <http://www.ancient-wisdom.com/turkeynevali.htm>.

286 <http://www.ancient-wisdom.com/turkeynevali.htm>.
287 Walter, *National Geographic*, 55.
288 Walter, *National Geographic*, 55.
289 Walter, *National Geographic*, 55.
290 <http://ngm.nationalgeographic.com/2011/06/gobekli-tepe/mann-text>.
291 <http://ngm.nationalgeographic.com/2011/06/gobekli-tepe/mann-text>.
292 <http://www.britannica.com/topic/Magdalenian-culture>.
293 Cauvin, *The Birth of the Gods and the Origins of Agriculture*, 54.
294 <http://www.ancient-wisdom.com/turkeynevali.htm>.
295 "Stone Age wells found in Cyprus," *BBC News* (June 2009), accessed August 14, 2010, <http://news.bbc.co.uk/2/hi/europe/8118318.stm>.
296 <http://www.esd.ornl.gov/projects/qen/nerc130k.html>.
297 Budge, *Babylonian Life and History*, 221.
298 <http://www.esd.ornl.gov/projects/qen/nerc130k.html>.
299 Budge, *Babylonian Life and History*, 221.
300 Budge, *Babylonian Life and History*, 221.
301 Yong-Xiang Li et al, "Synchronizing a sea-level jump, final Lake Agassiz drainage, and abrupt cooling 8,200 years ago," *abstract-ScienceDirect* (January 2012), accessed January 15, 2012, <http://www.sciencedirect.com/science/article/pii/S0012821X11003177>.
302 <http://www.esd.ornl.gov/projects/qen/nerc130k.html>.
303 Richard N. Frye, "History of Mesopotamia," *Encyclopaedia Britannica* (2013), accessed November 3, 2013, <http://www.britannica.com/place/Mesopotamia-historical-region-Asia#ref361170>.
304 Budge, *Babylonian Life and History*, 221; ed. Petraglia, Allchin, *The Evolution and History of Human Populations in South Asia*, 6.
305 Budge, *Babylonian Life and History*, 7.
306 <http://www.esd.ornl.gov/projects/qen/nerc130k.html>.
307 Samuel Noah Kramer, *The Sumerians: Their History, Culture, and Character* (Chicago: University of Chicago Press, 1971), 8.
308 David Wilcock, *The Source Field* (Kindle edition: Penguin, 2011), Chapter 16.
309 Wilcock, *The Source Field*, Chapter 16.
310 Budge, *Babylonian Life and History*, 210-211; About 1,600 years ago, in the fourth century CE, Hillel II created a perpetual calendar.
311 Budge, *Babylonian Life and History*, 14.
312 Russell, *History of Western Philosophy*, 24.
313 Minoan Civilization," *Minoan*, accessed November 30, 2015, <http://minoan.com/>; Russell, *History of Western Philosophy*, 24.
314 Evans Andrews, "9 Things You May Not Know About the Ancient Sumerians," *History* (December 2015), accessed December 17, 2015, <http://www.history.com/news/history-lists/9-things-you-may-not-know-about-the-ancient-sumerians>.
315 Kramer, *The Sumerians*, 328-330.

316 Kramer, *The Sumerians*, 328-330.
317 Budge, *Babylonian Life and History*, 257.
318 <http://www.smithsonianmag.com/history-archaeology/gobekli-tepe.html#ixzz2TImivFwK>.
319 Linda M. Howe, *Earthfiles Report Part 1: Mysterious 12,000-Year-Old Gobekli Tepe* (January 2013), accessed May 2, 2013, <http://www.earthfiles.com/headlines.php?category=Science>.
320 "The Indus Valley And The Genesis Of South Asian Civilization Edited By: R. A. Guisepi," *International World History Project* (2007), accessed March 22, 2014, <http://history-world.org/indus_valley.htm>.
321 <http://www.ancient-egypt.org/index.html>.
322 Andrew Kitchen, et al, "Bayesian phylogenetic analysis of Semitic languages identifies an Early Bronze Age origin of Semitic in the Near East," T*he Royal Society Publishing Proceedings B* (June 2009), accessed June 14, 2013, <http://rspb.royalsocietypublishing.org/content/276/1668/2703>.
323 Budge, *Babylonian Life and History*, 30-31.
324 <http://www.esd.ornl.gov/projects/qen/nerc130k.html>.
325 Budge, *Babylonian Life and History*, 30-31.
326 ed. Petraglia, Allchin, *The Evolution and History of Human Populations in South Asia*, 6.
327 Budge, *Babylonian Life and History*, 30-31.
328 "Why It's Called Hebrew," *Jewish Treats* (November 2011), accessed November 2, 2014, <http://www.jewishtreats.org/2011/11why-its-called-hebrew.html>.
329 Jo Marchant, "The Golden Warrior," *Smithsonian*, January-February 2017, 44.
330 <http://www.cnn.com/2013/04/19/world/meast/israel-ancient-structure-mystery/>.
331 Fox, *The Five Books of Moses*, 106.
332 "Parashat Shemot Part I," *Sephardic Institute* (2009), accessed December 25, 2013, <http://judaicseminar.org/bible/shemot1.pdf>.
333 Fox, *The Five Books of Moses*, 199.
334 <http://judaicseminar.org/bible/shemot1.pdf>.
335 <http://judaicseminar.org/bible/shemot1.pdf>.
336 <http://judaicseminar.org/bible/shemot1.pdf>.
337 "Hyksos," *Encyclopeadia Britannica* (2013), accessed December 6, 2013, <http://www.britannica.com/EBchecked/topic/279251/Hyksos#ref756992>.
338 Jacques Kinnaer, *Ancient Egypt: 2nd Intermediate Period* (June 2013), accessed December 20, 2013, <http://www.ancient-egypt.org/index.html>.
339 Nathan Ausubel, *The Book of Jewish Knowledge* (New York: Crown Publishers, Inc., 1964), 43.
340 Ausubel, *The Book of Jewish Knowledge*, 43.
341 Ausubel, *The Book of Jewish Knowledge*, 213-214.
342 <http://www.ancient-egypt.org/index.html>.

343 Jacques Kinnaer, *Ancient Egypt: 14th Dynasty* (June 2013), accessed December 20, 2013, <http://www.ancient-egypt.org/index.html>.
344 <http://www.ancient-egypt.org/index.html>.
345 <http://www.britannica.com/EBchecked/topic/279251/Hyksos#ref756992>.
346 Ausubel, *The Book of Jewish Knowledge*, 40.
347 Russell, *History of Western Philosophy*, 59; Marchant, *Smithsonian*, January-February 2017, 47-48.
348 <http://www.ancient-egypt.org/index.html>; <http://www.britannica.com/EBchecked/topic/279251/Hyksos#ref756992>.
349 Jacques Kinnaer, *Ancient Egypt: 15th Dynasty* (June 2013), accessed December 20, 2013, <http://www.ancient-egypt.org/index.html>.
350 Jacques Kinnaer, *Ancient Egypt: 17th Dynasty* (June 2013), accessed December 20, 2013, <http://www.ancient-egypt.org/index.html>.
351 <http://www.ancient-egypt.org/index.html>.
352 <http://www.britannica.com/EBchecked/topic/279251/Hyksos#ref756992>.
353 <http://www.britannica.com/EBchecked/topic/279251/Hyksos#ref756992>.
354 Jacques Kinnaer, *Ancient Egypt: New Kingdom* (June 2013), accessed November 26, 2015, <http://www.ancient-egypt.org/history/new-kingdom/index.html>.
355 <http://www.ancient-egypt.org/history/new-kingdom/index.html>.
356 Israel Finkelstein, Neil Asher Silberman, *The Bible Unearthed: Archaeology's New Vision of Ancient Israel and the Origin of Its Sacred Texts* (New York: Touchtone, 2002), 55.
357 <http://www.ancient-egypt.org/history/new-kingdom/index.html>.
358 <http://www.britannica.com/EBchecked/topic/279251/Hyksos#ref756992>.
359 "Supply List," *Jewish Treats* (February 2011), accessed February 4, 2011, <http://www.jewishtreats.org/2011/02/supply-list.html>.
360 Simon Sehama, *The Story of the Jews: Finding the Words 1000 BC–1492 AD* (New York: HarperCollins Publishers, 2014), 8-9.
361 Marchant, *Smithsonian*, January-February 2017, 47-48.
362 "Just A Half Shekel," *Jewish Treats* (February 2014), accessed February 14, 2014, http://www.jewishtreats.org/2014/02/just-half-shekel.html>.
363 <http://www.jewishtreats.org/2011/02/supply-list.html>.
364 <http://www.jewishtreats.org/2011/02/supply-list.html>.
365 "The Divine Dwelling," *Jewish Treats* (February 2009), accessed February 26, 2009, <http://www.jewishtreats.org/2009/02/divine-dwelling.html>.
366 <http://www.ancient-egypt.org/history/new-kingdom/index.html>.
367 "The Flags of the Tribes," *Jewish Treats* (June 2011), accessed June 14, 2011, <http://www.jewishtreats.org/2011/06/flags-of-tribes.html>.

368 "Rueben," *Jewish Virtual Library*, accessed January 12, 2014, <https://www.jewishvirtuallibrary.org/jsource/judaica/ejud_0002_0017_0_16668.html>.
369 <http://www.jewishtreats.org/2011/06/flags-of-tribes.html>.
370 <http://www.jewishtreats.org/2011/06/flags-of-tribes.html>.
371 <http://www.jewishtreats.org/2011/06/flags-of-tribes.html>.
372 Max I. Dimont, *Jews, God and History* (New York: Signet Books, 1962), 49.
373 <https://www.jewishvirtuallibrary.org/jsource/judaica/ejud_0002_0017_0_16668.html>.
374 "Joshua ben Nun," *Jewish Virtual Library*, accessed January 12, 2014, <https://www.jewishvirtuallibrary.org/jsource/biography/joshua.html>.
375 <https://www.jewishvirtuallibrary.org/jsource/judaica/ejud_0002_0017_0_16668.html>.
376 <http://www.jewishtreats.org/2011/06/flags-of-tribes.html>.
377 Danny Danon, *Israel: The Will to Prevail* (New York: Palgrave Macmillan, 2012), 108.
378 <http://www.jewishtreats.org/2011/06/flags-of-tribes.html>.
379 "The Tribe of Zebulan," *Jewish Treats* (February 2014), accessed March 14, 2014, <http://www.jewishtreats.org/2014/02/the-tribe-of-zebulun.html>.
380 "The Tribe of Dan," *Jewish Treats* (August 2013), accessed August 15, 2013, <http://www.jewishtreats.org/2013/08/the-tribe-of-dan.html>.
381 The story of the Danites acquiring Laish (or Leshem) is found in biblical texts Joshua 19:47 and in Judges 18:39.
382 Ausubel, *The Book of Jewish Knowledge*, 40.
383 Ishaan Tharoor, "Was Moses real?," *Washington Post* (December 10, 2014), accessed December 31, 2015, <https://www.washingtonpost.com/news/worldviews/wp/2014/12/10/was-moses-real/>.
384 <http://www.ancient-egypt.org/history/new-kingdom/index.html>.
385 Ausubel, *The Book of Jewish Knowledge*, 346.
386 Baron, et al, *Great Ages and Ideas of the Jewish People*, 30-31.
387 Amos Nura, Eric H. Clineb, "Poseidon's Horses: Plate Tectonics and Earthquake Storms in the Late Bronze Age Aegean and Eastern Mediterranean," *Science Direct* (January 2000), accessed December 13, 2013, <http://www.sciencedirect.com/science/article/pii/S0305440399904314>.
388 <http://www.sciencedirect.com/science/article/pii/S0305440399904314>.
389 Noah Wiener, "Bronze Age Collapse: Pollen Study Highlights Late Bronze Age Drought," *Bible History Dailey* (October 2013), <http://www.biblicalarchaeology.org/daily/ancient-cultures/ancient-near-eastern-world/bronze-age-collapse-pollen-study-highlights-late-bronze-age-drought/>.
390 Robert Drews, *The End of the Bronze Age* (New Jersey: Princeton University Press, 1993), 3.
391 Drews, *The End of the Bronze Age*, 3.
392 Russell, *History of Western Philosophy*, 59.
393 Drews, *The End of the Bronze Age*, 3.
394 Cristian Violatti, "Greek Dark Age," *Ancient History Encyclopedia*

(January 2015), accessed November 27, 2015, <http://www.ancient.eu/Greek_Dark_Age/>.
395 Drews, *The End of the Bronze Age*, 3.
396 Joshua J. Mark, "Sea Peoples," *Ancient History Encyclopedia*, accessed November 26, 2015, <http://www.ancient.eu/search/?q=Sea+Peoples&sa.x=15&sa.y=10>.
397 Nasser O. Rabbat, "Damascus," *Encyclopaedia Britannica* (2015), accessed November 15, 2015, <http://www.britannica.com/place/Damascus/History>.
398 <http://www.ancient-egypt.org/history/new-kingdom/index.html>.
399 Dimont, *Jews, God and History*, 49.
400 "Ancient Jewish History: The Hebrew Monarchy," *Jewish Virtual Library*, accessed June 14, 2014, <http://www.jewishvirtuallibrary.org/jsource/History/monarchy.html>.
401 "Saul," *The unedited full-text of the 1906 Jewish Encyclopedia*, accessed March 11, 2014, <http://www.jewishencyclopedia.com/articles/13224-sault>.
402 "The Tribe of Naphtali," *Jewish Treats* (November 2013), accessed November 19, 2013, <http://www.jewishtreats.org/2013/11/the-tribe-of-naphtali.html>.
403 "Philistines," *The unedited full-text of the 1906 Jewish Encyclopedia*, accessed March 11, 2014, <http://www.jewishencyclopedia.com/articles/12107-philistines>.
404 Ausubel, *The Book of Jewish Knowledge*, 346.
405 Dimont, *Jews, God and History*, 49.
406 "The Book of Malachim I (King 1): Chapter 9," *Jewish Virtual Library*, accessed September 14, 2012, <http://www.jewishvirtuallibrary.org/jsource/Bible/Kings9.html>.
407 Ausubel, *The Book of Jewish Knowledge*, 346.
408 Ausubel, *The Book of Jewish Knowledge*, 346.
409 Ausubel, *The Book of Jewish Knowledge*, 416-417.
410 Dimont, *Jews, God and History*, 50-51.
411 Dimont, *Jews, God and History*, 50-51.
412 "The Cochin Jews of India," *Jewish Treats* (August 2012), accessed August 15, 2012, <http://www.jewishtreats.org/2012/08/the-cochin-jews-of-india.html>.
413 "Jeroboam," *Jewish Virtual Library*, accessed August 10, 2014, <https://www.jewishvirtuallibrary.org/jsource/judaica/ejud_0002_0011_0_10083.html>.
414 <https://www.jewishvirtuallibrary.org/jsource/judaica/ejud_0002_0011_0_10083.html>.
415 Dimont, *Jews, God and History*, 54-55.
416 "Omri," *Jewish Virtual Library*, accessed August 10, 2014, <https://www.jewishvirtuallibrary.org/jsource/judaica/ejud_0002_0015_0_15101.html>.
417 <https://www.jewishvirtuallibrary.org/jsource/judaica/ejud_0002_0015_0_15101.html>.

418 "Ahab," *Jewish Virtual Library*, accessed August 14, 2013, <https://www.jewishvirtuallibrary.org/jsource/biography/Ahab.html>.
419 <https://www.jewishvirtuallibrary.org/jsource/biography/Ahab.html>.
420 Dimont, *Jews, God and History*, 54-55.
421 Ausubel, *The Book of Jewish Knowledge*, 3.
422 Dimont, *Jews, God and History*, 54-55.
423 Dimont, *Jews, God and History*, 57.
424 <http://www.jewishtreats.org/2013/11/the-tribe-of-naphtali.html>.
425 "Assyrian Exile," *Jewish Virtual Library*, accessed June 4, 2011, <https://www.jewishvirtuallibrary.org/.../ejud_0002_0006_0_06182.html>.
426 Jon Entine, "Israeli Researcher Challenges Jewish DNA links to Israel, Calls Those Who Disagree Nazi Sympathizers," *Forbes* (May 16, 2013), <http://www.forbes.com/sites/jonentine/2013/05/16/israeli-researcher-challenges-jewish-dna-links-to-israel-calls-those-who-disagree-nazi-sympathizers/>.
427 "The Bnei Menashe of India," *Jewish Treats* (August 2013), accessed August 14, 2013, <http://www.jewishtreats.org/2013/08/the-bnei-menashe-of-india.html>.
428 Dimont, *Jews, God and History*, 57.
429 "What's in the Book: Kings II (Part 2)," *Jewish Treats* (June 2010), accessed June 10, 2010, <http://www.jewishtreats.org/2010/06/whats-in-book-kings-ii-part-2_10.html>.
430 Dimont, *Jews, God and History*, 59.
431 "Babylonia," *Jewish Virtual Library*, accessed December 2, 2013, <http://www.jewishvirtuallibrary.org/jsource/judaica/ejud_0002_0003_0_01807.html>.
432 <http://www.jewishtreats.org/2012/08/the-cochin-jews-of-india.html>.
433 Sehama, *The Story of the Jews*, 8-9.
434 Eva Hoffman, *Shtetl: The Life and Death of a Small Town and the World of Polish Jews* (New York: Houghton Mifflin Company, 1997), 28.
435 "Book of Ezra," *The unedited full-text of the 1906 Jewish Encyclopedia*, accessed November 3, 2012, <http://www.jewishencyclopedia.com/articles/5968-ezra-book-of#anchor5>.
436 <http://www.jewishencyclopedia.com/articles/5968-ezra-book-of#anchor5>.
437 <http://www.jewishencyclopedia.com/articles/5968-ezra-book-of#anchor5>.
438 "Tu B'Av and the Offering of Wood," *Jewish Treats* (August 2012), accessed August 3, 2012, <http://www.jewishtreats.org/2012/08/tu-bav-and-offering-of-wood.html>.
439 <http://www.jewishtreats.org/2012/08/tu-bav-and-offering-of-wood.html>.
440 Russell, *History of Western Philosophy*, 331.
441 "The Sadducees," *Jewish Treats* (January 2010), accessed January 14, 2010, <http://www.jewishtreats.org/2010/01/sadducees.html>.

442 David C. Young, "Olympic Games," *Encyclopaedia Britannica* (2015), accessed November 5, 2015, <http://www.britannica.com/sports/Olympic-Games>.
443 Donald L. Wasson, "Philip II of Macedon," *Ancient History Encyclopedia* (August 2014), accessed November 5, 2015, <http://www.ancient.eu/search/?q=Philip+II&sa.x=23&sa.y=19>.
444 <http://www.ancient.eu/search/?q=Philip+II&sa.x=23&sa.y=19>.
445 Sehama, *The Story of the Jews*, 8-9.
446 "Alexander the Great," *International World History Project* (2007), accessed March 22, 2014, <http://history-world.org/alexander_the_great1.htm>.
447 "Chanukah and Divine Order," *Jewish Treats* (December 2015), accessed December 8, 2015, <http://www.jewishtreats.org/2015/12/chanukah-and-divine-order.html>.
448 Dimont, *Jews, God and History*, 79.
449 Dimont, *Jews, God and History*, 111, 114.
450 Dimont, *Jews, God and History*, 86.
451 "Ancient Jewish Cities & Regions: Idumea/Edom," *Jewish Virtual Library*, accessed August 14, 2013, <http://www.jewishvirtuallibrary.org/jsource/Society_&_Culture/geo/edom.html>.
452 "Yannai (Janneaus) Alexander," *Jewish Virtual Library*, accessed February 2, 2014, <https://www.jewishvirtuallibrary.org/jsource/judaica/ejud_0002_0021_0_21193.html>.
453 Nissan Mindel, "Queen Salone Alexandra," *Chabad.ORG*, accessed December 4, 2015, <http://www.chabad.org/library/article_cdo/aid/112049/jewish/Queen-Salome-Alexandra.htm>.
454 Rabbi Joseph Telushkin, *Jewish Literacy*, revised (New York: HarperCollins 2008), 114-115.
455 Telushkin, *Jewish Literacy*, revised, 114-115.
456 Simcha Jacobovici, "Time to Fight the Jew Haters," *Times of Israel* (June 2015), accessed June 2, 2015, <http://www.timesofisrael.com/author/simcha-jacobovici/>.
457 "Mourning Jerusalem II: A Brief History of the Second Temple," *Jewish Treats* (July 2012), accessed July 26, 2012, <http://www.jewishtreats.org/2012/07/mourning-jerusalem-ii-brief-history-of.html>.
458 Kevin MacDonald, *Separation and its Discontents: Toward an Evolutionary Theory of Anti-Semitism* (Westport: Praeger Publishers, 1998), 89.
459 Dimont, *Jews, God and History*, 111, 114.
460 "Herod," *Jewish Virtual Library*, accessed July 13, 2012, <https://www.jewishvirtuallibrary.org/jsource/biography/Herod.html>.
461 <http://www.jewishtreats.org/2012/07/mourning-jerusalem-ii-brief-history-of.html>.
462 "Han Dynasty," *Encyclopaedia Britannica*, accessed January 20, 2015, <http://www.britannica.com/topic/Han-dynasty>.
463 Ausubel, *The Book of Jewish Knowledge*, 215-216.
464 Ausubel, *The Book of Jewish Knowledge*, 215-216.

465 "Palestine, Jewish origins, and the Eastern Jews," *Society for Nordish Physical Anthropology* (July 2006), accessed September 28, 2014, <http://www.theapricity.com/snpa/index2.htm>.
466 "Archaeology in Israel: Crusader Fortress of Tiberias, *Jewish Virtual Library*, accessed April 24, 2014, <http://www.jewishvirtuallibrary.org/jsource/Archaeology/fortress_tiberias.html>.
467 Telushkin, *Jewish Literacy*, revised, 131.
468 <timesofisrael.com/author/simcha-jacobovici/>.
469 <http://www.jewishtreats.org/2012/07/mourning-jerusalem-ii-brief-history-of.html>.
470 Telushkin, *Jewish Literacy*, revised, 131-132.
471 Dimont, *Jews, God and History*, 76.
472 Anthony Everitt, *Hadrian and the Triumph of Rome* (New York: Random House, 2009), preface xi.
473 "Ancient Jewish History: the Bar-Kokhba Revolt," *Jewish virtual Library*, accessed January 31, 2015, <https://www.jewishvirtuallibrary.org/jsource/Judaism/revolt1.html>.
474 "The Second Uprising," *Jewish Treats* (July 22, 2015), accessed July 23, 2015, <http://www.jewishtreats.org/2015/07/the-second-uprising.html>.
475 <http://www.jewishtreats.org/2015/07/the-second-uprising.html>.
476 <https://www.jewishvirtuallibrary.org/jsource/Judaism/revolt1.html>.
477 <https://www.jewishvirtuallibrary.org/jsource/Judaism/revolt1.html>.
478 <https://www.jewishvirtuallibrary.org/jsource/Judaism/revolt1.html>.
479 Ausubel, *The Book of Jewish Knowledge*, 215-216.
480 Dimont, *Jews, God and History*, 184.
481 Dimont, *Jews, God and History*, 123.
482 Dimont, *Jews, God and History*, 76, 113.
483 Richard Gottheil, Hermann Vogelstein, "Constantine I (Flavius Valerius Aurelius Constantinus)," *The unedited full-text of the 1906 Jewish Encyclopedia*, accessed November 20, 2014, <http://www.jewishencyclopedia.com/articles/4620-constantine-i-flavius-valerius-aurelius-constantinus>.
484 Stewart Henry Perowne, "Julian, Roman Emperor," *Encyclopaedia Britannica*, accessed November 3, 2015, <http://www.britannica.com/biography/Julian-Roman-emperor>.
485 <http://www.britannica.com/biography/Julian-Roman-emperor>.
486 MacDonald, *Separation and its Discontents*, 89.
487 "Eudocia: Byzantine Empress," *Encyclopaedia Britannica*, accessed June 28, 2013, <http://www.britannica.com/biography/Eudocia>.
488 Will Wyeth, "Emperor Justinian I," *Jewish Encyclopedia*, accessed June 28, 2013, <http://www.ancient.eu/Justinian_I/>.
489 Dimont, *Jews, God and History*, 184.
490 Dimont, *Jews, God and History*, 208-209.
491 Dimont, *Jews, God and History*, 158.

492 Dimont, *Jews, God and History*, 394.
493 Mary Rowlatt, "Alexandria," *Encyclopaedia Britannica* (June 3, 2014), accessed July 18, 2015, <http://www.britannica.com/place/Alexandria-Egypt>.
494 Dimont, *Jews, God and History*, 394.
495 "Fatimids," *Jewish Virtual Library*, accessed June 2, 2014, <https://www.jewishvirtuallibrary.org/jsource/judaica/ejud_0002_0006_0_06300.html>.
496 "Ancient Jewish History: The Khazars," *Jewish Virtual Library*, accessed October 19, 2014, <https://www.jewishvirtuallibrary.org/jsource/Judaism/khazars.html>.
497 "Ashkenaz," *Jewish Virtual Library*, accessed June 3, 2014, <http://www.jewishvirtuallibrary.org/jsource/judaica/ejud_0002_0002_0_01461.html>.
498 "China," *Jewish Virtual Library*, accessed August 12, 2013, <http://www.jewishvirtuallibrary.org/jsource/vjw/chinajews.html#d>.
499 Telushkin, *Jewish Literacy*, 172-173.
500 Hoffman, *Shtetl*, 29.
501 <https://www.jewishvirtuallibrary.org/jsource/judaica/ejud_0002_0006_0_06300.html>.
502 Hoffman, *Shtetl*, 28.
503 <https://www.jewishvirtuallibrary.org/jsource/judaica/ejud_0002_0006_0_06300.html>.
504 David Attenborough, *The First Eden: The Mediterranean World and Man* (Boston: Little, Brown and Company, 1987), 148.
505 Attenborough, *The First Eden*, 151-152.
506 "Modern Jewish History: The Crusader Period," *Jewish Virtual Library*, accessed February 7, 2015, <http://www.jewishvirtuallibrary.org/jsource/History/Crusader.html>.
507 <http://www.jewishtreats.org/2012/08/the-cochin-jews-of-india.html>.
508 Ephraim Z. Buchwald, "Accepting the Inscrutable," *NJOP* (June 2015), accessed June 22, 2015, <http://rabbibuchwald.njop.org/category/numbers/chukat/>.
509 <http://rabbibuchwald.njop.org/category/numbers/chukat/>.
510 Jacob R. Marcus, *The Jew in the Medieval World* (New York: Atheneum, 1969), 24, 28.
511 Hoffman, *Shtetl*, 30.
512 Telushkin, *Jewish Literacy*, revised, 193.
513 Telushkin, *Jewish Literacy*, revised, 193.
514 "Kublai Khan Biography," *Biography.com* (2014), accessed December 2, 2014, <http://www.biography.com/people/kublai-khan-9369657>.
515 Ausubel, *The Book of Jewish Knowledge*, 219.
516 Hoffman, *Shtetl*, 35.
517 Isidore Singer, M. Franco, "Theodora," *The unedited full-text of the 1906 Jewish Encyclopedia*, accessed October 18, 2012, <http://jewishencyclopedia.com/articles/14358-theodora>.
518 Ole J. Benedictow, "The Black Death: The Greatest Catastrophe Ever,"

History Today (March 2005), accessed January 8, 2015, <http://www.historytoday.com/ole-j-benedictow/black-death-greatest-catastrophe-ever>.
519 Marcus, *The Jew in the Medieval World*, 47.
520 <http://jewishencyclopedia.com/articles/14358-theodora>.
521 Hoffman, *Shtetl*, 35.
522 <http://www.historytoday.com/ole-j-benedictow/black-death-greatest-catastrophe-ever>.
523 Dimont, *Jews, God and History*, 394-395.
524 Hoffman, *Shtetl*, 39.
525 Anatole Andro, *The 1421 Heresy* (Bloomingdale: Author House, 2005), Kindle chapter: Seven voyages to the Western Ocean.
526 Andro, *The 1421 Heresy*, Kindle chapter: Seven voyages to the Western Ocean.
527 "The End of the Inquisition," *Jewish Treats* (July 2015), accessed July 15, 2015, <http://www.jewishtreats.org/2015/07/the-end-of-inquisition.html>.
528 Dimont, *Jews, God and History*, 208-209.
529 Dimont, *Jews, God and History*, 208-209.
530 "If You Thought the Spanish Expulsion Was Bad...," *Jewish Treats* (January 2012), accessed January 17, 2012, <http://www.jewishtreats.org/2012/01/if-you-thought-spanish-expulsion-was.html>.
531 <http://www.jewishtreats.org/2012/01/if-you-thought-spanish-expulsion-was.html>.
532 <http://www.jewishtreats.org/2012/01/if-you-thought-spanish-expulsion-was.html>.
533 <http://www.jewishtreats.org/2012/08/the-cochin-jews-of-india.html>.
534 "Historical Earthquakes in China," *Disaster Pages of George Pararas-Carayannis* (March 2013), accessed June 24, 2015, <http://www.drgeorgepc.com/EarthquakesChina.html>.
535 Dimont, *Jews, God and History*, 394-395.
536 http://www.jewishvirtuallibrary.org/jsource/Archaeology/fortress_tiberias.html>.
537 Ausubel, *The Book of Jewish Knowledge*, 343.
538 Hoffman, *Shtetl*, 57.
539 Hoffman, *Shtetl*, 28.
540 Ausubel, *The Book of Jewish Knowledge*, 343.
541 The Reader's Digest Association, *How Did It Really Happen*, 93.
542 "A Ship's Tale," *Jewish Treats* (September 2012), accessed September 17, 2012, <http://www.jewishtreats.org/2012/09/a-ships-tale.html>.
543 "Prussia," *Encyclopaedia Britannica*, accessed July 17, 2014, <http://www.britannica.com/place/Prussia>.
544 <http://www.jewishtreats.org/2015/07/the-end-of-inquisition.html>.
545 "The French and Indian War," *US history.org* (2015), accessed December 4, 2015, <http://www.ushistory.org/declaration/related/frin.htm>.

546 "The Indigo Guy of South Carolina," *Jewish Treats* (May 2014), accessed May 23, 2014, <http://www.jewishtreats.org/2014/05/the-indigo-guy-of-south-carolina.html>.
547 <http://www.ushistory.org/declaration/related/frin.htm>.
548 <http://www.ushistory.org/declaration/related/frin.htm>.
549 <http://www.jewishtreats.org/2014/05/the-indigo-guy-of-south-carolina.html>.
550 <http://www.jewishtreats.org/2012/09/a-ships-tale.html>.
551 "Louisiana Purchase," *History* (2016), accessed January 23, 2016, <http://www.history.com/topics/louisiana-purchase>.
552 "A Constitutional Congregation," *Jewish Treats* (May 2014), accessed May 14, 2014, <http://www.jewishtreats.org/2014/05/a-constitutional-congregation.html>.
553 "Timeline of the Revolutionary War," *US history.org* (2015), accessed December 23, 2015, <http://www.ushistory.org/declaration/revwartimeline.htm>.
554 Hoffman, *Shtetl*, 61.
555 Hoffman, *Shtetl*, 70.
556 "The Pale of Settlement," *Jewish Virtual Library*," accessed December 8, 2015, <http://www.jewishvirtuallibrary.org/jsource/History/pale.html>.
557 Herman Rosenthal, "Pale of Settlement," *The unedited full-text of the 1906 Jewish Encyclopedia*, accessed March 11, 2014, <http://jewishencyclopedia.com/articles/11862-pale-of-settlement>.
558 "Napoleon Bonaparte," *Jewish Virtual Library*, accessed April 25, 2014, <https://www.jewishvirtuallibrary.org/jsource/biography/napoleon.html>.
559 <http://www.history.com/topics/louisiana-purchase>.
560 "Napoleon Bonaparte I," *Encyclopaedia Britannica* (2015), accessed May 12, 2015, <http://www.britannica.com/biography/Napoleon-I>.
561 <https://www.jewishvirtuallibrary.org/jsource/biography/napoleon.html>.
562 Pogroms took place in Russia from 1821 through 1906, in newly independent Ukraine in 1920, and British-backed Pogroms occurred from 1920-1939 in Israel during British occupation. A Pogrom is state-sponsored, a pogrom is a civilian (nongovernmental sanctioned) act of extreme violence against a minority ethnic or religious group. Use of the world genocide began in 1944.
563 Telushkin, *Jewish Literacy*, 172-173.
564 Ausubel, *The Book of Jewish Knowledge*, 344.
565 Ausubel, *The Book of Jewish Knowledge*, 344.
566 Baron, et al, *Great Ages and Ideas of the Jewish People*, 332.
567 Baron, et al, *Great Ages and Ideas of the Jewish People*, 332.
568 Baron, et al, *Great Ages and Ideas of the Jewish People*, 427.
569 <http://www.jewishtreats.org/2015/07/the-end-of-inquisition.html>.
570 Baron, et al, *Great Ages and Ideas of the Jewish People*, 437.

571 "Irish Potato Famine," *The History Place* (2000), accessed November 1, 2015, <http://www.historyplace.com/worldhistory/famine/america.htm>.

572 "The Jews' Hospital of New York," *Jewish Treats* (May 2013), accessed June 11, 2013, <http://www.jewishtreats.org/2013/05/the-jews-hospital-of-new-york.html>.

573 "Taiping Rebellion," *Encyclopaedia Britannica* (2014), accessed April 27, 2014, <http://www.britannica.com/event/Taiping-Rebellion>.

574 "Jerusalem, the Old City," *Jewish Virtual Library*, accessed July 18, 2014, <http://www.jewishvirtuallibrary.org/jsource/vie/Jerusalem2.html#Jewish>.

575 Bret Stevens, *America in Retreat* (New York: Penguin Group USA, LCC, 2014), 130-131.

576 Baron, et al, *Great Ages and Ideas of the Jewish People*, 357, 443.

577 William Seward, *William H. Seward's Travels Around the World* (New York: D. Appleton and Company, 1873), 635-645.

578 David Fromkin, *Europe's Last Summer: Who Started the Great War in 1914* (New York: Random House, Inc., 2004), 70.

579 Fromkin, *Europe's Last Summer*, 70.

580 "Immigration to Israel: The first Aliyah," *Jewish Virtual Library*, accessed November 28, 2014, <https://www.jewishvirtuallibrary.org/jsource/Immigration/First_Aliyah.html>.

581 "About World ORT," *ORT and the Displaced Person Camps* (2010), accessed September 15, 2014, <http://dpcamps.ort.org/about-us/>.

582 Ausubel, *The Book of Jewish Knowledge*, 344.

583 Ausubel, *The Book of Jewish Knowledge*, 345.

584 "Kingdom of Serbs, Croats, and Slovenes," *Encyclopaedia Britannica* (2014), assessed November 8, 2014, <http://www.britannica.com/place/Kingdom-of-Serbs-Croats-and-Slovenes>.

585 Fromkin, *Europe's Last Summer*, 5.

586 Edwin Black, "When Germany Came to Africa," *San Diego Jewish Journal* (July 2016): 50-51.

587 Black, *San Diego Jewish Journal* (July 2016): 50-51.

588 Fromkin, *Europe's Last Summer*, 57.

589 Fromkin, *Europe's Last Summer*, 5, 57.

590 Susan Zucotti, *Under His Very Windows: The Vatican and the Holocaust in Italy* (New Haven: Yale University Press, 2000), introduction.

591 Baron, et al, *Great Ages and Ideas of the Jewish People*, 440.

592 "A National Poet," *Jewish Treats* (January 2014), accessed January 9, 2014, <http://www.jewishtreats.org/2014/01/a-national-poet.html>.

593 Telushkin, *Jewish Literacy*, 249.

594 Baron, et al, *Great Ages and Ideas of the Jewish People*, 441.

595 Shmuel Katz, *The Aaronsohn Saga* (New York: Gefen Books, 2007), 7, 9.

596 Ronald Florence, *Lawrence and Aaronsohn* (New York: Penguin Group USA Inc., 2008), 29.

597 Katz, *The Aaronsohn Saga*, 7, 9.
598 Ausubel, *The Book of Jewish Knowledge*, 536.
599 Danon, *Israel*, 157.
600 Florence, *Lawrence and Aaronsohn*, 6.
601 Ausubel, *The Book of Jewish Knowledge*, 534-535.
602 Florence, *Lawrence and Aaronsohn*, 29.
603 "American Jewish Organizations: Joint Distribution Committee (JDC)," *Jewish Virtual Library*, accessed March 3, 2015, <http://www.jewishvirtuallibrary.org/jsource/Orgs/jdc.html>; The JDC (Joint Distribution Committee) continued its vital work after the close of WWI. JDC helped Jews fleeing the Nazis before and during WWII, and provided aid to Jews in Displaced Persons camps after the war ended. For over 100 years the organization has given aid to Jews all over the world in times of crisis. JDC expanded after WWII to provide humanitarian aid to victims of global disasters.
604 Florence, *Lawrence and Aaronsohn*, 29.
605 Katz, *The Aaronsohn Saga*, 335, 337.
606 David Fromkin, *A Peace to End All Peace: the Fall of the Ottoman Empire and the Creation of the Modern Middle East* (New York: Henry Holt and Company, LLC, 2009), 136.
607 Florence, *Lawrence and Aaronsohn*, 29.
608 Katz, *The Aaronsohn Saga*, 337.
609 Katz, *The Aaronsohn Saga*, 340.
610 Samuel Katz, *Battleground: Fact and Fantasy in Palestine* (New York: Bantam Books, 2002), 64-65.
611 Yehuda Lapidot, "The Establishment of the Irgun," *Jewish Virtual Library* (2000), accessed October 7, 2014, <http://www.jewishvirtuallibrary.org/jsource/History/irgun1.html>.
612 "The Haganah," *Jewish Virtual Library* (2000), accessed October 7, 2014, <http://www.jewishvirtuallibrary.org/jsource/History/haganah.html>.
613 Jacqueline Shields, "Arab Riots of the 1920's," *Jewish Virtual Library* (2008), accessed October 7, 2014, <http://www.jewishvirtuallibrary.org/jsource/History/riots29.html>.
614 Telushkin, *Jewish Literacy*, 247.
615 Danon, *Israel*, 158-159.
616 Fromkin, *A Peace to End All Peace*, 267.
617 Fritz Fisher, *Germany's Aims in the First World War* (New York: W. W. Norton & Company, Inc., 1968), introduction.
618 Fisher, *Germany's Aims in the First World War*, introduction.
619 "The Holocaust: The Mufti and the Fuhrer," *Jewish Virtual Library*, accessed October 7, 2014, <http://www.jewishvirtuallibrary.org/jsource/History/muftihit.html>.
620 "Ex-Mufti, Criminal Ally: State Dept. Conceals Promised White," *Children of Jewish Holocaust Survivors* (New York Post February 23, 1948) by Observer, accessed December 8, 2014, <http://cjhsla.org/2014/12/08/

ex-mufti-criminal-ally-state-dept-conceals-promised-white-new-york-post-monday-feb-23-1948-by-observer/#sthash.qg4mL2az.dpuf>.

621 Katz, *Battleground*, 72.
622 Danon, *Israel*, 162-163.
623 David Horowitz, *Why Israel is the Victim* (Sherman Oaks: David Horowitz Freedom Center, 2013), 22.
624 Baron, et al, *Great Ages and Ideas of the Jewish People*, 449.
625 Benjamin Netanyahu, *A Durable Peace: Israel and Its Place Among the Nations* (New York: Warner Books, 2000), 449.
626 Hoffman, *Shtetl*, 157.
627 Telushkin, *Jewish Literacy*, 247.
628 "Pre-State Israel: The 1936 Arab Riots," *Jewish Virtual Library*, accessed December 1, 2013, <http://www.jewishvirtuallibrary.org/jsource/History/riots36.html>.
629 Telushkin, *Jewish Literacy*, 285.
630 Fisher, *Germany's Aims in the First World War*, introduction.
631 "Holocaust Studies: Historical Background: Rise of Hitler," *Aish* (December 1969), accessed October 7, 2014, <http://www.aish.com/ho/o/48971576.html>.
632 "About Bank of International Settlements," *Bank for International Settlements* (June 2015), accessed July 23, 2015, <http://www.bis.org/about/>.
633 <http://www.aish.com/ho/o/48971576.html>.
634 Peter Levenda, *The Hitler Legacy: The Nazi Cult in Diaspora: How it was Organized, How it was Funded, and Why it Remains a Threat to Global Security in the Age of Terrorism* (Lake Worth: Ibis Press, 2014), 32.
635 Levenda, *The Hitler Legacy*, 32.
636 Diana West, *American Betrayal* (New York: St. Martin's Press, 2013), 94, 97.
637 West, *American Betrayal*, 193.
638 West, *American Betrayal*, 94.
639 <http://www.aish.com/ho/timeline/Timeline-of-the-Holocaust.html>.
640 "The Holocaust: Timeline of Jewish Persecution," *Jewish Virtual Library*, accessed October 9, 2014, <http://www.jewishvirtuallibrary.org/jsource/Holocaust/chron.html>.
641 Janet Levy, "Op-Ed: The Vatican Against Israel: Review of New Meotti Book," *Israel National News* (July 2014), accessed July 10, 2014, <http://www.israelnationalnews.com/Articles/Article.aspx/14158#.U_Y9XmdATIW>.
642 Baron, et al, *Great Ages and Ideas of the Jewish People*, 449.
643 "Celtic Tribes in Switzerland," *History of Switzerland* (2004), accessed February 27, 2014, <http://history-switzerland.geschichte-schweiz.ch/history-celtic-helvetians-switzerland.html>.
644 The Nazi elite apparently took seriously the Adolf Hitler as the new Messiah component of their revised version of Christianity because Michael Phayer records an entry in the diary of Joseph Goebbels in his book, *The Catholic*

Church and the Holocaust: 1930-1965 (Chapter 7, endnote 1) wondering if Hitler's true identity was the Messiah or John the Baptist.

645 Baron, et al, Roth, *Great Ages and Ideas of the Jewish People*, 449; Joe Sharkey, "Word for Word/The Case Against the Nazis; How Hitler's Forces Planned To Destroy German Christianity," *New York Times* (January 2002), accessed June 2, 2014, <http://www.nytimes.com/2002/01/13/weekinreview/word-for-word-case-against-nazis-hitler-s-forces-planned-destroy-german.html>; <http://www.jewishvirtuallibrary.org/jsource/Holocaust/chron.html>.

646 Telushkin, *Jewish Literacy*, revised, 385.

647 <http://www.jewishvirtuallibrary.org/jsource/Holocaust/chron.html>.

648 Katz, *Battleground*, 71.

649 <http://www.jewishvirtuallibrary.org/jsource/History/riots36.html>.

650 Israel's four holiest cities are Jerusalem, Hebron, Safed, and Tiberias.

651 Telushkin, *Jewish Literacy*, 285.

652 <http://www.jewishvirtuallibrary.org/jsource/History/riots36.html>.

653 <http://www.jewishvirtuallibrary.org/jsource/History/riots36.html>.

654 Kitty Werthmann, "How a democracy beset by creeping socialism became Nazi Germany," <http://clashdaily.com/2013/03/85yr-old-austrian-lived-under-hitler-says-were-screwed/#ixzz2QfK7bb1s> (Viewed at American Freedom Alliance conference on The Globalization of California, Los Angeles, California, June 2014), <http//www.youtube.com/watch?v=baApAqBk82Q>.

655 <http://clashdaily.com/2013/03/85yr-old-austrian-lived-under-hitler-says-were-screwed/#ixzz2QfK7bb1s>.

656 "DP Camps in Austria," *ORT and the Displaced Person Camps* (2010), accessed September 15, 2014, <http://dpcamps.ort.org/dp-camps/austria/dp-camps-in-austria/>.

657 Katz, *Battleground*, 77-75.

658 Ausubel, *The Book of Jewish Knowledge*, 538.

659 "Milestones," *Saudi Aramco* (2016), accessed January 20, 2016, <http://www.saudiaramco.com/en/home/about/history/milestones/1930s.html>.

660 <http://www.aish.com/ho/timeline/Timeline-of-the-Holocaust.html>.

661 Scott Thompson, "The Nazi Roots of the House of Windsor," *American Almanac*, August 25, 1997, from The New Federalist Newspaper, accessed November 5, 2003, <http://members.tripod.com/~american_almanac/naziroots.htm>.

662 Katz, *Battleground*, 213.

663 <http://www.aish.com/ho/timeline/Timeline-of-the-Holocaust.html>.

664 Golabek, Cohen, *The Children of Willesden Lane*, 16-17, 24.

665 <http://www.aish.com/ho/timeline/Timeline-of-the-Holocaust.html>.

666 <http://www.aish.com/ho/timeline/Timeline-of-the-Holocaust.html>; There are many individuals, Jewish and non-Jewish, who were heroic in their efforts to save European Jewry in the wake of Nazi mass murder and

terrorism before, during, and after WWII until the establishment of modern Israel.
667 <http://www.aish.com/ho/timeline/Timeline-of-the-Holocaust.html>.
668 <http://www.aish.com/ho/timeline/Timeline-of-the-Holocaust.html>.
669 Rafael Medoff, "Who Shut America's Doors To Jewish Refugees?," *Children of Jewish Holocaust Survivors New Holocaust Resistance* (October 2014), accessed October 5, 2014, <http://www.cjhsla.org/2014/10/03/who-shut-americas-doors-to-jewish-refugees-by-rafael-medoff-part-1- medoff-?utm_source=wysija&utm_medium=email&utm_campaign=Whitewashing+FDR#sthash.JgQnZYNc.dpuf>.
670 <http://www.aish.com/ho/timeline/Timeline-of-the-Holocaust.html>.
671 Telushkin, *Jewish Literacy*, revised, 392-393.
672 <http://www.aish.com/ho/timeline/Timeline-of-the-Holocaust.html>; Levenda, *The Hitler Legacy*, 14.
673 Katz, *Battleground*, 74-75.
674 <http://www.aish.com/ho/timeline/Timeline-of-the-Holocaust.html>.
675 Eli E. Hertz, *This Land is My Land* (New York: Myths and Facts, Inc., 2008), Kindle edition, chapter 5.
676 Hoffman, *Shtetl*, 200.
677 Hoffman, *Shtetl*, 213.
678 Gitta Sereny, "Stolen Children," *Jewish Virtual Library*, accessed January 5, 2011, <http://www.jewishvirtuallibrary.org./jsource/Holocaust/children.html>.
679 Hoffman, *Shtetl*, 189.
680 David Faber, *Because of Romek: A Holocaust Survivor's Memoir* (La Mesa: Faber Press, 2006), 203-204.
681 "Great Britain & the Holocaust: The Kindertransport," *Jewish Virtual Library*, accessed October 8, 2014, <http://www.jewishvirtuallibrary.org/jsource/Holocaust/kinder.html>.
682 Norman Berdichevsky, "The Legacy of the Three International Brigades," *Outpost* (June 2015), accessed May 29, 2015, <http://afsi.org/Outpost/2015/Outpost_2015_06.pdf>.
683 "The Jews of Finland," *Jewish Treats* (December 2011), accessed December 6, 2011, <http://www.jewishtreats.org/2011/12/jews-of-finland.html>.
684 "Today in Jewish History: Tishrei 11," *Aish*, accessed October 5, 2014, <http://www.aish.com/dijh/Tishrei_11.html>.
685 <http://www.aish.com/ho/timeline/Timeline-of-the-Holocaust.html>.
686 Michael Phayer, *The Catholic Church and the Holocaust: 1930-1965* (Bloomingdale: Indiana University Press, 2000), 41.
687 <http://www.jewishvirtuallibrary.org./jsource/Holocaust/children.html>.
688 West, *American Betrayal*, 258.
689 Hertz, *This Land is My Land*, chapter 5.
690 <http://www.jewishvirtuallibrary.org/jsource/History/muftihit.html>.
691 <http://www.jewishvirtuallibrary.org/jsource/History/muftihit.html>.

692 <http://cjhsla.org/2014/12/08/ex-mufti-criminal-ally-state-dept-conceals-promised-white-new-york-post-monday-feb-23-1948-by-observer/#sthash.qg4mL2az.dpuf>.
693 <http://members.tripod.com/~american_almanac/naziroots.htm>.
694 <http://dpcamps.ort.org/dp-camps/austria/dp-camps-in-austria/>.
695 Mona Golabek, Lee Cohen, *The Children of Willesden Lane* (New York: Grand Central Publishing, 2003), 6.
696 <http://dpcamps.ort.org/dp-camps/austria/dp-camps-in-austria/>.
697 David Kopel, *Armed Resistance to the Holocaust*, Journal on Firearms and Public Policy (2007), Volume Nineteen, 149-150.
698 "Holocaust Maps: Ghettos & Concentration Camps," *Jewish Virtual Library*, accessed November 3, 2014, <https://www.jewishvirtuallibrary.org/jsource/Holocaust/ccmaptoc.html>; <http://www.israelnationalnews.com/Articles/Article.aspx/14158#.U_Y9XmdATIW>.
699 <http://cjhsla.org/2014/12/08/ex-mufti-criminal-ally-state-dept-conceals-promised-white-new-york-post-monday-feb-23-1948-by-observer/#sthash.qg4mL2az.dpuf>; Until historians and scholars are permitted full access to the Vatican archives on the Shoah/Holocaust, the Vatican's actions during the Jewish (and Catholic) massacres before and during WWII remain incomplete.
700 Rafael Mendoff, "Exposing Auschwitz," *Aish* (2009), accessed October 5, 2014, <http://www.aish.com/ho/i/48967096.html>.
701 Faber, *Because of Romek*, 132.
702 Telushkin, *Jewish Literacy*, revised, pg 394, 354-335; <http://www.aish.com/ho/i/48967096.html>; Faber, *Because of Romek*, 134.
703 <http://www.aish.com/ho/timeline/Timeline-of-the-Holocaust.html>.
704 Danon, *Israel*, 196.
705 <http://www.jewishtreats.org/2011/12/jews-of-finland.html>.
706 Telushkin, *Jewish Literacy*, 288.
707 Faber, *Because of Romek*, 208.
708 Faber, *Because of Romek*, 208.
709 "Auschwitz-Birkenau: Living Conditions, Labor & Executions," *Jewish Virtual Library*, accessed September 1, 2013, <http://www.jewishvirtuallibrary.org/jsource/Holocaust/auconditions.html>.
710 <http://www.aish.com/ho/timeline/Timeline-of-the-Holocaust.html>.
711 <https://www.jewishvirtuallibrary.org/jsource/Holocaust/ccmaptoc.html>.
712 <http://cjhsla.org/2014/12/08/ex-mufti-criminal-ally-state-dept-conceals-promised-white-new-york-post-monday-feb-23-1948-by-observer/#sthash.qg4mL2az.dpuf>; <http://www.jewishvirtuallibrary.org/jsource/History/muftihit.html>.
713 Telushkin, *Jewish Literacy*, revised, 303-304.
714 Levenda, *The Hitler Legacy*, 14.

715 Levenda, *The Hitler Legacy*, 14.
716 "The SS (Schutzstaffel): Organization of Former SS Members (ODESSA), *Jewish Virtual Library*, accessed July 22, 2015, <http://www.jewishvirtuallibrary.org/jsource/Holocaust/odessa.html>.
717 Julian J. Landau, *Israel and the Arabs: A Handbook of Basic Information* (Tel Aviv: Israel Communications, 1971), 173.
718 Levenda, *The Hitler Legacy*, 14.
719 <http://clashdaily.com/2013/03/85yr-old-austrian-lived-under-hitler-says-were-screwed/#ixzz2QfK7bb1s>.
720 <http://clashdaily.com/2013/03/85yr-old-austrian-lived-under-hitler-says-were-screwed/#ixzz2QfK7bb1s>.
721 The Soviet occupation lasted ten years. For six weeks Russian troops prepared for their return to the Soviet Union, during which time Russian soldiers targeted Austrian women and girls. Women and girls hid in basements or secret underground rooms as long as they could. When they had to come out of hiding for food and water the Russians murdered them. A monument in Vienna is dedicated to them.
722 <http://dpcamps.ort.org/dp-camps/austria/dp-camps-in-austria/>.
723 Katz, *Battleground*, 29.
724 <http://www.jewishtreats.org/2011/12/jews-of-finland.html>.
725 Telushkin, *Jewish Literacy*, revised, 193.
726 <http://www.jewishvirtuallibrary.org/jsource/History/muftihit.html>.
727 West, *American Betrayal*, 258.
728 Hertz, *This Land is My Land,* chapter 5.
729 "Paris Peace Conference," *Encyclopaedia Britannica*, accessed October 2, 2014, <http://www.britannica.com/event/Paris-Peace-Conference>.
730 <http://clashdaily.com/2013/03/85yr-old-austrian-lived-under-hitler-says-were-screwed/#ixzz2QfK7bb1s>.
731 Joshua Muravchik, *Making David into Goliath: How the World Turned Against Israel* (New York: Encounter Books, 2014), 5; Phayer, *The Catholic Church and the Holocaust*, 159.
732 Telushkin, *Jewish Literacy*, 288.
733 Telushkin, *Jewish Literacy*, 288.
734 <http://www.jewishtreats.org/2015/04/he-was-best-man-we-had.html>.
735 Baron, et al, *Great Ages and Ideas of the Jewish People*, 448.
736 Telushkin, *Jewish Literacy*, 289.
737 Telushkin, *Jewish Literacy*, 289.
738 "Israeli War of Independence: Background & Overview," *Jewish Virtual Library*, accessed March 3, 2015, <http://www.jewishvirtuallibrary.org/jsource/History/1948_War.html>.
739 Fromkin, *A Peace to End All Peace*, 267.
740 <http://www.jewishtreats.org/2015/04/he-was-best-man-we-had.html>.
741 <http://afsi.org/Outpost/2015/Outpost_2015_06.pdf>.

742 <http://www.jewishtreats.org/2015/04/he-was-best-man-we-had.html>.
743 Danon, *Israel*, 108.
744 Horowitz, *Why Israel is the Victim*, 22.
745 "He Was the Best Man We Had," *Jewish Treats* (April 2015), accessed April 23, 2015, <http://www.jewishtreats.org/2015/04/he-was-best-man-we-had.html>; "The War of Independence: Arab Armies Invade," *Jewish Virtual Library*, accessed April 18, 2013, <http://www.jewishvirtuallibrary.org/jsource/History/Invade.html>.
746 Danon, *Israel*, 107.
747 Telushkin, *Jewish Literacy*, 292.
748 <http://afsi.org/Outpost/2015/Outpost_2015_06.pdf>.
749 Horowitz, *Why Israel is the Victim*, 9-10.
750 Danon, *Israel*, 104.
751 Danon, *Israel*, 107.
752 Horowitz, *Why Israel is the Victim*, 24.
753 Lucette Lagnado, "When the Arab Jews fled," *The Wall Street Journal*, October 13, 2012, sec. Review, C3.
754 "The Exodus of the Syrian Jews," *Jewish Treats* (March 2013), accessed March 14, 2013, <http://www.jewishtreats.org/2013/03/the-exodus-of-syrian-jews.html>.
755 Horowitz, *Why Israel is the Victim*, 9; Dennis Prager, Joseph Telushkin, *Why The Jews* (New York: Touchstone, 2003), 112-113; Israel stretches 263 miles from north to south, and its width varies from 71 miles to 26 miles Including Judah and Samaria).
756 Horowitz, *Why Israel is the Victim*, 25.
757 "Bankrupting terrorism one lawsuit at a time," *Israel Law Center* (March 2016), accessed March 22, 2016, <http://www.israellawcenter.org>.
758 "ZOA Retracts its 2011 Qualified Support of Daniel Shapiro to be US Ambassador to Israel," ZOA President Morton A. Klein press release (New York, January 20, 2016), *Zionist Organization of America*, accessed January 20, 2016, <http://zoa.org/category/news/>; <http://zoa.org/category/news/>; The US State Department and successive American presidents reject moving the US Embassy to Jerusalem because, as part of a foreign policy platform, they refuse to recognize Jerusalem as part of Israel. The US government and the media began referring to eastern Jerusalem as East Jerusalem and suggesting Jerusalem may be divided sometime in the future to satisfy Palestinian demands.
759 Mark Sherman, "Jerusalem Passport Case Divides Court," *San Diego Union-Tribune*, November 4, 2014, A8.
760 Baron, et al, *Great Ages and Ideas of the Jewish People*, 443; Stevens, *America in Retreat*, 128-130.
761 Horowitz, *Why Israel is the Victim*, 4.
762 "From the Land of the Czars: Escape from the Pogroms," *Jewish Virtual Library*, accessed May 21, 2014, <https://www.jewishvirtuallibrary.org/jsource/loc/czars1.html>.

763 <http://cjhsla.org/2014/12/08/ex-mufti-criminal-ally-state-dept-conceals-promised-white-new-york-post-monday-feb-23-1948-by-observer/#sthash.qg4mL2az.dpuf, (accessed 12/8/2014)>; "Haj Amin al-Husseini and Nazi Racial Policies in the Arab World," *Children of Jewish Holocaust Survivors New Holocaust Resistance* (December 2014), accessed December 9, 2014, <http://cjhsla.org/2014/12/08/haj-amin-al-husseini-and-nazi-racial-policies-in-the-arab-world/>, see more at: <http://cjhsla.org/2014/12/08/haj-amin-al-husseini-and-nazi-racial-policies-in-the-arab-world/#sthash.lZaQBw1R.dpuf>.

764 <http://zoa.org/2014/10/10263180-zoa-condemns-u-k-parliament-recognizing-hamasfatah-terrorist-dictatorship-as-palestine/>.

765 <http://zoa.org/2014/10/10263180-zoa-condemns-u-k-parliament-recognizing-hamasfatah-terrorist-dictatorship-as-palestine/>.

766 "Documents Reveal Arafat's Person Role in Terror Campaign," *ADL archive website* (April 2002), accessed June 19, 2016, <http://archive.adl.org/israel/israel_documents.html>; Many Jews refer to the Oslo Accords as the Oslo Betrayal and to the Jews who participated in its secrecy as traitors. Crowds of angry Israelis protested the secrecy after the Accords were announced by the media. An infuriated Israeli assassinated Rabin in November, 1995 (Jewish calendar: 5756), for signing the Oslo Accords.

767 "Jerusalem Must Stay a United City," Detroit Jewish News Editorial on January 7, 2016, *Zionist Organization of America*, accessed January 12, 2016, <http://zoa.org/2016/01/10309945-detroit-jewish-news-editorial-extensively-quotes-zoas-views-on-jerusalem/>; Siddhartha Mahanta, "Israel Decidedly Unhappy With Vatican-Palestine Treaty," *FP Passport* (June 26, 2015), accessed February 1, 2016, <http://foreignpolicy.com/2015/06/26/pope-francis-israel-palestine-treaty/>.

768 Katz, *Battleground*, 32.

769 Prager, Telushkin, *Why The Jews*, 10.

770 *Children of Jewish Holocaust Survivors New Holocaust Resistance* (2014), accessed October 23, 2014, <http://www.cjhsla.org/>.

771 <http://www.cjhsla.org/>.

772 Diana West, "Blinding History," *Children of Jewish Holocaust Survivors New Holocaust Resistance* (October 2014), accessed October 23, 2014, <http://www.cjhsla.org/2014/10/03/blinding-history-by-diana-west/#sthash.oZEcbDjN.dpuf>.

773 Neil A. Abrams, M. Steven Fish, "How Western aid enables graft addiction in Ukraine," *Washington Post* (May 5, 2016), accessed May 10, 2016, <https://www.washingtonpost.com/news/monkey-cage/wp/2016/05/05/how-western-aid-enables-graft-addiction-in-ukraine/?wpisrc=nl_az_most>.

774 "Biography," *Nostradamus* (2005), accessed January 20, 2016, <http://www.nostradamus.org/>.

775 "The Nobel Prize in Physics 1921," *Nobelprize.org* (2016), accessed April 20, 2016, <http://www.nobelprize.org/nobel_prizes/physics/laureates/1921/>; The Reader's Digest Association, *How Did It Really Happen*, 117.

776 Dan Vergano, "One EMP and the world goes dark," *USA Today* (October 2010), accessed April 6, 2015, <http://usatoday30.usatoday.com/tech/science/2010-10-26-emp_N.htm>.
777 Ferris, *National Geographic* (June 2012): 52.
778 <http://usatoday30.usatoday.com/tech/science/2010-10-26-emp_N.htm>.
779 Hawks, *The Rise of Humans*, 117, 122.
780 <http://news.yahoo.com/could-major-discovery-astrophysicists-planning-announce-today-135308336.html>.

BIBLIOGRAPHY

Andro, Anatole. *The 1421 Heresy*. Bloomingdale: Author House, 2005.

Attenborough, David. *The Mediterranean World and Man*. Boston: Little, Brown and Company, 1987.

Ausubel, Nathan. *The Book of Jewish Knowledge*. New York: Crown Publishers, Inc, 1964.

Barber, Elizabeth Wayland. *Woman's Work: The First 20,000 Years, Women, Cloth, and Society in Early Times*. New York: W.W. Norton and Company, 1994.

Baron, Salo W., and et al. *Great Ages and Ideas of the Jewish People*. New York: Random House, Inc., 1956.

Budge, E.A. Wallis. *Babylonian Life and History*. New York: Barnes and Noble Books, 1993.

Cauvin, Jacques. *The Birth of the Gods and the Origins of Agriculture*. New York: Cambridge University Press, 2000.

Copa, Alfredo, and et al. "Newly recognized Pleistocene human teeth from Tabu Cave, Israel." *Journal of Human Evolution*, 2005: 301-305.

Dalley, Stephanie. *Myths from Mesopotamia: Creation, the Flood, Gilgamesh, and Others*. Oxford: Oxford University Press, 1991.

Dalrymple, G. Brent. "The age of the Earth in the twentieth century: a problem (mostly) solved." *Geological Society Special Publication*, January 1, 2001: 205-221.

Danon, Danny. *Israel: The Will To Prevail*. New York: Palgrave MacMillian, 2012.

Dawkins, Richard. *The Blind Watchmaker*. New York: W.W. Norton & Company, 1996.

Dimont, Max I. *Jews, God and History*. New York: Signet Books, 1962.

Drews, Robert. *The End of the Bronze Age*. New Jersey: Princeton University Press, 1993.

Eyles, Nick, and Andrew Miall. *Canada Rocks: The Geologic Journey*. Markham: Fitzhenry & Whiteside, 2010.

Faber, David. *Because of Romek: A Holocaust Survivor's Memoir*. La Mesa: Faber Press, 2006.

Feltman, Rachel. "Find Called Crucial to Human Evolution." *San Diego Union-Tribune*, March 5, 2015: A10.

—. "Neanderthals Possible Inventors of Jewelry." *San Diego Union-Tribune*, March 12, 2015: A10.

Ferris, Timothy. "Sun Struck." *National Geographic*, June 2012: 44.

Finkelstein, Israel, and Neil Asher Silberman. *The Bible Unearthed: Archaelology's New Vision of Ancient Israel and the Origin of its Sacred Texts.* New York: Touchstone, 2002.

Firestone, Richard, Allen West, and Simon Warwick-Smith. *The Cycle of Cosmic Catastrophes: How a Stone-Age Comet Changed the Course of World Culture.* Rochester: Bear & Company, 2006.

Fisher, Fritz. *Germany's Aims in the First World War.* New York: W.W. Norton & Company, Inc., 1968.

Florence, Ronald. *Lawrence and Aaronsohn.* New York: Penguin Group USA, Inc., 2008.

Fromkin, David. *A Peace to End All Peace: the Fall of the Ottoman Empire and the Creation of the Modern Middle East.* New York: Henry Holt and Company, LLC, 2009.

—. *Europe's Last Summer: Who Started the Great War in 1914.* New York: Random House, 2004.

Golabek, Mona, and Lee Cohen. *The Children of Willesden Lane.* New York: Grand Central Publishing, 2003.

Gross, Jenny. "Fossil Discovery Clouds Human Origin Story." *The Wall Street Journal*, May 28, 2015: A9.

Hall, Brian K., and Benedikt Hallgrimsson. *Strickberger's Evolution.* Sudbury: Jones & Gartlett, 2008.

Hawks, John. *The Rise of Humans: Great Scientific Debates .* Virginia: The Great Courses, 2011.

Hertz, Eli E. *This Land is My Land.* New York: Myths and Facts, 2008.

Hodges, Glenn. "The first face of the first Americans." *National Geographic*, January 2015: 132-133.

Hoffman, Eva. *Shtetl: The Life and Death of a Small Town and the World of Polish Jews.* New York: Houghton Miffin Company, 1997.

Horowitz, David. *Why Israel is the Victim.* Sherman Oaks: David Horowitz Freedom Center, 2013.

Katz, Samuel. *Battleground: Fact and Fantasy in Palestine.* New York: Bantam Books, 2002.

Katz, Shumel. *The Aaronsohn Saga.* New York: Gefen Books, 2007.

Kopel, David. "Armed Resistance to the Holocaust." *Journal on Firearms and Public Policy*, 2007: 149-150.

Kramer, Samuel Noah. *Sumerian Mythology*. (Philadelphia: University of Pennsylvania Press, 1972.

—. *The Sumerians: Their History, Culture, and Character*. Chicago: University of Chicago Press, 1971.

Lagnado, Lucette. "When the Arab Jews fled." *The Wall Street Journal*, October 13, 2012: C3.

Landau, Julian J. *Israel and the Arabs: A Handbook of Basic Information*. Tel Aviv: Israel Communications, 1971.

Lange, Ian M. *Ice Age Mammals of North America*. Missoula: Mountain Press Publishing, 2002.

Levenda, Peter. *The Hitler Legacy: The Nazi Cult in Diaspora: How it was Organied, How it was Funded, and Why it Remains a Threat to Global Security in the Age of Terrorism*. Lake Worth: Ibis Press, 2014.

Lincoln, Don. *The Large Hadron Collider*. Baltimore: John Hopkins University Press, 2014.

MacDonald, Kevin. *Separation and its Discontents: Toward an Evolutionary Theory of Anti-Semitism*. Westport: Praeger Publishers, 1998.

Malkowski, Edward F. *Ancient Egypt 39,000 BCE: The History, Technology, and Philosophy of Civilization X*. Vermont: Bear & Company, 2010.

Marcus, Jacob R. *The Jew in the Medieval World*. New York: Atheneum, 1969.

McKie, Robin. "How a hobbit is rewriting the history of the human race." *The Observer*. February 20, 2010. http://www.guardian.co.uk/science/2010/feb/21/hobbit-rewriting-history-human-race (accessed July 2013).

McMenamin, Mark A. S., and Dianna L. Schulte McMenamin. *The Emergence of Animals: The Cambrian Breakthrough*. New York: Columbia University Press, 1990.

Muravchik, Joshua. *Making David into Goliah: How the World Turned Against Israel*. New York: Encounter Books, 2014.

Netanyahu, Benjamin. *A Durable Peace: Israel and Its Place Among the Nations*. New York: Warner Books, 2000.

Oswmanagich, Semir. *Pyramids Around the World*. Kindle Edition: New Era Times Press, 2012.

Pettitt, Paul. *The Palaeolithic Orgins of Human Buriel*. New York: Routledge, 2010.

Phayer, Michael. *The Catholic Church and the Holocaust: 1930-1965.* Bloomingdale: Indiana University Press, 2000.

Plato. *The Timaeus and Critias or Atlanticus of Plato: The Thomas Taylor Translation.* New Jersey: Princeton University Press, 1968.

Prager, Dennis, and Joseph Telushkin. *Why the Jews.* New York: Touchstone, 2003.

Rabinovich, Abraham. "Scholars decipher oldest Bible text." *Jerusalem Post International Edition,* June 28, 186: Back section.

Redfern, Nick. *Bloodlines of the Gods.* New Jersey: The Career Press, Inc., 2015.

Russell, Bertrand. *History of Western Philosophy.* New York: Simon and Schuster, 1972.

Sehama, Simon. *The Story of the Jews: Finding the Words 1000 BC-1492 AD.* New York: HarperCollins Publishers, 2014.

Seward, William. *William H. Seward's Travels Around the World.* New York: D. Appleton and Company, 1873.

Sherman, Mark. "Jerusalem Passport Case Divides Court." *San Diego Union-Tribune,* November 4, 2014: A8.

Sitchin, Zecharia. *Twelfth Planet: Book I of the Earth Chronicles.* Vermont: Bear & Company, 1991.

—. *Divine Encounters (New York: Avon Books, 1996).* New York: Avon Books, 1996.

Spinney, Laura. "Archaeology: The lost world." *Nature454,* July: 151-154.

Stanford, Dennis J., and Bruce A. Bradley. *Across Atlantic Ice: The Origins of America's Clovis Culture.* Berkeley: University of California Press, 2012.

Stevens, Bret. *America in Retreat.* New York: Penguin Group USA, 2014.

Telushkin, Joseph. *Jewish Literacy, revised.* New York: HarperCollins, 2008.

—. *Jewish Literacy: The Most Important Things to Know About the Jewish Religion, Its People, and Its History.* New York: William Morrow and Company, Inc., 1991.

Trompf, G. W. *The Idea of Historical Recurrence in Western Thought.* California: University of California Press, 1979.

Urquhart, Frank. "Doggerland: The real Atlantis, just off Scotland." *The Scotsman,* March 7, 2012: 1.

Walter, Chip. "First Artists." *National Geographic,* January 2014: 45.

West, Diana. *American Betrayal.* New York: St. Martin's Press, 2013.

Wilcock, David. *The Source Field.* Kindle Edition: Amazon, 2011.

Wilford, John Noble. "On Crete, New Evidence of Very Ancient Mariners." *New York Times*, February 16, 2010: D1.

Wilson, Marjorie. "Central Atlantic passive margins." *Geo Science World*, June 1997: 491-495.

Woolley, C. Leonard. *The Sumerians*. New York: W. W. Norton & Company, Inc., 1965.

Zitchin, Zechariah. *There Were Giants Upon the Earth: Gods, Demigods, and Human Ancestry*. Vermont: Bear & Company, 2010.

Zucotti, Susan. *Under His Very Windows: The Vatican and the Holocaust in Italy*. New Haven: Yale University Press, 2000.

Websites Utilized

A quick background to the last ice age, <http://www.esd.ornl.gov/projects/qen/nerc130k.html>
ABC Science Online, <http://www.abc.net.au/science/>
about education, physics.about.com
ADL archive website, archive.adl.org/israel/israel_documents.html.
Aggsbach's Paleolithic Blog, www.aggsbach.com
Aish, <http://www.aish.com>
American Almanac, <http://members.tripod.com/~american_almanac.htm>
American Physical Society, <http://phys.org/news>
Ancient Egypt, <http://www.ancient-egypt.org/index.html>
Ancient History Encyclopedia, <http://www.ancient.eu>
Ancient Wisdom, <http://www.ancient-wisdom.com>
Anthropark, <http://www.anthropark.htm>
Bad Astronomy, <http://www.slate.com/blogs/bad_astronomy/>
Bank for International Settlements, <http://www.bis.org/about/>
BBC News, <http://news.bbc.co.uk>
Bible History Dailey, <http://www.biblicalarchaeology.org>
Biography.com, <http://www.biography.com>
BMC Evol Biol, <http://bmcevolbiol.biomedcentral.com/>
Bonedigger, <http://bonedigger.lefora.com>
Bradshaw Foundation, <http://www.bradshawfoundation.com/>
Bulletin of the Geological Society of America, <http://dx.doi.org/10.1130/0016-7606(1953)64[865:EOTNAM]2.0.CO;2>
California Academy of Sciences, <http://www.calacademy.org/newsroom/>
Chabad.ORG, <http://www.chabad.org>
Children of Jewish Holocaust Survivors New Holocaust Resistance, <http://cjhsla.org>
CNN, <http://www.cnn.com>

Debates in World Archaeology, <http://www.anthropology.hawaii.edu/>
Disaster Pages of George Pararas-Carayannis, <http://www.drgeorgepc.com>
Dr. Robert M. Schoch, <http://robertschoch.com/>
Earthfiles Report <http://www.earthfiles.com>
Encyclopaedia Britannica Online, <http://www.britannica.com/>
eNotes, <http://www.enotes.com>
Forbes, <http://www.forbes.com>
FP Passport, <http://foreignpolicy.com>
Geological Society of America Memoirs, <http://memoirs.gsapubs.org/>
Geology, <http://geology.gsapubs.org/>
Geotimes, <http://www.geotimes.org/>
Graham Hancock, <https://grahamhancock.com>.
Healing Crystals, Healing Stones, <http://www.healing-crystals-healing-stones.com>
History of Switzerland, <http://history-switzerland.geschichte-schweiz.ch>
History Today, <http://www.historytoday.com>
History, <http://www.history.com>
in5d Esoteric Metaphysical Spiritual Database, <http://in5d.com/>
International World History Project, <http://history-world.org>
Iran Review, <http://www.iranreview.org>
Israel Law Center, <http://www.israellawcenter.org>
Israel National News, <http://www.israelnationalnews.com>
Jewish Treats, <http://www.jewishtreats.org>
Jewish Virtual Library, <http://www.jewishvirtuallibrary.org>
Live Science, <http://www.livescience.com>
MichaelHeiser.com, <http://www.michaelsheiser.com>
NASA News, <http://www.nasa.gov/home/hqnews>
National Geographic Genographic Project, <https://genographic.nationalgeographic.com/>
National Geographic Magazine, <http://ngm.nationalgeographic.com/>
National Geographic News, <http://news.nationalgeographic.com/news/>
nature geosciences, <http://www.nature.com/ngeo/journal/.html>
Nature International Journal of Science, <http://www.nature.com/nature/>
Nature News, <http://www.nature.com/news/>
Nature, <http://adsabs.harvard.edu/abs/1995Natur.377..203G>
New World Encyclopedia, <http://www.newworldencyclopedia.org>

New York Times, <http://www.nytimes.com>
NJOP, <http://rabbibuchwald.njop.org>
Nobelprize.org, <http://www.nobelprize.org>
Nostradamus, <http://www.nostradamus.org/>
ORT and the Displaced Person Camps, <http://dpcamps.ort.org>
Outpost, <http://afsi.org/Outpost>
Proceedings of the National Academy Science, <http://www.pnas.org/>
Questa Trusted online research, <https://www.questia.com/>
Ray Techniques Ltd, <http://www.nanodiamond.co.il>
Saudi Aramco, <http://www.saudiaramco.com>
Science Direct, <http://www.sciencedirect.com/>
Science, <http://www.sciencemag.org/>
Sephardic Institute, <http://judaicseminar.org/bible>
Smithsonian, <http://www.smithsonianmag.com>
Society for Nordish Physical Anthropology, <http://www.theapricity.com/snpa/index2.htm>
Space Daily, <http://www.spacedaily.com/>
tekitites.com.uk, <http://www.tektites.co.uk/>
The Atlantic, <http://news.yahoo.com>
The Big Hole Kimberley, <http://www.thebighole.co.za/thebighole.php>.
The Electronic Text Corpus of Sumerian Literature, <http://etcsl.orinst.ox.ac.uk/>
The Encyclopedia of Earth, <http://www.eoearth.org/>
The History Place, <http://www.historyplace.com>
The Neanderthal theory of autism, Asperger, and ADHD, <http://www.rdos.net/eng/asperger.htm>
The Observer, <http://www.guardian.co.uk/science/>
The Royal Society Publishing Proceedings B, <http://rspb.royalsocietypublishing.org>
The unedited full-text of the 1906 Jewish Encyclopedia, <http://www.jewishencyclopedia.com>
Times of Israel, <http://www.timesofisrael.com>
UC Berkeley News, <http://www.berkeley.edu/news/media/releases/>
University of California Museum of Paleontology, <http://www.ucmp.berkeley.edu/>
University of Georgia Libraries, <http://*www.libs.uga.edu*/>

US history.org, <http://www.ushistory.org>
USA Today, <http://usatoday30.usatoday.com>
Virginia Tech News, <http://www.vtnews.vt.edu/articles/>
Vredefort Dome.org, <http://www.vredefortdome.org/index.html>
Washington Post, <https://www.washingtonpost.com/news/>
Women In Green, <http://www.womeningreen.org>
Zionist Organization of America, <http://zoa.org>

INDEX

Aaron (biblical), 122-124
Aaronsohn, Aaron, 195-197
Aaronsohn, Sara, 195-196
Aboriginals (Australia), 43
Abraham, Jewish Patriarch, long life, 93
  "ten generations," 92-93
  in Sumeria, 107-108
  in Promised Land, 108-109, 132, 202
  in Egypt, 109
  as dynast, 114, 118, 126
  legacy of, 129, 244
Abydos, 62, 116, 117
Adam, (biblical), father of humanity, 89
  long life, 93, 104
  "ten generations," 92-93
Aegean mainland, prehistoric, 46, 48
  ancient, 133-135
Aegean Sea supervolcano –see Thera
Aelia Capitolina, 158, 160
Afghanistan, ancient, 100, 145, 150
Africa, formation, 16-17, 20-21
  prehistoric, 23-26, 30-31, 37-38, 49, 64, 72, 99
  ancient, 101, 105, 117, 149, 153
  CE, 158, 160, 164, 166
  modern, 188, 230, 233, 235
Ahab, King of Israel, 142-143
Ahmose, King/Pharaoh, 116-117
Akhenaten, Pharaoh of Egypt, 132
Akhet-Aton (Amarna, or Amana), 132
Akiva ben Joseph, Rabbi, 158
Akkad/Akkadia, 105, 107, 143-144
Albania, 193
Aleppo, 128, 136, 144
Alexander the Great, 149-150
Alexander, Ivan, Tsar of Russia, 170
Alexandria, 155, 164
al-Husayni, Mohammad Amin,
  as British operative, 197
  as Mufti, 200, 202, 206
  as Nazi, 216-217, 219, 222
  as war criminal, 229, 239

Allenby, Edmund, 195-196
Allied Powers (Allies), 189, 196-197, 199, 204, 219, 223, 229
America –see United States
Amsterdam, 169
  New Amsterdam –see New York
Anatolia, prehistoric, 66-67
  ancient, 78, 100, 117, 135-136, 149-150, 153
  CE, 163, 171
Andean-Saharan Ice Age, 18
Annu, 9
Antarctica, 17, 19, 58
anti-Semitism/Jew hatred,
  in ancient Egypt, 116
  in Roman Empire, 161-162
  in Europe, 168-171, 179, 181,183, 228
  in Russia, 179, 181-182, 189-190
  in America, 183, 204
  in British Palestine, 197, 201, 222
  in Vatican City, 189, 218-219, 251
  causes of, 170-171, 181-182, 204, 244, 249-253
  Arab–Israeli Conflict, 244
Apophis, King of Hyksos Egypt, 116
Arabian Peninsula, 20, 99, 117, 160, 162-163
Arafat, Yasser, 251
Archaic Homo sapiens, 23, 28, 30, 41, 43
  Denisovan, 43
  H. heidelbergensis, 28
  Red Deer Cave People, 28, 52, 72
Arctic, 14
Arctic Ocean, 19, 58-59
Ark of the Covenant, 124, 127-128
Armenian, 190-191, 195-196
Armenian Genocide, 190-191, 196
Ashkenaz Jews, 49, 144, 165-166, 187, 243
Ashkenaz, son of Gomer, 165
Ashur-bani-pal Palace Library, 5, 101, 103
Asia, prehistoric, 23, 26, 28, 43, 45

desertification of, 72, 105,
  CE, 170-171
  modern, 227, 261
  –also see China
Assyria, 142-145
Assyrian Exile, 131, 144-145
asteroid belt, 82
Aswan, 122
Athens, 149-150, 243
Athenian Empire, 148-149
Atlantic Ocean, 13, 19, 51, 57, 59-60, 65, 78, 100
Atlantis, 2, 48, 50, 55-60, 64-65, 78-79, 90, 177
Atlas Mountains, 20, 57
Augustus, Philip, King of France, 168
Aurignacian culture, 39, 42-49, 51-52, 73, 97-98
Australia, 17, 43, 74, 180
Australopithecus afarensis, 23-24
Austria, prehistoric, 44-47,
  Austria-Syria, 168
  Holy Roman Empire, 178, 180-181
  Austrian Empire, 181, 186
  Austria-Hungry, 189, 193-194
  Austria-Germany, 207- 210, 218, 221
  Russian invasion, 227-229
Avaris, 113, 115-119, 121
Azores Archipelago, 56, 59-60, 79
  Platform, 59-60, 66, 78-79, 177
Babi Yar Massacre, 215-216
Babylon/Babylonia, 95, 142, 145, 147, 162
Babylonian Exile, 131, 147-148
Bahamas, 62, 65-66
Balfour Declaration, 195-198, 235
Balfour, James Arthur, 194-196
Balkan Wars, 193
Balkans, prehistoric, 29, 44, 46, 48
  CE, 170-171
  Nazi occupied, 213, 215-216, 219, 221
  Displaced Persons Camps, 233
Bank for International Settlements (BIS), 202, 211, 223-224
Bar Kokhba, Shimon, 158
Bar Kokhba Revolt, 158-159, 252
Barber, Elizabeth Wayland, 47
Belarus, 182, 187, 215

Belgium, prehistoric, 49
  modern, 193, 209-211, 214-215
Ben-Gurion, David, 231, 239
bene ha'elohim, 85
Berlin, 178, 204, 216-217, 219, 254
Betar, 157, 159, 162
Bevin, Ernest, 234
Bialik, Chaim Nachman, 190
Big Bang Theory, 11
Bilha (Rachel's maid), 110
Bimini, Road/Wall, Islands, 62, 65-66
Black Sea region, prehistoric, 29, 44
  ancient, 145-146, 149
  CE, 164-165, 180, 182
  modern, 223
Blombos Cave, 31, 37-39
Bolsheviks, 196
Bonaparte, Napoleon, 181
Bosnia, 68, 186, 190, 193, 219
Bradley, Bruce, 51
Britain/England/United Kingdom,
  prehistoric, 50
  ancient, 158
  CE, 169, 171, 178, 183, 187
  modern, 188, 193-194, 202, 209-210, 221, 236, 241, 250-251
  WWII, 213, 216, 219, 223, 229, 233-235
Bronze Age, 32, 95, 102
Bronze Age Collapse, 131, 133-135, 137-138, 148
bubonic plague (Black Death), 170-171, 257
Bulgaria, Bulgarians, 134, 170, 186, 194, 221
Bush, George W., 245
Byblos –see Gebal
Caesar, Gaius Julius, 153
Cairo, 57, 164
Cambodia, 68, 188
Cambrian Explosion, 18
Canaan (descendent of Noah), 102
Canaan, prehistoric, 23, 28, 30, 41, 49, 53, 58, 66, 72
  ancient, 95-100, 103, 105
Canada, Canadian Shield, 13, 16, 17
Canary Archipelago, 58, 68
carbon dating, 80, 81
Carrington Event, 259

Catherine, Empress of Russia, 180
Caucasus Mountain region, 25-26, 100, 146, 165, 201
Cayce, Edgar, 64, 65
Cenozoic Era, 18, 20
Chamberlain, Neville, 211
Central Powers (Axis), 189, 229
Chicxulub extinction event, 19-20
China, prehistoric, 26-28, 31, 41, 49, 52, 72
  ancient, 68, 100, 105, 145
  CE, 155, 165-166, 169-172, 175
  modern, 216, 229, 254, 258
Churchill, Winston, 196, 207, 211, 216
Civilization X, 2, 55, 58, 79
Cleopatra, 152
Clinton, Bill, 245
Clovis culture, 51, 72
Cochin, 141, 146, 168, 173
Colonial War, 178-179
Columbia supercontinent –see Nuna
Columbus, Christopher, 172-173
Communism, 203
Communists, 207, 225, 254
concentration camps, German, 188, 204, 228, 230, 234
  Nazi, 209, 214-215, 217-222, 228, 230
  British, 228, 230-234
  Soviet/Russian, 203, 215, 254
Congress of Berlin –see Treaty of Berlin
Constantine, Emperor of Rome, 161-162
Constantinople, 163, 171
Council of Four Lands, 180
Crete Island, prehistoric, 30, 102
  ancient, 100, 102-103, 108, 115, 135, 138, 143
Crimea, Crimean Mountains, 45-46, 146, 164-165, 170, 180, 182, 203, 215
Croatia, 29, 170, 186, 229
  Croatian Nazis, 229
Cro-Magnon, in Early Canaan, 23, 28, 30-32, 38-39, 41-42
  in Morocco, 30-31, 47
  in China, 31, 41, 49, 72
  in South Africa, 37-38
  in India, 39
  in Europe/Russia, 41, 43-45, 52, 72
  in Anatolia, 97
  interbreeding with Neandertals, 30, 42-43, 47
Crusades, Crusaders, 167-169, 186
Cuba (archipelago), 65, 210
Cyprus Island, 95, 99-100, 230-231, 233-235, 238, 241
Cyrene, 155
Cyrus, King of Persia/Babylonia, 147
Czech Republic/Czechoslovakia, prehistoric, 46, 97
  modern, 208-209, 211, 228, 237
Dammeseq, 136-137, 139, 142
Dan (Laish/Leshem), 128
Darius, King of Persia/Babylonia, 147
David, King of Israel, 38, 103, 131, 138-142, 147, 151
De Beers brothers, 75
Dead Sea, 24, 27, 73, 86-87, 127, 134, 148
Dead Sea Scrolls, 87, 148
Deborah, Jewish Prophetess, 128
Deluge –see Great Flood
Denmark, 50, 178, 205, 221, 226
Diaspora, 160-161, 164, 166, 168, 207, 212, 214, 236, 246, 252
Displaced Persons Camps, 230, 233
Doggerland, 50, 53, 79, 177
Dominican Republic, 208
Dryas stadials, Oldest, 49-53
  Older, 53, 66, 71
  Younger, 71-72, 77-79, 81, 83, 88-89, 92, 94-98, 246, 260
Early Modern Human (EMH) –see Cro-Magnon
East India Company, 177-178
Edward I, King of England, 169, 228
Egypt, ancient, xiii, 100-103, 109-118, 121, 125, 131-135, 145
  CE, 155, 158, 164
  modern, 175, 181, 187, 224, 239-242
Eichmann, Adolf, 217, 224
Einstein, Albert, 12, 196, 257, 262
El Khiam culture, 73, 98-99
Elam, 105
England –see Britain
Enoch (biblical), 93
Entebbe Raid, 242-243
Epigravettian culture, 48, 53
Eritrea, 230-231

Essenes, 86-87, 148
Ethiopia, 24, 30
Eudocia, Empress of Rome, 162
Euphrates River, 99, 139
European Union, xii, 224, 252, 258
Eve/Havva (biblical), "mother of humanity," 89
   long life, 93
Ever (grandson of Noah), 107
Evian-les-Bains Conference, 207-208, 210
Exodus, 121-126, 132, 134, 137, 142
Exodus, Book of, 111, 129
Exodus—1947, 233-234, 241
Ezra, 147-148
Fatah (Al Aqsa Martyrs Brigade), 251
Fatimid Dynasty, 165-166
Feinstein, Dianne, 245
Ferdinand II of Aragon, 172-173
Ferdinand, Franz, Austrian Archduke, 193
Final Solution –see Wannsee Conference
Finland, 180, 214-215, 221, 228, 235
Firestone, Richard, 81
First Aliyah, 186
First Opium War, 183
First World War –see World War I
Flanders, 49, 67
Flavius, Josephus, 114
Florida, 65, 179, 210
Flores Island, 25-26, 37
Florence, 171
Fourth Reich, 225
France, prehistoric, 27, 29-30, 46-49, 51-52
   CE, 163, 166-168, 171-172
   French Revolution, 180-181
   Nazi occupied, 211, 213, 215-216, 218, 220, 224
   modern, 187-189, 225, 227
Frank, Anne, 210
Franz Joseph I, Austrian Emperor, 186
Frederick, Duke of Austria and Syria, 168
Frederick I, King Prussia, 178
French and Indian War, 178-179
Fukishima nuclear disaster, 259
Gaul –see France

Gebal, 128, 136-137, 142, 146
Geminga pulsar, 81-82
genetic bottleneck theory, 35-36
Geneva Convention of 1925, 214
George, Lloyd David, 194-195, 235
Germany, prehistoric, 29, 45, 48, 52, 74
   Germania, 159, 163, 165-166, 170, 173
   Holy Roman Empire, 176-178
   German Empire, 185-189, 193-194, 196, 197
   German Republic, 202-204
   Nazi Germany, 204-211, 213-214, 216-221, 223, 249, 257
   post-war Germany, 227-228, 234
   West Germany, 242
   Germany (reunified), 257
giants, Book of Giants, 87
   Anaks, 124
   Goliath, 139
Gilgal, 138-139
Gilgamesh, 87
   Epic of Gilgamesh, 87-88
Giza Plateau, 62, 66
Göbekli Tepe, 3, 61, 66-69, 97-99, 104
Golan Heights –see Israel
Goshen, 111, 118, 124
Grand Mufti –see al-Husayni
Gravettian culture, 45-46, 52, 73, 98
Great Depression of 1929, 202
Great Famine, 183
Great Flood (the Deluge), 85-94, 96, 104, 109, 124, 131
Great Oxygenation Event, 15
Great Pyramid, 61-62, 65, 68
Great Revolt of 66 CE, 86, 156-157
Great Rift Valley, 21, 23-25, 30, 37
Great Sphinx, 57, 63-65, 68
Greece, 46, 134-135, 150, 155
Greenland, 17, 260
Hadrian, Aelius, Emperor of Rome, 157-160
Hadrian's Wall, 158
Haganah, 197, 206-207, 231-232, 234
Ham ben Noah, 96, 102, 131-132
Hamas, 251
Harappa culture, 99, 105
Ha-Shomer, 190
He, Zheng, 172, 175

Hebraic culture, 38, 88, 96, 144, 246, 249
Hebron, Patriarch/Matriarch Cave, 109, 111, 118, 124
  Israelite settlement, 127
  British/Arab Pogroms, 197, 201, 202
  British occupation, 206
Herod, King of Judea, 152-153, 155
Hertz, Joseph, Chief Rabbi of England, 194
Herzl, Theodor, 189
Hezbollah, 243
Himmler, Heinrich, 217
Hindenburg, Paul von, 204
Hindu Kush, 100, 143-144
Hispaniola, 65
Hitler, Adolf, rise to power, 203-204, 207-208, 211
  as Messiah, 205
  during WWII, 213, 215-217
Holland, 209-211, 214
Holocaust –see Shoah
Holocene Period, 260
Holy Roman Empire –see Germany
Homo erectus, 23, 26-27, 39, 43
  Peking Man, 27
Homo floresiensis, 23, 25, 37, 72
Homo habilis, 23, 25- 26
Homo sapiens idaltu, 23, 30
Homo sapiens Neandertalensis, in Early Canaan, 23, 28-29, 32, 39, 42-43
  in Europe, 29, 39, 43-44, 47-48
  in China, 41, 43
  in Morocco, 47-48
Homo sapiens sapiens –see Cro-Magnon
Hopkins, Harry, 216
House of Hanover, 185
Howiesons Poort culture, 39
Hungary, 189, 219, 222, 228-229
Huronian Ice Age, 16
Iceland, 48, 59
India, prehistoric, 26-27, 39, 68, 100
  ancient, 104-105, 141, 143, 145-146
  CE, 155, 160, 166, 168, 173, 177
  modern, 235
Indonesia, ancient, 23, 25-27, 36-37, 72
  modern, 224
Ionia, 78
Iran, x, 145, 250, 254, 258

Iraq, x, 5, 87, 101, 103, 144, 239, 241-242
Irgun (National Defense), 231-233
Iron Age, 134
Isaac, Jewish Patriarch, 93, 109
Isabella I of Castile, 172-173
Isaiah the Prophet, 144
Israel, prehistoric sites, 27-28, 31-32, 38, 42, 53
  Promised Land, 107-109, 128, 131, 157
  ancient Gaza, 127, 135, 138, 151
  ancient Galilee, 128, 139, 156, 159, 162
  ancient Golan (Heights), 128, 151
  ancient Jezreel Valley, 99, 128, 138
  ancient Judah, 127-128, 141-142, 144-147, 150-153
  ancient Samaria, 142-144
  ancient Negev, 108-109, 127
  CE, 156, 158-159, 161-167, 173, 175-177
  War of Independence 1948, 239-240
Italy, prehistoric, 43, 46, 48
  ancient, 150, 163, 166, 171, 181
  modern, 194, 221, 228
Jabotinsky, Zeev, 194, 197
Jacob, Jewish Patriarch, 93, 109-112, 117-118
Jakbim, King of Hyksos Egypt, 115
Japan, 196, 202, 204, 216, 223
  Fukishima disaster, 259
Jericho, 72-73, 95, 97, 99, 127, 142
Jerusalem, ancient, 119, 122, 127, 131, 133, 139, 141
  Babylonians in, 146-147
  Macedonians in, 149
  Romans in, 152, 156-159
  CE, 161-164, 166-167, 173
  modern, 90, 173, 184, 195-198, 232, 236, 238, 242
Jerusalem Embassy Act of 1995, 245-246
Jewish calendar, ix, 101-102
  Calendar of Nineveh, ix, 11, 101
Jezebel, Queen of Israel, 142
Joao II, King of Portugal, 172-173
Jordan, 241-242, 245
  Transjordan, 201, 238-242
Jordan River, 27, 72-73, 97, 127-129, 201

Jordan Valley, prehistoric, 43-44, 73, 100
   ancient, 109, 126-127, 151
   CE, 175
   modern, 195-196, 198, 200-201
Josephus, Flavius, 114
Julian, Emperor of Rome, 161-162
Judah, 241-242, 246, 251
Kaifeng, 165
Kalahari Desert, 188
Kamose, King of Egypt, 116-117
Kaptara –see Crete
Karnak, 117
Karoo Ice Age, 18
Kazimierz III (Casimir), King of Poland, 170
Kebaran culture, 41, 49, 53, 98-100
Khafre, Pharaoh of Egypt, 63
Khan, Kublai, 169
Khazaria, 164-165
Kindertransport Program, 209-210, 214, 229
King List, Egyptian, 113
King List, Sumerian, 103-104
Kish, 101, 103, 105
Kishinev (massacre), 190
Kissinger, Henry, 243
Klein, Morton A., 250
Kristallnacht, 208-211
Kubaba, King of Sumeria, 103, 115
Kuiper Belt, 82
Kurdistan, 145, 175
La Garita supervolcano, 20-21
Lagash, 105
Lake Agassiz, 71-72, 100
Lake Kinneret, 24, 68, 108, 127-128, 155- 156
Lamech (biblical), 93
Laos, 188
Lascaux Cave paintings, 52
Last Glacial Maximum, 45-46, 48, 50, 78, 104
Laurentia –see North America
Laurentide Ice Sheet, 32-33, 60, 71, 73, 100
League of Nations, 197-198, 200-201, 206, 211, 215, 229, 238
Leah, Jewish Matriarch, 93, 110-111
Lebanon, modern, 43, 239, 242, 245

Lend-Lease Program, 216, 229, 235
Libby, Willard, 80
Libya, 155, 243
Lindo, Moses, 178-179
Linear A-B script, 123
Linz, 217
Lisbon, 173
Lithuania, 178, 180, 187
Little Ice Age, 169, 175, 179, 181, 183, 188
London, 194, 197, 200, 211, 227, 236
Louis XI, King of France, 168
Lubeck, 234
Luther, Martin, 173
Maccabee family, 151-152, 190
MacDonald, Malcolm, 211
Macedonia, 136, 148-150, 152
Magdalenian culture, 48-49, 52-53, 98
Manchuria, 233
Manetho, 114, 119
Manuel I, King of Portugal, 173
Mari, 95, 100-102, 105, 108
Marinoan (Elatina) Ice Age, 17-18
matriarchal societies, 44
May Laws (Russia), 187
Maya culture, 74, 166
Maya Calendar, 11
Megiddo, 128, 146
Mesoproterozoic Era, 16
Mesozoic Era, 19
Methuselah (biblical), 93
Mid-Atlantic Ridge, 19, 56, 58-60, 78, 177
Milankovitch, Milutin, 25
Milky Way Galaxy, 80
Miriam (biblical), 122-123
Mongolia, 43, 160
Morocco, prehistoric, 27, 31, 47-48, 56
   ancient, 144, 155
   CE, 164-165
   modern, 241
Moses, 89, 122-126
   Mosaic Law, 140
Mount Ararat, 88-89, 91
Mount Carmel, 31-32, 42, 128
Mount Moriah, 139, 148, 152, 157, 159, 162
Mount Olympus, games of, 149
Mount Sinai, 89, 123-124

Movius, Hallam (Movius Line), 26
Munich Agreement, 208
Muslim Brotherhood, 240
Mycenaean culture, 115, 122-123, 135
National Reich Church, 205
National Socialists, 207
Natufian culture, 41, 53, 72, 97, 100
Nazism, 188, 203-205, 216, 223-224, 250, 254
Nebuchadnezzar II, King of Babylon, 146-147
Nefertiti, 132
nefilim, 85-86
Negev Desert –see Israel
Neoproterozoic Era, 17
Netanyahu, Benjamin, 255
Netanyahu, Yonatan, 243
Nevah Cori, 97-99, 104
New Amsterdam, 177
New York, 178-179, 183, 227, 254
New York Stock Exchange, 224
Nicolas I, Tsar of Russia, 187
Nicolas II, Tsar of Russia, 196
Nili Spies, 195-196
Nineveh, 101, 104, 143
North Africa –see Africa
North America, formation, 17, 24, 74
   prehistoric, 28, 33, 39, 45, 71-73
   end of the Ice Age, 76-79, 82, 91
   ancient, 100
   CE, 166, 177
North Atlantic Current, 59, 72
Norway, Nazi occupied, 215, 220
Nostradamus, 257
Nuna supercontinent, 16
Nuremberg Laws, 205
Nuremberg Trials, 222
Obama, Barack, 242
Octavian, Emperor of Rome, 153
Odessa, 182, 186
Odessa (Nazi Brotherhood), 224
Omo National Park, 30
Omri, King of Israel, 141-142, 151
Oort cloud, 82
Oslo Peace Accords, 251
Pacific Ocean, 24
Palace of Nestor, 123
Pale of Settlement, 180, 182, 187

Paleoproterozoic Era, 15
Paleozoic Era, 18
Pangaea supercontinent, 19
Paris, 201, 216, 227
Paris Peace Conference of 1919, 196,198
Paris Peace Conference of 1946, 229
patriarchal societies, 44
Peking Man –see *H. erectus*
Perón, Juan, 224
Persia, 149-150, 155, 162-164
Petlura, Simon, 198, 201
Pharisees, 148, 151
Philip II, King of Macedonia, 149
Philo of Alexandria, 155
Pillars of Hercules, 55, 60, 78
Pius X (Giuseppe Sarto), Pope, 189
Pius XII (Eugenio Pacelli), Pope, 219
Plato, Atlantis story, 2, 55, 57-58, 60, 78-79, 90
   Helios story, 77-78, 90
Poland, prehistoric, 48
   ancient, 146
   CE, 165, 168-171, 176-177
   modern, 180, 196, 228
   Nazi occupied, 213-215, 217, 220, 222
Pompey, Gnaeus, 152
Portugal, prehistoric, 44, 46-48, 51
   CE, 172-173
   modern, 183
Prussia, 165, 168, 173, 178, 180
Quaternary Ice Age, 23-24, 260
Qumran, 86-87, 148
Quraish Arabs, 160
Rachel, Jewish Matriarch, 93, 110, 116
Ramban (Moshe ben Nahman), 93-94
Ramesses I, Pharaoh of Egypt, 133
Rebecca, Jewish Matriarch, 93, 109
Red Cross, 230
Red Sea, prehistoric, 24, 49
   ancient, 134, 139
   modern, 230-231, 242
Reed Sea (Sea of Reeds), 123
Refugee Conference of 1957, 251-252
Renaissance, 171
Rock of Gibraltar, 60
Roman Republic, 131, 152-153
   Empire, 155-157, 160-163
Rodinia supercontinent, 17

Romania, 176, 216, 222, 228
Roosevelt, Franklin Delano, 203, 210, 216
Rothschild, Lord Walter, 194, 196, 277
Rufus, Titus, 158
Russia, prehistoric, 26, 41, 44, 46, 48
   CE, 165, 170, 175
    Tsarist Russia, 176, 178, 179
    Russian Empire, 180-182, 186-187, 189, 190, 193, 196
    USSR, 201, 203, 213, 215-216, 235
    Russian Federation, 254, 258
SS *St. Louis*, 210
Sadducees, 148
Safed, 173, 176
Sahara Desert –see Africa
Saladin, Kurdish ruler, 167
Samaria, 241-242, 246, 251
Samuel, Jewish prophet, 138-139
Samuel, Sir Herbert, 194
San Carlos de Bariloche, 224
San Remo, 197-200
Sanhedrin, 137-138, 157, 159
Sarah, Jewish Matriarch, long life, 93
   in Sumeria, 102, 107-108
   in Promised Land, 108-109, 132, 202
   in Egypt, 109
   as dynast, 114, 118, 126
   legacy of, 128-129, 246
Sarajevo, 193
Sargon II, King of Assyria, 144
Sargon of Akkad, King of Sumeria, 105
Sassanid Empire, 162, 164
Saudi Arabia, 203, 207-208, 239
Saul ben Kish, King of Israel, 138, 140-141
Schoch, Robert M., 64, 82, 93-94
Schonfeld, Rabbi Solomon, 209-210
Schwartzbard, Sholem, 201
Sea of Galilee –see Lake Kinneret
Sea Peoples, 135-137
Second Aliyah, 189-190
Second World War –see World War II
Seleucid Greeks –see Syrian Greeks
Serbia, 161, 187, 193
Seward, William H., 186
Shaanxi Province earthquake, 175
Shechem, 108, 125-126, 128, 139, 141-142

shekel, 124
Shem ben Noah, 96, 107
Shlomtzion Alexandera, King of Jerusalem, 151-152
Shoah (Holocaust), 211, 214, 230
   survivors of, 230, 234, 236
   underlying cause, 253
Siberia, prehistoric, 17-18, 39, 43, 45
   modern, 180, 213, 260
Sidon, 128, 136, 137, 142, 146
Silk Road, 165
Sinai Desert, ancient, 73, 114, 123-125, 139
   CE, 164
   modern, 242
Six Day War, 242
Slovakia, 46, 215
Sobekneferu, King of Egypt, 113-114
Solomon, King of Israel, 103, 122, 139-141, 146
Solon, Athenian Lawgiver, 57-58, 77, 79, 90
Solutrean culture, 38, 48-52, 72
South Africa, 75,
South America, prehistoric, 24
   CE, 166, 177
   modern, 224
Soviet Union –see Russia
Spain, prehistoric, 28-29, 44-46, 48, 51-52
   CE, 93, 163, 172-173, 183
   modern, 188, 224
Spanish Inquisition, 172, 177, 183
Sphinx –see Great Sphinx
Stalin, Joseph, 203, 213
Stanford, Dennis, 51
Still Bay culture, 39
Strait of Gibraltar, 21, 78, 177
Struma, 223
Sturtian Ice Age, 17
Sudetenland, 211
Sumer/Sumeria, settlement of, 9, 95-97, 100
   confederation of, 101-103, 105
   fall of, 107, 246
Swabia, prehistoric, 45-46, 52
Sweden, 178, 215, 221
Switzerland, 98, 178, 202, 205, 209, 224
Syria, ancient, Egyptians in, 132

Assyrians in, 145
Macedonians in, 150
Romans in, 152-153, 155-156
  CE, Austria/Syria, 168
  modern, Turks in, 176, 186, 191
Syrian Arab Republic, 239, 242-243, 251, 252
Syrian Desert, 44, 191
Syrian Greeks, 150-151
Tel Aviv, 190, 234, 238-240, 243, 245
Temple Mount –see Mount Moriah
Terror Famine, 203
Tethys Ocean, 21
The Third Reich –see Germany
Thebes, 115-117, 132, 145-146
Thera (Aegean) supervolcano, 56, 113, 115-118, 134
Theodora, Queen of Bulgaria, 170
Theodosius I, Emperor of Rome, 162
Thrace, 134-135, 148-150
Tiberias, 155-156, 159-160, 176
Tiglath-Pilesar II, King of Assyria, 143
Toba supervolcano, 1, 23, 35, 38
Transjordan –see Jordan
Treaty of Berlin-Congo Congress, 186, 188
Treaty of Paris (1783), 179
Treaty of Versailles, 197, 199-200, 202, 204
Triple Alliance –see Central Powers
Triple Entente –see Allied Powers
Troy, 136, 143
Truman, Harry, 235
Trump, Donald J., 246
Turkey, prehistoric, 26, 66, 68, 88, 97-98
  ancient, 135
  CE, 163, 171, 173
  modern, 144-145, 190-191, 195, 197-198, 230
Turkmenistan, 166, 171
Tyre, 128, 136-137, 139, 142, 146
Ukraine, prehistoric, 44-45
  CE, 164-165, 180, 182
  modern, 187, 196, 201, 203, 215, 220-221, 254
United Kingdom –see Britain
United Nations, formation of, 197-198, 216, 229
  on Israel, 235, 238-240
  on social change, xii
United States of America, settlement of, 172, 177-179
  American Revolution, 179-181
  Expansion of, 186
  Civil War, 185
  WWI, 195-196
  creation of BIS, 202
  Soviet (USSR) recognition, 203
  WWII, 209-210, 216, 219-220, 223, 227, 229
  creation of UN, 227
  immigration to, 183, 189, 224
  anti-Semitism in, 179, 183, 190, 204, 207-208, 210
  on Israel, 232, 237, 240, 242, 245-246
Ur, 9, 101, 105, 107-108, 144
Ur supercontinent -see Vaalbara
Urban II (Ortho de Lagery), Pope, 167
Uris, Leon, 241
Uruk, 103, 105
Vaalbara (Ur) supercontinent, 14
Vatican, The, during Armenian Genocide, 191
  during Third Reich, 204, 218-219, 224, 251
  on Jews/Judaism, 189, 219, 252
  on Israel, 251
Venus figurines, *H. erectus*, 27-28
  Aurignacian, 44-46, 97
  Gravettian, 46-47
  Magdalenian, 52, 97
  at Göbekli Tepe/Nevah Cori, 97-98
  ancient, 73, 98-99, 104-105
Vespasian, Titus, Emperor of Rome, 156-157
  Arch of Titus, 157
Victoria, Queen Alexandrina, 183, 185
Vienna, 168-169, 207, 209
Vietnam, 188
von Bismarck, Otto, 185-186, 188
Wagner-Rogers Bill, 210
Wannsee Conference (Final Solution), 217
Warsaw Ghetto –see Poland
Warwick-Smith, Simon, 81
Weizmann, Chaim, 194-197

West, Allen, 81
Western Wall, 123, 156, 186
White Paper of 1939, 211, 229, 235
Wilhelm II, 188-189
World War I, 193-196
World War II, 213-223
Xia Dynasty, 105
Yannai Alexander, King of Israel, 151
Y'annui, King of Hyksos Egypt, 115
Yarmuti, 105
Yavneh, 157, 160-162
Yebu, 122, 146, 149-150
Yefet ben Noah, 96, 132, 165,
Yellowstone National Park, 20, 259
Yellowstone supervolcano, 20, 28, 259

Yemen, 239, 241
Yochanan ben Zakkai, 157, 161
Yom Kippur War, 242
Younger Dryas –see Dryas stadials
Yucatán Peninsula, prehistoric, 19-20, 56 CE, 166
Zeus, 102
Zerubabel, 147
Zhiren Cave, 32
Zichron Ya'akov, 195
Zilpa (Leah's maid), 110
Zipporah (biblical), 123
Zionist Federation of Britain and Ireland, 196

www.ingramcontent.com/pod-product-compliance
Lightning Source LLC
Chambersburg PA
CBHW031427160426
43195CB00010BB/642